NEW DEVELOPMENTS IN STATISTICS FOR PSYCHOLOGY AND THE SOCIAL SCIENCES

EDITED BY
A. D. LOVIE

New Developments in Statistics for Psychology and the Social Sciences

Edited by

A. D. LOVIE

Lecturer in the Department of Psychology
University of Liverpool

The British Psychological Society and
Methuen, London and New York

The British Psychological Society and
Methuen, London and New York

© The British Psychological Society, 1986

First edition published in 1986 by The British Psychological Society, St Andrews
House, 48 Princess Road East, Leicester LE1 7DR, in association with Methuen
& Co. Ltd, 11 New Fetter Lane, London EC4 4EE, and in the USA by Methuen,
Inc., 29 West 35th Street, New York, NY 10001.

British Library Cataloguing in Publication Data

New developments in statistics for psychology
  and the social sciences
  1. Psychometrics
  I. Lovie, A. D.
  519.5′02415   BF39

ISBN 0-901715-46-8

Library of Congress Cataloging in Publication Data

New developments in statistics for psychology
  and the social sciences

  Includes bibliographies and index.
  1. Social sciences—Statistical methods—Addresses, essays, lectures.
  2. Psychology—Statistical methods—Addresses, essays, lectures.
  I. Lovie, A. D. (Alexander D.)
  HA29.N4535   1985   300′.1′5195   85-15347

ISBN 0-901715-46-8

Computer-Filmset and printed in Great Britain by Adlard & Son Ltd,
Bartholomew Press, Dorking, Surrey.

Contents

To the memory of
B.S., S. and M.

Foreword

FREDERICK MOSTELLER

Today's researchers in the social sciences ordinarily have a greater command of statistical techniques than professional statisticians had when I was a graduate student. At the same time that the researchers learn and use more statistics, partly because of better training and understanding of their needs and partly because of the help given by computers and software, statistics itself has been advancing, and so scholars have much more to command.

As a consequence, social scientists require continuing education in statistical techniques as well as in other parts of their subject. In reviewing the chapters of this book, I have been impressed with the extent of development of the new fields of statistics and with the editor's selection of courses from the feast of innovations.

Were it only that new techniques have been invented, perhaps the advances could be expected to be handled by research assistants alone with senior investigators liberated from this new knowledge. Instead, much of the thinking and many of the attitudes about quantitative analysis have changed. The ideas of confirmatory data analysis (tests of significance, confidence limits, general statistical inference including decision theory) tended to tyrannize the careful researcher because problems of selection effects and of multiplicity made it seem immoral to explore one's data thoroughly. Those undesirable effects were and are real and the careful worker was wise to be concerned. At the same time, it is intolerable not to use one's data to the hilt. Distinguishing as we do now among conditions appropriate for description, confirmation, and exploration, puts the researcher into a more satisfactory position for both analysing and reporting results. The need for stating in advance hypotheses to be tested has become part of the protocol of many researchers. The idea of openly reporting how much and what kind of data-dredging has been done has become respectable and desirable. And in some areas, one can have one's cake and eat it too because methods of simultaneous multiple comparisons give us a way to control significance levels in the face of having chosen the largest, say, of many possible outcomes or, more generally, at having peeked at the data before choosing the analysis. This new understanding has put confirmatory data analysis in a more reasonable perspective.

At the same time, the whole discipline of exploratory data analysis has grown up, giving us new systematic methods of analysing data, methods that defend themselves against the failure of assumptions about distribution shape and yet are able to squeeze out most of the information contained in the data (Chapter 2, P. R. Jackson). Some of these new methods, like the jackknife and bootstrap, contribute as well to confirmatory data analysis by giving us measures of variability that do not depend on delicate assumptions that may be violated or on approximate mathematics with unknown error structure.

The research scientist will want to be acquainted with these new attitudes and these new approaches because they make the new quantitative techniques more relevant to daily work. This book presents, often in spritely fashion, brief expositions of new methods of presenting and analysing data including graphics (Chapter 1, A. Seheult), robust and resistant methods (Chapter 2, P. R. Jackson), and outlier analysis (Chapter 3, P. Lovie).

The weakest preparation in beginning statistics courses comes in learning to appraise the power (the strength) of the study for detecting differences or other departures from null models. Although a small study too weak to stand on its own may occasionally be justified, how matters are reported may make a difference. For example, some people argue that confidence limits given at the close of a study eliminate the need for discussing power. At the same time that one applauds the offering of confidence limits, one must remember that a small weak study is likely to produce 'no significant differences'. When such a null effect is reported, it discourages further work in a field. If, however, a report is accompanied by such information as: 'The study had only one chance in ten of detecting a 50 per cent gain', the reader is alerted in a very direct way to the weakness of the study. Why might a weak study be justified at all? Sometimes targets of opportunity present themselves and valuable data that might otherwise be lost can be preserved. If adequately reported, they may be combined, through techniques of meta-analysis, with results from other studies to reach strong conclusions as data accumulate. A new exposition of this important neglected topic, power, is most welcome (Chapter 7, B. R. Singer, A. D. Lovie, and P. Lovie).

Over the last 25 years, the analysis of contingency tables (cross-classifications with cell entries composed of counts) has advanced in many directions from merely carrying out the chi-squared test for independence in a table with r rows and c columns. These new methods are so extensive that whole textbooks are being written about them. The analyses of these tables has become a specialty of its own. Chapter 4 (G. J. G. Upton) gives an introduction to these new methods.

Similarly the field of longitudinal studies (Chapter 5, I. Plewis), studies where investigators measure individuals repeatedly through time, has taken on a life of its own. The appropriate regression methods, matching, and special modelling efforts offer ways to analyse the data and avoid or reduce the bias inherent in some techniques of analysis.

Sometimes it is profitable to regard sets of data as arising from mixtures of subpopulations. Each subpopulation has its own distribution, and the total population is formed as a weighted sum of the subpopulations. One then may wish to use the data to estimate the weights associated with the subpopulations and/or the parameters of the subpopulations. Chapter 6 (B. S. Everitt) explains how to do this for a variety of circumstances and models, one being called latent class analysis.

Although analysis of variance tells us whether means of populations tend to differ, in many instances the key question is which population is the best (has the largest mean, say). Because this question is so clearly the one we want to answer in many experimental situations – What variety of wheat gives farmers the most for their money? What method of teaching spelling produces the highest scores for 8-year-olds? – we must remember that, except when we have only two treatments, this question is one that the classical analysis of variance does not treat. Very recently, this question has generated the substantial new statistical research reported on in Chapter 8 (A. D. Lovie).

In Chapter 9, the editor tells us how these new methods could be introduced into the curriculum.

Each chapter has a substantial set of references that will carry eager readers the further steps along the way that their research may require. Because some of this material is likely to be unfamiliar, I would recommend a scanning of chapters to make sure that something very central is not missed merely because the names do not sound relevant or friendly. Inevitably the question will arise, were there other techniques that might have been included? And just as inevitably, the answer would have to be 'yes'. And so when the editor finds out how this work is used and whether there are ways to improve the exposition, perhaps he will devote another volume to these additional areas. It is well to keep a book to a size that the wrist can manage.

15 February 1985

Introduction

John W. Campbell, Jr, the best editor that *Astounding Science Fiction* ever had, once defined a paradox as the warning smell in a logical system. So try this paradox for size: psychology is one of the biggest consumers of statistics of all the social and behavioural sciences, yet all teachers of statistics are faced by an epidemic of maths phobia and statistics turn-off. There are also large numbers of researchers thumbing through the index of the latest edition of 'Winer' or 'Keppel' or 'Kirk' trying to find a design that fits their current experiment on the effects of high temperature and 120 dB heavy metal rock on the ability of dancing mice to whistle 'Swanee' while balancing on one leg on a shock grid.

This book attacks one of the aspects of this paradox, which is that there is too slow a movement of new statistical ideas into psychology and other social sciences with too great an emphasis on tailored and cook-book solutions to statistical problems. Of course, it is difficult for a non-statistician to view statistics in the same creative, questioning way employed by the professional, but a lively awareness that statistics does change and some aquaintance with those changes is of considerable value even to the lay statistician. This book, therefore, provides a sampler of new ideas, attitudes and techniques of actual or potential use to social scientists. In other words, I am not claiming that this book is either exhaustive or the final word on statistics in the large or even of any of the topics contained herein. Rather it covers recent topics of use to psychology and other social sciences which by and large have not been well covered elsewhere in the literature. However, I will admit to one major omission; regression and the linear model were excluded partly because of the sheer volume of contemporary work but also because the recent texts by Weisberg (1980), McCullagh & Nelder (1983), Cook & Weisberg (1983), Belsley *et al.* (1980) and Fox (1984) provide modern and accessible treatments of the area.

The chapters in this text also reflect recent statistical themes. In particular, these include an increased emphasis on mathematical models and descriptions of data and situations; a comparative neglect of the formal aspects of statistical inference; a hankering for the flexible and the informal; a blurring of the boundaries between inference and description; a suspicion of the parametric; a movement into the tails of the distribution and beyond; a clear rejection of the null in favour of the much more seductive alternative hypothesis; plus, of course, an obsession with von Neumann and Turing's little toys.

What all of this means in terms of the contents of the present text is chapters on pictures and graphical methods (Seheult), robust statistics (Jackson) and outliers (Lovie), while the chapters on log-linear models (Upton) and mixtures (Everitt) show the direction in which recent attempts to model experimental situations

1

have gone, as does the chapter on comparative statistics (Plewis) where the statistical *background* has now been brought into the model and the analysis. Finally the chapters on power (Singer *et al.*) and selection tests (Lovie) show some of the effort that is currently being expended in exploring the flip side of the null hypothesis.

One other reason why there is so much variety on offer in the statistical market-place is that so many of the statistician's wares are the result of collaboration with their applied clients whose widespread demands have produced some interesting but highly divergent solutions. Statistics is, after all, a branch of *applied* mathematics and as such has to be client driven.

The book, therefore, mixes attitude, theory and practice in about equal parts. Perhaps this is the best way of presenting statistics: more than a collection of cook-book routines; rather the exploration of many divergent world views using a varying set of mathematical and logical tools. Ultimately, statistical analysis reflects the times and the society in which it is embedded. Perhaps there lies the creative well springs of the topic.

Some of the points made in this introduction will be taken up and amplified in the final chapter when I return to the vexed problem of how to incorporate this recent statistical work into today's crowded statistics courses. Finally, although most of the techniques in this book are illustrated by examples from psychology, the diversity of the applications indicates the relevance of these methods to the social sciences in general.

I would like to thank the following people for their patience and help with the rather lengthy genesis of the text: first, all the contributors; second, Chris Leach and Joyce Collins for The British Psychological Society whose collective skill with the executive editing knife was so good that I never even saw the blood; third, my Department's efficient typists, Dorothy Foulds and Anne Halliwell; and finally, of course, Pat, my constant goad, comforter and retriever of irretrievably lost manuscripts. As some readers may know, one of my contributors, Bernard Singer, died before completing his chapter. I hope that our version of Bernard's work would have pleased him.

References

BELSLEY, D.A., KUH, E. & WELSCH, R.E. (1980). *Regression Diagnostics*. New York: Wiley.

COOK, R.D. & WEISBERG, S. (1982). *Residuals and Influence in Regression*. New York: Chapman and Hall.

FOX, J. (1984). *Linear Statistical Models and Related Methods, with Applications to Social Research*. New York: Wiley.

McCULLAGH, P. & NELDER, J.A. (1983). *Generalized Linear Models*. New York: Chapman and Hall.

WEISBERG, S. (1980). *Applied Linear Regression*. New York: Wiley.

Sandy Lovie
Liverpool

1
Simple Graphical Methods for Data Analysis

ALLAN SEHEULT

I write as a statistician attempting to modify the way in which psychologists may choose to think about, analyse and present data from experimental or observational studies. One aspect of this concerns the use of graphical methods, whether for analysis or presentation of results. Rather than attempt a complete coverage, I will concentrate here on a few simple but effective techniques. Thus, for example, the important and rapidly developing area of graphical methods for multiple response data will hardly be considered. However, the recent book *Graphical Methods for Data Analysis* by Chambers *et al.* (1983), henceforth referred to as *GMDA*, is a valuable reference for the whole field of graphical methods. Wainer & Thissen (1981) also give a very readable and useful review of many aspects of graphical data analysis, including some novel two-way displays for multiple response data.

The graphical techniques described and used in this chapter are not original and are accessible elsewhere; for example, see *Exploratory Data Analysis* by Tukey (1977) or *Applications, Basics, and Computing of Exploratory Data Analysis* by Velleman & Hoaglin (1981), henceforth referred to as *EDA* and *ABC* respectively. My aim is to try to encourage psychologists to use routinely techniques such as those described here in a guided but unrestrained way to enable them to uncover important features of their hard-earned data that may otherwise be disguised or distorted by too rigid analysis. Rather than present a list of techniques, I will discuss their use in analysing part of the data from a current experimental programme in the Psychology Department at Durham University. In this way I hope the reader will be better placed to assess the potential utility of the methodology used in the analysis.

The reader will find very little discussion here on the science and philosophy of graphical methods; these aspects are fully covered in the references cited. The main emphasis here is on the usefulness of the techniques.

Discussions with psychologists suggest that having carried out a careful study they often do not have the energy or inclination to think too hard about statistical analysis but hope that some appropriate standard method – most often analysis of

3

Table 1. Perpendicular errors in degrees for 36 subjects: see text for complete description

Subject	Vertical							Horizontal							Oblique						
	150°	30°	135°	45°	120°	60°	90°	150°	30°	135°	45°	120°	60°	90°	150°	30°	135°	45°	120°	60°	90°
								Long baseline													
1	10	−14	15	0	−19	−9	5	72	22	57	16	36	9	5	38	−10	29	20	8	4	15
2	18	−1	8	0	−13	−16	5	16	−4	−5	−14	−7	−18	−2	4	8	−5	13	2	12	−8
3	−16	28	−23	6	−34	−6	20	38	40	32	50	21	35	4	5	8	0	50	−20	62	29
4	4	16	−11	2	−19	10	13	36	−16	26	−34	0	20	8	11	−15	17	2	−12	−25	10
5	123	3	−5	−20	−30	0	14	5	−13	−7	−25	−37	60	5	48	23	−7	88	0	51	0
6	−12	18	−22	8	−32	−30	5	4	20	−2	−9	−5	15	4	−10	109	21	94	33	21	−5
7	1	6	1	0	−16	−23	3	21	31	12	2	−10	−7	−3	21	26	10	7	8	−5	0
8	−7	34	−4	38	−13	24	4	−5	17	26	7	20	24	−10	16	25	24	24	−8	51	12
9	10	15	13	5	22	−19	−5	28	19	13	12	14	3	−6	14	−5	−15	−15	39	−37	−6
10	7	8	−4	−16	−18	12	4	44	34	46	18	24	16	−2	27	51	24	51	13	44	15
11	126	14	7	−6	8	15	13	15	26	14	114	−5	1	3	14	31	15	104	41	−42	6
12	38	7	36	−18	−6	15	−27	105	15	96	0	56	−28	−1	56	95	19	96	−13	89	35
13	−17	−14	−31	−29	26	−23	−3	−8	15	14	7	−16	15	3	−13	31	−2	34	8	−44	0
14	−2	3	−6	6	2	−7	5	1	−4	−1	−10	−20	−28	6	10	−15	−15	49	−36	22	−13
15	−1	20	−11	−3	−11	−9	3	3	37	4	7	−17	8	2	19	−7	21	−11	17	10	14
16	15	5	−4	−11	−8	−23	−5	4	25	−9	25	−21	11	3	10	11	−1	6	−12	41	45
17	15	5	13	3	2	−13	−1	21	14	3	13	−7	−5	−1	9	4	10	−5	6	−1	−12
18	29	19	15	2	−9	2	1	17	10	27	7	5	1	−5	23	−2	15	4	7	27	−7
								Short baseline													
19	5	−7	−5	−10	−15	−9	−4	10	−10	14	−20	2	−26	−2	10	−8	−5	−5	−5	6	0
20	5	−6	−7	−25	−27	−33	8	11	−4	8	3	−9	−5	−5	5	2	3	0	−11	−8	28
21	3	29	−4	1	−27	−14	10	17	19	10	3	0	−9	−8	18	1	13	−19	−23	51	49
22	2	2	−13	−9	−6	−11	3	31	11	7	8	−2	−8	−7	23	12	11	−13	16	6	−12
23	10	−19	−8	−28	−24	−37	60	91	17	0	4	3	−13	−44	−3	42	6	−15	1	−16	−10
24	−4	0	−3	−19	−19	−22	5	22	11	7	3	−8	86	−8	5	13	−18	−18	84	−10	−15
25	−7	−1	−29	−16	−18	−14	4	21	8	10	3	−8	−22	6	10	7	6	6	1	84	31
26	−4	2	−15	0	−28	19	−3	−1	−5	−2	−15	−29	−44	0	7	−10	−18	−19	84	−44	47
27	7	−3	−4	−6	−27	−18	−1	11	12	33	−4	−14	−30	−4	23	18	−8	−7	−18	19	−3
28	35	16	3	2	2	19	7	40	35	33	19	46	6	−10	25	29	28	37	−20	69	10
29	4	−8	3	−17	1	−16	−6	−14	19	−8	15	−15	−31	1	16	−10	−2	−15	−8	21	17
30	−1	11	−10	−18	−1	−8	−5	10	26	−10	17	−11	−6	−29	2	−12	46	−1	3	57	18
31	−13	63	50	39	4	24	6	39	47	29	55	16	20	2	59	71	1	50	14	34	7
32	−4	−5	9	−19	−32	−20	6	2	17	6	6	2	−38	−2	6	−1	18	−22	8	5	8
33	19	−10	−5	6	−13	−1	8	26	23	19	8	6	−10	−5	28	−14	1	−10	−1	15	12
34	42	−14	22	−17	4	−29	−1	−3	12	−23	121	−32	−35	−1	−5	34	18	3	84	−27	13
35	13	9	13	3	2	−13	5	52	45	31	32	24	15	2	50	−2	−34	−23	5	−35	13
36	13	−5	15	−10	−2	−30	10	44	26	27	28	24	14	−12	14	−4	12	16	17	31	−6

variance – will satisfy a conservative editor! If this account encourages psychologists to accept that valid indications from data can often be scientifically more valuable than formal inference then it will have succeeded in its purpose.

EXPERIMENT AND DATA

The data in Table 1, which are used to illustrate the graphical techniques employed in this chapter, derive from an experiment on young children's drawing conducted by Dr Charles Crook of the Psychology Department at Durham University. Thirty-six five-year-olds each copied seven angles *30, 45, 60, 90, 120, 135* and *150 degrees* on to each of three predrawn baseline orientations – *vertical, horizontal* and *45 degrees oblique*. One group, subjects 1–18, drew on a *long baseline (140 cm)* and the remaining group of 18 drew on a *short baseline (75 cm)*. Following Crook's account, the pairs *30/150, 45/135* and *60/120* will be referred to sometimes as *acute/obtuse 30, 45* and *60 degrees*, respectively. Thus, in all, each child copied 21 angles on to predrawn baselines: for the purposes of this chapter, the three 90 degree angles will not be included in the analysis. Figure 1 illustrates three such tasks for children in the short baseline group.

Each entry in Table 1 is the copying error from the target angle: it is positive when the angle is drawn towards the perpendicular to the baseline and negative when the angle is drawn away from this perpendicular. The entries −14 and 8 for

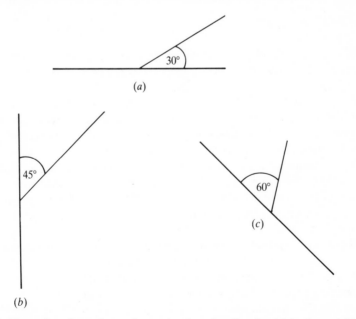

Figure 1. Examples of copying tasks on the short baseline for (*a*) horizontal 30 degree acute, (*b*) vertical 45 degree obtuse, and (*c*) oblique 60 degree obtuse angles.

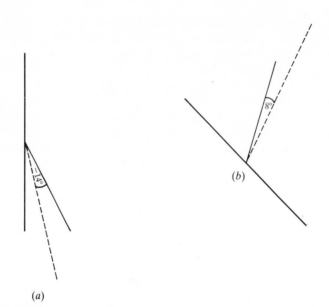

(b)

(a)

Figure 2. Examples of perpendicular errors for subject 1: (a) −14 degree for 30 degree acute angle on the vertical baseline and (b) +8 degree for 60 degree obtuse angle on the oblique baseline: dashed line indicates subject's attempt at reproducing the solid line angle.

subject 1 under the headings *vertical 30 degree acute* and *oblique 60 degree obtuse* are illustrated in Figure 2: they correspond to drawn angles of 16 and 112 degrees, respectively.

The experiment was motivated by the research of Ibbotson & Bryant (1976) which demonstrated a tendency for children to make 45 degree angles approach the perpendicular – *the perpendicular error* – except when they are drawn on a vertical baseline – *the vertical effect*. Thus, positive errors support the perpendicular error hypothesis, whilst small errors on the vertical baseline support the vertical effect hypothesis. Crook's experiment extends the conditions studied by Ibbotson & Bryant and therefore can address wider questions. Is the perpendicular effect present for all angles and, if so, is the size of the effect related to the size of the target angle? Is the vertical really a privileged baseline orientation or does it merely support different kinds of biases? In the next section these and other questions will be examined using simple graphical displays.

A common feature in the construction of these displays is the use, for example, of the median rather than the mean as a measure of location and the interquartile range rather than the standard deviation as a measure of dispersion. However, this does not imply that the displays cannot be drawn using means and standard deviations. The median and interquartile range are generally preferred because they are *resistant* to the presence of a few outliers; that is, they are largely unaffected by large changes in a small part of the data. On the other hand, the mean and standard deviation are not resistant and consequently standard methods based on them, such as the analysis of variance required to summarize Crook's data, can be seriously affected by the presence of a few outliers. More importantly, outliers themselves may be of particular interest to the experimenter and, therefore, their detection and identification should be a primary part of analysis and summary, whether graphical or numerical. Outliers are not so readily detected by non-resistant methods; on the contrary, such methods tend to mask them.

SOME GRAPHICAL DISPLAYS

The main purpose of a graphical display should be to aid the data analyst or viewer to get a feel for data by seeing it. Displaying data graphically often involves a loss of information but this is usually offset by gains in insight and understanding. Distributional shape, location, dispersion, outliers and comparison are generally easier to perceive from a graphical display than from the data or numerical summaries alone. However, it should be noted that important graphical considerations are involved in producing effective tabular presentation, including choice of row and column spacings, the use or not of horizontal and vertical lines, headings, underlining and emboldening. Excellent accounts of this important part of data presentation can be found in Ehrenberg (1978, 1982).

It is useful to distinguish between *working displays* and *presentation displays*. The former are used as part of the process of exploring and analysing data: they are often rough and ready and personal to the user. Such displays should be quick and easy to draw and effective in gaining possible insight into data. The *stem-and-leaf plot* in Figure 3, to be described later, is a good example of a particularly useful working display that I frequently use in the process of analysing data, especially in examining residuals from a fitted statistical model. Carefully drawn versions of working displays can be used for final presentation of data. A presentation display should be uncluttered by unnecessary lines and numerical detail. Moreover, to assimilate the information that it is intended to convey should not require great intellectual effort. Wainer (1984) gives an amusing and instructive account of how to draw bad graphical displays.

Most of the displays used in this chapter were developed by John W. Tukey and can be found in his book, *Exploratory Data Analysis* (1977). Another interesting but perhaps lesser-known article, specifically concerned with graphical display, is Tukey (1972). There, Tukey discusses the idea of a semi-graphical display: one which combines both 'table' and 'graph'. A prototype example which employs this once heretical combination is the stem-and-leaf plot. Figure 3 offers an example for the errors of the 18 children attempting to reproduce the 150 degree angle on the long vertical baseline, given in the upper part of column 1 in

Table 1. Its construction uses the simple observation that each entry in Table 1 has a *stem* (the number of *tens*) and a *leaf* (the number of *units*) and that leaves of entries having the same stem can be stacked up alongside the corresponding stem; for example, the errors 10, 18, 10 and 15 made by subjects 1, 2, 10 and 17 give the line 1|0805 in Figure 3. The line −0|721 summarizes the errors −7, −2 and −1 by subjects 9, 15 and 16. To construct the complete display, set out the stems vertically and run through the data writing down the leaves against their appropriate stems. Further details, especially with regard to sensible quick choices of stem width and rounding strategy can be found in *EDA*, *ABC* and Hoaglin *et al.* (1983).

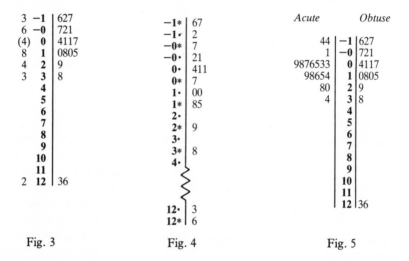

Fig. 3	Fig. 4	Fig. 5

Figure 3. Stem-and-leaf plot of perpendicular errors for the 30 degree obtuse angle on the long vertical baseline: leaf unit 1 degree.

Figure 4. Stretched version of the plot in Figure 3: stem width 5 degrees.

Figure 5. Back-to-back stem-and-leaf plot to compare perpendicular errors for the 30 degree acute and obtuse angles on the long vertical baseline: leaf unit 1 degree.

The display in Figure 4 is a stretched version of the one in Figure 3: leaves 0–4 appear on stems marked '·' and leaves 5–9 appear on stems marked '*'. Note that either display can be constructed from the other so that if an initial choice of stem width produces a display which is too smooth or too rough in appearance then the required change can be readily implemented.

The display in Figure 3 has the visual impact of an histogram on its side and, in addition, retains all the numerical detail of the original data but in more compact form; subject identification with data values is, in this case, the only information not directly available from display.

Note that the construction of the stem-and-leaf plot partially orders the data allowing important summaries to be easily read from the display with the aid of the column of cumulative counts given to the left of the main display. Accumulation of counts to the stem containing the median make it easy to 'count in' to any desired depth from either end. Thus, the quartiles at depth 5 are −2 degrees and 18 degrees, and the median at depth 9.5 is 5.5 degrees, the average of 4 degrees and 7 degrees. Ordering leaves within stems orders the data completely to produce a presentation version.

Two gross outliers, 123 degrees and 126 degrees, for subjects 5 and 12 are readily apparent in the stem-and-leaf plot. These errors correspond to angles of 27 degrees and 24 degrees which are closer to the 30 degrees acute version of the attempted 150 degree angle. Perhaps these two children were mistakenly shown the 30 degree acute angle, or perhaps they have a visuomotor deficit. Certainly subject 12 experiences difficulty with several angles but the general difficulty is less marked with subject 5. Such gross errors are of interest to the investigation and deserve special attention both scientifically and statistically. The mean of all 18 errors is 18.2 degrees and is 4.9 degrees without the two outliers: the median of all 18 errors is 5.5 degrees. The discrepancy of some 13 degrees between the two location measures is substantial: the mean value supports the perpendicular error hypothesis on the vertical baseline, hence denying the vertical effect hypothesis of Ibbotson & Bryant. On the other hand, the median value, while lending a little support to the perpendicular error hypothesis, does not refute the vertical effect hypothesis. The median of the 16 'clean' values is 2.5 and lends further support to the vertical effect hypothesis. While on the subject of resistance to outliers, it should be noted that the standard deviation of all 18 errors is 41.2 degrees which is reduced approximately three-fold to 15.2 degrees when the two outliers are removed. The interquartile range as a measure of dispersion is not so affected. Thus, another effect of the outliers is to inflate the error term in the 'bottom line' of the analysis of variance, possibly leading to false conclusions.

Another important statistical activity is *comparison*. Here, for example, two immediately come to mind: comparison of the distributions of errors for different angles on the same baseline, and comparing the same angles on different baselines.

A display with stem-and-leaf plots for each experimental condition soon overpowers the information processing capabilities of the eye/brain system. However, when only two experimental conditions are to be compared a back-to-back stem-and-leaf plot, such as the one depicted in Figure 5 comparing the 30 degree and 150 degree angles on the long vertical baseline, can sometimes be a useful device. Apart from the outliers, we see that average behaviour for the two conditions is similar. It might be argued that acute and obtuse versions of the same angle on a given baseline present the same problem for a given child and therefore the child's errors ought to be similar. This hypothesis is not supported for this example by the scatter plot in Figure 6 where the outliers have been set aside and have not been allowed to dominate the horizontal scale. The correlation coefficient is −0.14 and without the two outliers is −0.11, a result which, because of the fortuitous position of the outliers, does not demonstrate the general non-resistant behaviour of this standard measure of linear dependency; either coefficient supports the graphical assessment from Figure 6. Non-resistant versions of the correlation coefficient are available: see Gnanadesikan & Kettenring (1972) for work in this area, especially in relation to the many statistical multivariate techniques which depend so heavily on correlation matrices.

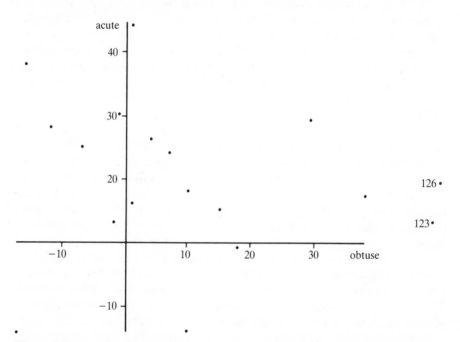

Figure 6. Scatter plot of perpendicular errors for the 30 degree acute and 30 degree obtuse angles on the long vertical baseline.

When comparing several batches of data in display form, a simple graphical summary of each batch is required which occupies less space than the stem-and-leaf plot but nevertheless captures its essential features. Figure 7 offers three different graphical summaries of the stem-and-leaf plot in Figure 3: the *boxplot*, the *midgap plot* of Tufte (1983) and the *schematic plot*. The ends of the box in Figures 7a and 7c are positioned at the quartiles so that the length of the box, the interquartile range, gives a visual impression of dispersion, and the position of the median, the bar within the box, gives information about location and symmetry. The arms of the display in 7a extend to the extremes of the data values and give an impression of outliers or a stretched-tail distribution. The midgap plot in Figure

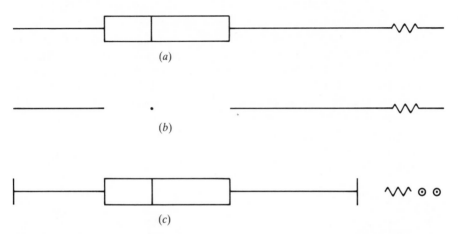

Figure 7. (*a*) Boxplot, (*b*) midgap plot and (*c*) schematic plot for the 30 degree obtuse angle on the long vertical baseline.

7*b* is an economical version of the boxplot and is particularly useful for comparison of several batches. The schematic plot in Figure 7*c* is an embellished version of the boxplot: each arm of the display extends to the last data value within one-and-a-half interquartile ranges of the corresponding quartile and approximates the three standard deviation limits of the Gaussian distribution. Values outside these arms are designated as outliers. The outlier rule is necessarily somewhat arbitrary but, in practice, successfully draws attention to obvious straggling values. The midgap version of the schematic plot is used in Figures 8 and 9.

In Figure 8 parallel midgap plots are arranged vertically in order to compare the errors for the six angles on the long vertical baseline. A scale is given to the left of the main display with emphasis given to the zero degree error line. Approximately equal dispersions, reasonable symmetry, and outliers are readily apparent in the display. Another noteworthy feature is the near equality of corresponding acute and obtuse medians. Figure 9, drawn on the same vertical scale for the same six angles on the long oblique baseline, conveys somewhat different impressions: median errors are all positive and dispersion is generally larger than that in Figure 8, especially for each of the three acute angles. It might be significant that all three target obtuse angles on the oblique baseline are no more than 15 degrees from the 'true' vertical whereas the acute angles are within the same limits of the 'true' horizontal.

It would seem important to relate errors to the actual drawings the children were asked to copy, especially for presentation purposes. Figure 10 offers such a display for *all* 36 children for each of the other 3×6=18 conditions: thus, baseline length has been ignored. Special difficulties are encountered in designing a display which attempts to capture both the circular nature of the data and its relation to the actual drawing task. Unfortunately concentric circles, while useful

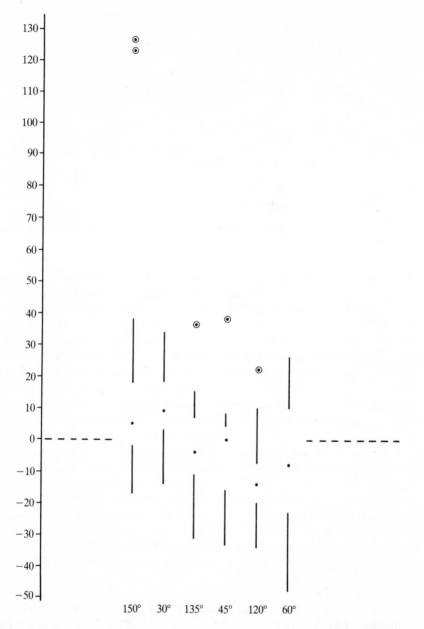

Figure 8. Comparison plot of perpendicular errors on the long vertical baseline for the 30 degree obtuse/acute, 45 degree obtuse/acute and 60 degree obtuse/acute angles.

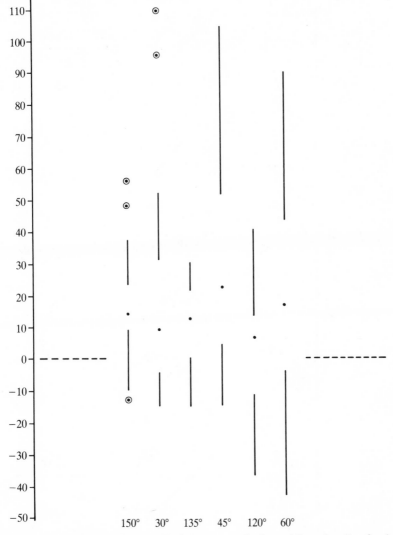

Figure 9. Comparison plot of perpendicular errors on the long oblique baseline for the 30 degree obtuse/acute, 45 degree obtuse/acute and 60 degree obtuse/acute angles.

for comparing location, make comparison of dispersion awkward. The main difficulty is that because a circle occupies equal amounts of horizontal and vertical space there is little opportunity to stretch scales to obtain more resolution, especially when several batches are to be compared. Perhaps Figure 10 is an unsatisfactory solution to this problem; suggestions for better alternative displays would be most welcome. If interest focuses on location only then Figure 11 relates

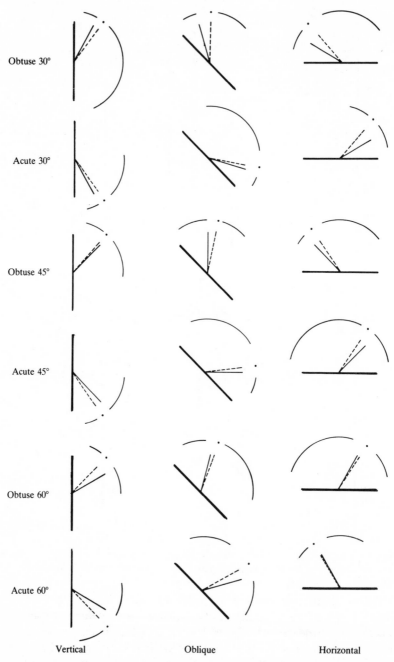

Figure 10. Circular midgap plots and drawing tasks of all 3×6 baseline/angle conditions for 36 children: baseline length ignored. Dashed line points to median attempted angle.

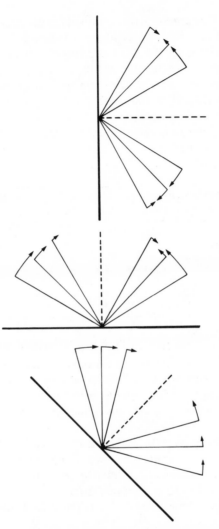

Figure 11. Direction and magnitude of median errors from target angles of 36 children for the vertical, horizontal and oblique baselines: baseline length ignored.

median error to the target angle and emphasizes the direction of the shift for each of the 3×6 conditions. Comparison of results for the horizontal and vertical baselines in Figure 11 suggests that perhaps the natural vertical and horizontal are the appropriate coordinates against which errors should be assessed. Certainly, when baseline orientation is ignored, the errors associated with the 150, 135 and 120 degree angles on the vertical baseline are similar to those associated with the 60, 45 and 30 degree angles on the horizontal baseline, respectively. This observation will be discussed further.

I now consider how graphical displays might throw light on the relationship, if any, between angle and baseline orientation. Although there are some differences in detail for the errors on the short and long baselines, the general pattern is similar. I therefore ignore baseline length in the remainder of this chapter and summarize over all 36 children; the extra replication should give more stable indications of 'average' error than with just 18 children, provided the baseline assumption is not unreasonable.

Table 2, below, gives the two-way array of medians, rounded to the nearest integer, for the 3×6 conditions.

Table 2. Median perpendicular errors over 36 children for different angle and baseline orientation

Baseline orientation	Acute			Obtuse		
	30°	45°	60°	30°	45°	60°
Vertical	4	−7	−13	4	−4	−14
Horizontal	17	7	−2	17	10	−1
Oblique	7	4	13	14	8	2

One of the simplest descriptions of this two-way table is to fit each entry as the sum of three parts – a *common term*, a *baseline effect* and an *angle effect* – called its *fitted value*. The remainder, the difference between any entry and its fitted value, represents the extent to which a simple main effects description fails to describe that entry and is that entry's contribution to the overall baseline × angle interaction.

The least squares fit given in Table 3 is that used in the analysis of variance. The fit is obtained by 'sweeping out' row and column means in Table 2 to obtain the 3×6 array of interaction effects and then adjusting the two sets of marginal main effects so that they each have zero mean.

Thus, for example, the entry −14 in the NE corner of Table 2 can be decomposed as:

$$-14 = 4 + (-9) + (-8) + (-1)$$

entry = common + orientation + angle + interaction.

The inequality of this decomposition for some entries is due to rounding error.

The mean squares for baseline orientation, angle, and baseline × angle interaction in the analysis of variance are each proportional to the sum of squares of the corresponding effects in Table 3.

Table 4 shows the decomposition obtained when we successively sweep out row and column medians instead of means and where the marginal effects are arranged to have zero medians: see *EDA* or *ABC* for details.

Table 3. Mean decomposition of Table 2 showing baseline effects, angle effects and baseline × angle effects: entries rounded to the nearest degree

	Acute			Obtuse			
	30°	45°	60°	30°	45°	60°	
Vertical	3	0	−4	1	0	−1	**−9**
Horizontal	3	1	−6	1	1	−1	**4**
Oblique	−7	−2	9	−2	−1	2	**4**
	6	**−2**	**−4**	**8**	**1**	**−8**	**4**

Table 4. Median decomposition of Table 2 showing baseline effects, angle effects and baseline × angle effects: entries rounded to the nearest degree

	Acute			Obtuse			
	30°	45°	60°	30°	45°	60°	
Vertical	0	0	0	0	−1	0	**−11**
Horizontal	0	1	−2	0	0	0	**2**
Oblique	−8	0	15	−1	0	5	**0**
	9	**−2**	**−8**	**9**	**2**	**−9**	**6**

The median decomposition is 'cleaner' than the one based on means. The excellent fit for both the vertical and horizontal baselines, as evidenced by the relatively small interaction effects in the corresponding rows, is not so apparent in the mean analysis, where the relatively large interaction effects for the 30 and 60 degree angles on the oblique baseline, as pinpointed in the median analysis, have been 'smeared' over the other interaction effects and into the main effects in the margins. The angle effects from the median analysis show the near equality of error for corresponding acute and obtuse angles. The anomalous behaviour of the oblique baseline, particularly for acute angles, has been noted previously and is also apparent here; but the fact that the 45 degree angle is horizontal might explain the correspondingly small interaction term if it were hypothesized that horizontal lines are easier to reproduce.

Turning our attention to the orientation effects, we note once again the approximate 13 degree difference between the horizontal and vertical baselines and the near equality of the horizontal and oblique baselines. In the final section, I discuss some implications of these indications for possible lines of future research into children's drawings.

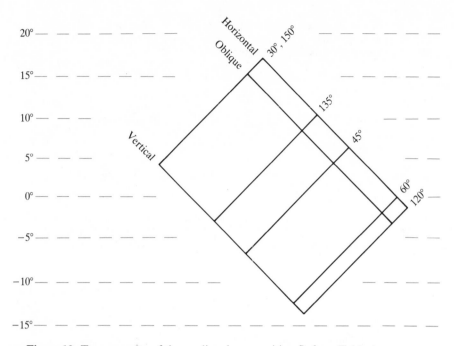

Figure 12. Two-way plot of the median decomposition fit from Table 4: see text.

Understanding the results of the analysis of a small table, like the one under consideration here, is relatively easy from the numerical output alone; this will not in general be the case with large tables, particularly where an audience may not have enough time to assimilate detailed numerical results. We now consider what graphical displays might help here. Tukey (1972; and also in *EDA*) suggested the *two-way plot*. Figure 12 is the two-way plot for the *fit* from the median analysis in Table 4 and Figure 13 is similar except that the interaction terms, coded by sign and size, are placed at the intersections of the two orthogonal sets of parallel lines. The height above the horizontal of each intersection represents the fitted value for the corresponding combination of baseline orientation and angle. Only the vertical scale is relevant: the horizontal coordinate is introduced only to provide space for the display but is otherwise forgotten.

Constructing a two-way plot is simple. A brief description will suffice here: the details can be found in *EDA* or Tukey (1972). Any fitted value can be written as $x + y$, where x denotes one of the effects and y denotes the sum of the common term and the other effect. In our example we take x to be the orientation effect. We now plot on graph paper the pairs (x, y) for the 18 fitted values, add some 45 degree lines of constant fit, rotate the graph paper through 45 degrees, and trace the result to produce the display in Figure 12. The lines of constant fit now represent the vertical scale.

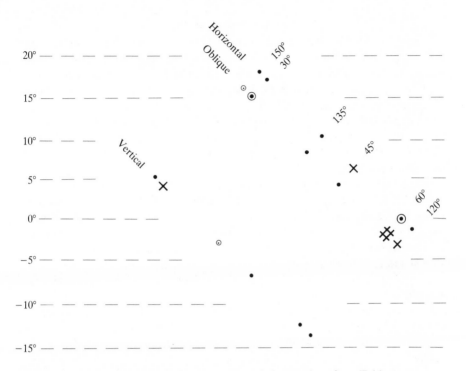

Figure 13. Coded two-way plot of baseline × angle interactions from Table 4: see text.

- `.` dot represents zero or near zero interaction
- `⊙` dot in small circle represents a small negative interaction
- `☉` dot in large circle represents a large negative interaction
- `+` plus sign represents a small positive interaction
- `#` double plus sign represents a large positive interaction

What can we see from this picture? First note that both sets of effects have been ordered: the baseline order now corresponds to natural rotation order. The horizontal and oblique baseline fits are similar. Subjects have little difficulty with acute/obtuse 60 degree angles on the horizontal baseline and acute/obtuse 30 degree angles on the vertical baseline. They have most difficulty with acute/obtuse 60 degree angles on the vertical baseline and acute/obtuse 30 degree angles on the horizontal baseline. The difficulty experienced with acute/obtuse 45 degree angles falls roughly half way between these two extremes. These statements must be tempered by the information in the interaction plot of Figure 13. There, circles of increasing size represent negative interactions of increasing magnitude, and correspondingly for plus signs: the dots represent zero or near zero interaction effects. Notice we have resisted the temptation to include fit and interaction details on the same display. To do so would have required the viewer to assess too much information.

CONCLUDING REMARKS

In retrospect, what started out to be a chapter on graphical methods now seems to be more like an exercise in data analysis. I offer no apologies for this outcome because the analysis suggests a possible new angle on this line of research into children's drawings! In particular, future experiments might use fixed angles to the vertical in combination with different baseline orientations, rather than the current approach which focuses on angles which are fixed relative to the baseline. Such experiments may throw light on the apparent dominance of the vertical over the horizontal and the extent to which these natural coordinate axes interact with baseline orientation.

In the light of the results of the present analysis, what is the status of the perpendicular error and vertical effect hypotheses referred to in the previous section? When averaged over all conditions, the median error is about 7 degrees towards the perpendicular and gives some overall support to the perpendicular error hypothesis. On the other hand, the vertical baseline results clearly refute the vertical effect hypothesis for all angles, whereas the horizontal and oblique baseline results lend support to the perpendicular error hypothesis for these orientations.

A common criticism of exploratory data analysis and graphical methods in particular is their general failure to involve the usual formal statistical processes such as confidence intervals, significance tests, and multiple comparison procedures. For those who might feel insecure without the support of these formal procedures the papers by Fisher (1983), Hettmansperger (1984) and McGill *et al.* (1978), which link some aspects of non-parametric inference with graphical methods, are very readable.

What topics have not been covered and where can you find them? *GMDA* has already been mentioned as a valuable reference, and the interested reader is strongly recommended to consult it. Main omissions in this chapter include probability quantile plots for assessing distributional assumptions, residual plots for regression diagnostics, plots for displaying multivariate data, and plots of smooth estimates of density and regression functions. All these and other topics are well covered in *GMDA*. Detailed considerations of the philosophy and science and technology of graphical methods are superbly treated in the splendidly scholarly works of Bertin (1983) and Tufte (1983).

Finally, a few remarks on computing are in order. All the displays in this chapter were originally drawn by hand, but much of the initial analysis was carried out interactively at a computer terminal using home-grown APL programs. While an interactive computing facility is certainly a useful asset, it is not essential for effective data analysis. The displays and routines used here were developed with the pencil and paper user in mind and will continue to be useful tools, especially when the computer is not close by. However, most of the displays and exploratory data analysis routines used in this chapter are part of the interactive package MINITAB which is widely accessible and now even available on certain microcomputers. No doubt other similar packages are available. Of course an ever present danger with computers is that their output can sometimes overwhelm careful thought: the balance should be right.

Acknowledgements

I am indebted to Charles Crook for kindly providing the data and for helpful discussions; also to Sandy Lovie and the Books and Special Projects Group of the British Psychological Society for their patience.

References

BERTIN, J. (1983). *Semiology of Graphics* (translated by W. Berg). Madison, Wisconsin: University of Wisconsin Press.

CHAMBERS, J.M., CLEVELAND, W.S., KLEINER, B. & TUKEY, P.A. (1983). *Graphical Methods for Data Analysis*. Belmont, California: Wadsworth.

EHRENBERG, A.S.C. (1978). *Data Reduction: Analysing and Interpreting Statistical Data*. New York: Wiley.

EHRENBERG, A.S.C. (1982). *A Primer in Data Reduction: An Introductory Statistics Textbook*. New York: Wiley.

FISHER, N.I. (1983). Graphical methods in nonparametric statistics: a review and annotated bibliography. *International Statistical Review, 51*, 25–58.

GNANADESIKAN, R. & KETTENRING, J.R. (1972). Robust estimates, residuals, and outlier detection with multiresponse data. *Biometrics, 28*, 81–124.

HETTMANSPERGER, T.P. (1984). Two-sample inference based on one-sample statistics. *Applied Statistics, 33*, 45–51.

HOAGLIN, D.C., MOSTELLER, F. & TUKEY, J.W. (1983). *Understanding Robust and Exploratory Data Analysis*. New York: Wiley.

IBBOTSON, A. & BRYANT, P.E. (1976). The perpendicular error and the vertical effect in children's drawing. *Perception, 5*, 319–326.

McGILL, R., TUKEY, J.W. & LARSEN, W.A. (1978). Variations of boxplots. *The American Statistician, 32*, 12–16.

TUFTE, E.R. (1983). *The Visual Display of Quantitative Information*. Cheshire, Connecticut: Graphics Press.

TUKEY, J.W. (1972). Some graphic and semigraphic displays. In: T. A. Bancroft (ed.) *Statistical Papers in Honor of George W. Snedecor*. Ames, Iowa: Iowa State University Press.

TUKEY, J.W. (1977). *Exploratory Data Analysis*. Reading, Massachusetts: Addison-Wesley.

VELLEMAN, P.F. & HOAGLIN, D.C . (1981). *Applications, Basics, and Computing of Exploratory Data Analysis*. North Situate, Massachusetts: Duxbury Press.

WAINER, H. & THISSEN, D. (1981). Graphical data analysis. *Annual Review of Psychology, 32*, 191–241.

WAINER, H. (1984). How to display data badly. *The American Statistician, 38*, 137–147.

2

Robust Methods in Statistics

PAUL R. JACKSON

Making sense of data is rather like putting up a tent in a gale. You get part of it fastened down and just as you are ready to deal with the next bit all that you have done comes apart and you have to start again. It requires several pairs of hands. Likewise, data analysis is an iterative process where assumptions made early on in order to make a start may turn out later to be unwarranted. They must then be undone and the first analysis repeated with the prior assumptions relaxed or modified in some way. The problem is that progress is bought by making assumptions, but that the cost of making those assumptions may well be hidden by the methods used to make progress.

Part of this initial work may involve exploratory graphical analysis of the kind discussed by Tukey (1977) and Seheult (Chapter 1); and there have been many recent developments in graphical displays which are highly informative (see for example, excellent discussions in Hoaglin *et al.*, 1983; Velleman & Hoaglin, 1981). The focus of this chapter, though, is on other procedures which aim to summarize data efficiently but with estimators which are cheap in assumptions, the area of robust statistics. This area of research has generated a number of sound principles to guide applied statistical work and a plethora of alternative methods and procedures. Some of them are of no more than theoretical interest, but a good many have proved themselves in real life.

Most of the methods to be discussed in this chapter are not routinely computed by the standard packages (though some can be incorporated into flexible packages such as GLIM or GENSTAT), so what is the point of talking about them? The answer is that robust methods are of great value, both to the beginner (or the unwary) and to the skilled analyst. The skilled analyst knows how much he or she can trust a set of data and the measures derived from it; and can use standard procedures with due disrespect, or non-standard techniques with due sensitivity. The beginner, on the other hand, needs a set of analytic tools which will do a fair job on a wide range of problems with large safety margins built in. In this chapter I hope to show that the routine use of linear statistics like means, standard deviations and so on does not give the right safety margin. So robust methods are invaluable to the beginner. They are also of value to the skilled since, when used alongside non-robust methods, they can reveal trouble spots in the data which may require attention before more detailed analysis can proceed.

The emphasis in this chapter is on robustness in model building. This may be an informal process as in the exploratory analysis of unfamiliar data, or it may be a formal process of detailed model fitting and statistical inference. The purpose at all stages is to aid understanding by the use of as simple a model as reasonably possible to describe salient features of the data.

Box (1980) described two facets of this model building process – estimation and criticism – and robustness is an important component of both. Estimation involves tentative fitting of a model to the data; criticism involves a close critical analysis of the adequacy of the model, its form and what it conceals (i.e. the analysis of residuals from a fitted model). Two main aspects of the estimation process to be considered below are first, the choice of robust and non-robust estimators; and second, the definition of confidence intervals for the precision of an estimate. Other important aspects will also be touched upon but in less detail – robustness in sampling design, and the role of transformations in robust model building. Robustness is important too in the process of model criticism, and will be considered briefly here.

First of all, then, it is necessary to say what is meant by the term robustness. Box (1979) defines it this way: 'the property of a procedure which renders the answers it gives insensitive to departures, of a kind which occur in practice, from ideal assumptions' (p. 201). In a similar manner, Huber (1981) says that robustness signifies 'insensitivity to small deviations from the assumptions' (p. 1). He expands on this definition, in terms of the desirable features of a robust procedure (p. 5):

(1) It should have a reasonably good (optimal or nearly optimal) efficiency at the assumed model.

(2) It should be robust in the sense that small deviations from the model assumptions should impair the performance only slightly, that is, the latter (described, say, in terms of the asymptotic variance of an estimate, or of the level and power of a test) should be close to the nominal value calculated at the model.

(3) Somewhat larger deviations from the model should not cause a catastrophe.

These definitions all imply a concern for sensitivity in critical areas (those we care about and want to include in a model), and insensitivity elsewhere. What kinds of things should a procedure be insensitive to? Two kinds of problem have been considered in research on robust estimation:

(1) Throwing in small amounts of gross contamination (outliers, gross errors, bad values);

(2) Changing slightly the values of all observations (by rounding, grouping, local inaccuracies in measuring instruments).

Systematic analysis of the effects of these different kinds of data contamination requires some method of diagnosing precisely their effect on an estimator. Such a diagnosis is provided by the influence function.

THE INFLUENCE CURVE

Influence functions have been developed as useful tools both for theoretical development in robust statistics (see Hampel, 1974) and for practical data analysis (see for example, Devlin *et al.*, 1975; Thissen *et al.*, 1981). Formal definitions vary slightly, but the aim is the same in each case, that of defining the effect of a single observation on an estimator calculated from a sample. One way of doing this is to derive an estimate from the total sample, and then recalculate it dropping each observation in turn. The influence of an observation is then the difference between the two estimates, and it is often written as

$$I_{-i}(y; \hat{\theta}).$$

As an example, consider the problem of estimating a regression coefficient. If the total sample estimate $\hat{\theta}$ is 0.35 and the coefficient changes to 0.15 when observation 1 is removed then the value of the sample influence function, $I_{-1}(y; \hat{\theta})$, for observation 1 is $0.35-0.15=0.20$. There is a close relation between the sample influence function and the jackknife technique for estimating the precision of an estimate (see later section).

One role for the sample influence function is as a diagnostic device in routine data analysis. Thissen *et al.* (1981) discuss simple methods of enhancing scatter plots in order to assess the influence of each observation on the sample correlation coefficient. They show how their proposals may easily be implemented by preparing plots on perspex sheets of influence contours for correlations of say 0.0, 0.25, 0.5 and 0.75. These may then be overlaid on line printer plots from standard packages such as SPSS or GLIM, provided that scales are equalized first (for example, by standardizing the variables defining both axes before plotting).

The role of influence functions as regression diagnostics is also becoming important (see Atkinson, 1982; Belsley *et al.*, 1980; Cook, 1977; Velleman & Welsch, 1981).

The main concern of this chapter, however, is with the sample influence function as a building block in robust estimation. Mosteller & Tukey (1977, pp. 351–356) give a simple example of the way influence functions can reveal the relative vulnerabilities of different estimators of location in a mathematically useful but intuitively appealing way. They consider a sample of 11 measurements in all, where 10 of them sum to zero and have fixed values. They then examine changes in the mean and the median as one observation travels through all possible values. Suppose that 10 of the observations have the values:

$$10, 7, 3, 3, 3, -2, -5, -5, -6, -8$$

which sum to zero (simply for convenience in the arithmetic). Because they sum to zero, the grand total including the 11th observation, x, must be x, and the sample mean is $x/11$. Thus, the sample influence curve for the sample mean (see Figure 1a) is a straight line with slope $1/11$. Because the sample has an odd number of observations, the middle observation is the median. If x is bigger than or equal to 3, the median is 3; if x is smaller than or equal to -2, the median is -2; and if x is between the two, the median is x. Thus the sample influence curve for the median (Figure 1b) is composed of three straight line segments, two of them parallel to the horizontal (x) axis, and the third connecting them. The distance between the parallel lines equals the distance between the two middle observations in the basic set of 10 (here, this distance is 5 units).

Several conclusions may be drawn from this simple example of an analysis of the influence function for two estimators. First of all, the influence of any single additional observation on the sample mean decreases with increasing sample size (in other words, the slope of the influence curve is shallower for larger sample sizes). One result of this is that the larger the sample size, the less we need to worry about the effect of a single outlier, however extreme it may be. Of course, the larger the sample size, the more outliers there are likely to be! Furthermore, for any fixed sample size, influence increases with the difference between the new observation and the original mean. Note, too, that the influence curve for the mean is unbounded – it goes off to infinity at both ends. This is the basis for the statistician's claim that the mean is non-robust.

The influence curve for the median is very different. The most obvious difference is that the curve is bounded, so that the median is totally insensitive to the actual value of the additional observation once that value goes outside the narrow range defined by the middle measurements. The curve is also very steep in the middle (remember that its slope here depends only on two adjacent values), and this can lead to problems for some robust methods (see below).

This informal analysis of the properties of well-known estimators of location serves to demonstrate the approach adopted in robust statistics and also to introduce the rest of this section. This presents three main classes of robust estimator, and intuitive requirements for good robust estimates. Finally, some illustrative examples are offered of the performance of robust estimators with real data.

TYPES OF ESTIMATOR

The investigation of robust estimators has been an active research area in statistics for some time (see, for example, the compendious simulation studies reported by Andrews *et al.*, 1972). Much of this work has been concerned with estimators of location, but some work has also been done on robust estimators of spread in univariate samples. Huber (1972) has distinguished between three types of estimator, L-estimators, M-estimators and R-estimators, and this serves to summarize the main results in this field.

L-estimators

If the observations in a random sample of size n are written down in an ordered form from smallest to largest, then the ordered observations are known as order statistics. They may be shown as:

$$x(1) \leqslant x(2) \leqslant \ldots \leqslant x(n).$$

An L-estimator is an estimator which is a linear combination of these order statistics:

$$\hat{\theta} = \sum a_i \, x(i),$$

where the a_i are weights applied to the ordered observations.

The main differences between the various L-estimators lie in these weights. The sample mean is formed by setting a_i equal to $1/n$ for all observations. A simple and intuitively appealing way of coping with the problem of outlying observations is to assign lower weights to observations in the extremes than to those in the main body of the data. The sample median does this in a rather drastic way by setting a_i equal to zero for all observations except the middle (or middle two for n even) order statistics. Between these two methods of weighting observations is the family of L-estimators known as trimmed means.

Trimmed means are formed by omitting a fixed proportion α of the lowest and highest sample values and calculating the mean of the remaining observations. Trimming the same proportion of observations from both ends of the distribution gives the family of estimators known as the α-trimmed means, where α is the percentage of trim. Trimmed means give equal weights to all observations in the middle $1-2\alpha$ per cent of the data and zero weight to the rest. The 25 per cent trimmed mean (the mean of the middle half of the data) is known, quite reasonably, as the midmean; and the median is approximately the 50 per cent trimmed mean. Common trim percentages are 5 and 10, although individual circumstances will dictate what is appropriate in each case.

Other L-estimators sometimes used include Winsorized means and those which are linear functions of just some of the order statistics. Winsorized means are defined in a similar way to trimmed means except that instead of omitting 2α per cent of observations, the sample values are replaced by the value of the nearest observation to remain unchanged. Thus the Winsorized mean is based on a transformed sample of size n. One example of an estimator based solely on a few order statistics is Tukey's trimean which is a weighted average of the first, second and third quartiles (with weights of 0.25, 0.50, and 0.25, respectively).

L-estimators are among the commonest robust estimators in everyday use and they have a number of advantages which make them particularly attractive in applied work. First of all, they are easy to calculate either by hand for small batches or by slight adaptations of existing computer programs for the sample mean. For this reason trimmed means and variances are often used in simulation studies as starting points for more sophisticated procedures (for example, Devlin

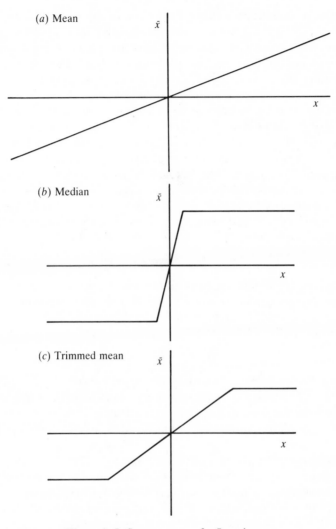

Figure 1. Influence curves for L-estimators.

et al., 1975). A disadvantage of both trimming and Winsorizing is that they down-weight the highest and lowest order statistics whether or not all observations are sound. Thus, a proportion of the data values are always either omitted altogether or have their values changed towards the centre of the distribution. Some statisticians argue that a more efficient procedure will reduce the influence of extreme observations only if not doing so would result in detrimental change in the estimate. It is shown below that M-estimators do precisely that, though the cost is a more complicated computation.

Inspection of the influence curves for several L-estimators (Figure 1) shows that the median and the α-trimmed mean both have bounded influence curves. In other words, there is in each case an upper limit to the amount of influence that a single observation can have on a sample estimate. The influence curve for the median (Figure 1b) has a jump in the middle; and the slope of the curve at that point depends only on the values of two-order statistics.

The α-trimmed mean behaves in the same way as the ordinary mean in the centre, in that the influence of an observation increases with increasing distance from the centre. However, the difference between the two estimators lies in the trim boundary beyond which the influence curve of the trimmed mean is horizontal, corresponding to constant influence. It is important to note that the influence of an extreme outlier on the trimmed mean is not zero as might be supposed. Omitting observations does not mean that they have zero influence; rather, they have influence equal to an additional observation at the trim boundary. This is the highest influence possible!

M-estimators

The second type of estimator includes those in which the influence attached to an observation changes gradually with the distance of the observation from the centre. Maximum likelihood type estimates or M-estimates are solutions T to an equation of the form

$$\sum \psi(x_i - T)/s = 0,$$

where s is a robust measure of spread, estimated either independently of the sample data or simultaneously with the estimate of location. The name M-estimator derives from the similarity between the defining equation above and the equation for obtaining the maximum likelihood estimate for the mean of the normal distribution.

Many different ψ functions have been proposed. They fall into two main classes. The first class includes an M-estimate due to Huber (1964) which is very similar to the trimmed means discussed earlier. For this estimator, $\psi(x)=x$ for all observations in the range $-k<x<k$; $\psi(x)=k$ for observations where $x>k$ and $\psi(x)=-k$ when $x<-k$. The effect of this influence function is to assign constant weight to observations which are more than a certain distance from the centre of the sample (here the distance is referred to as k). The influence curve for the Huber M-estimate is shown in Figure 2a, and the similarity with the influence function for the trimmed mean is obvious. As a consequence of this, it shares the property that the influence of an extreme observation is not zero: as before, omitting an observation does not assign it zero influence.

Recognition of this phenomenon led to the development of other, so called redescending, M-estimators, where the influence curve first increases and then decreases again with increasing distance from the centre. Eventually, the influence assigned to an extreme observation is zero. This type of estimator forms

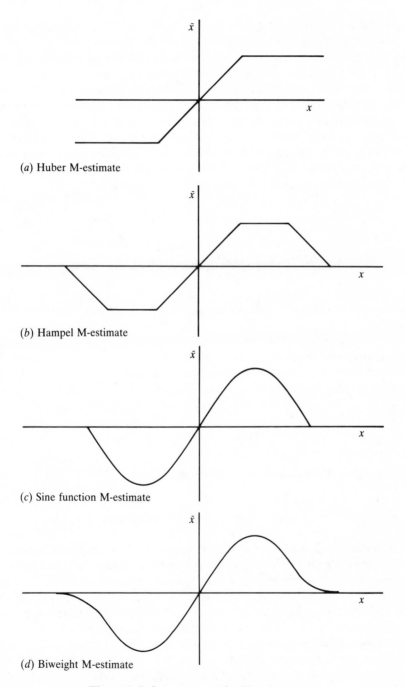

(*a*) Huber M-estimate

(*b*) Hampel M-estimate

(*c*) Sine function M-estimate

(*d*) Biweight M-estimate

Figure 2. Influence curves for M-estimators.

the second main class of M-estimator. Here again, several possibilities exist for the form of the ψ function, and three are presented here.

The simplest redescending adaptation of the Huber estimate is Hampel's (1974) three-part redescending M-estimate whose influence curve is shown in Figure 2b. In the centre of the distribution, the form of the Huber and Hampel estimates is the same. For observations in the range $\pm a$, influence increases with increasing distance from the centre; for observations between a and b, influence is a constant; for values between b and c, the influence of an observation decreases with increasing distance from the centre; while observations greater than c have zero influence and are effectively ignored completely. A formal statement of the ψ function for the three-part redescending estimate is as follows:

$$\psi(x)=\begin{cases} x, & |x|\leqslant a, \\ a\ \text{sgn}\ (x), & a<|x|\leqslant b, \\ a\{c\ \text{sgn}\ (x)-|x|\}/(c-b), & b<|x|\leqslant c, \\ 0, & |x|>c. \end{cases}$$

Reasonable values for a, b and c are suggested as 1.7, 3.4 and 8.5 by Hogg (1979); and Huber (1981) warns against using estimates which redescend too quickly (that is, too steep a slope between b and c).

Both of the M-estimators discussed so far consist of straight-line segments; but other smoother estimators have also been proposed. These include the sine function proposal of Andrews *et al.* (1972) where

$$\psi(x)=\begin{cases} \sin\ (x/d), & |x|<d\pi, \\ 0, & |x|>d\pi. \end{cases}$$

Finally here, Tukey's biweight is defined as

$$\psi(x)=\begin{cases} x(1-x^2)^2, & |x|\leqslant 1, \\ 0, & \text{otherwise.} \end{cases}$$

The influence curves for these two estimators are shown in Figures 2c and 2d.

A common feature of all M-estimators is that they require iteration, since the influence function relies on estimates of both location and spread which in turn depend on the influence function and so on. This makes them more expensive in time and effort than, for instance, the trimmed means described above. Computer programs for these estimators generally begin with simple robust estimates such as the median as an estimate of location and the median absolute deviation (see below) as an estimate of spread. Huber (1981) suggests that in practical work the improvement in performance through using redescending M-estimators is likely to be small compared with the more rough and ready procedures described earlier. If extreme outliers are present then these estimation procedures are certainly beneficial, but the cost of poorly tuned ψ functions may be higher than the gains involved. More experience in routine applied work is clearly required here.

One practical implication of this work on robust M-estimators is to emphasize the importance of the judicious use of transformations before applying any of the estimation procedures described here. Examination of the influence curves in Figure 2 shows that all of the curves are symmetric about the middle. This means that they may only be realistically used on data which are roughly symmetrical. As we know, many types of variable in everyday use in social science do not have this property of symmetry, either because of sampling fluctuations or because the underlying population distribution is not itself symmetrical. For example, measures of response times are generally positively skewed; and in cases such as this, a sensible precaution is to consider a transformation such as the log or square root before calculating M-estimators of location or spread.

Finally, M-estimators form the basis for a great deal of theoretical work on robust alternatives to the standard least squares methods in multivariate analysis, particularly in regression (see Huber, 1981, Ch. 7; Mosteller & Tukey, 1977; Huynh, 1982). Recent developments are thus leading to a coherent body of statistical theory linking robust estimation of location, spread and dependence, which can, in turn, be used in day-to-day work as an alternative to standard least squares methods.

R-estimators

R-estimators are formed from the ranks derived from the ordered sample observations. Replacing the order statistics by their ranks is the basis for many non-parametric tests for differences between groups (for example, the Mann–Whitney test). Other, more complex, R-estimators depend on normal scores formed from the integral of the normal distribution.

Although rank tests have a long history of use in social science, the corresponding family of R-estimators has received comparatively little attention. In part this arises because the other types of estimator (L-estimators and M-estimators) may be placed into broad families of related methods. However, recent work has gone a long way towards remedying this deficiency.

The commonest R-estimator is the Hodges–Lehmann estimator, which is calculated by forming the average of all possible pairs of observations and then taking the median of these $n(n+1)/2$ pairwise averages. Policello & Hettmansperger (1976) introduced an extension of this Hodges–Lehmann estimator which uses a simple weighting function. The result is a family of R-estimators analogous to trimmed means or the simpler M-estimators. The weighting function has the effect of deleting a proportion α of the highest and lowest order statistics and then forming the Hodges–Lehmann estimate from all possible pairwise averages of the remaining observations. The trim proportion may be varied to suit the individual circumstance; and higher trim proportions give additional protection at the cost of lower efficiency. The robustness properties of these R-estimates are rather similar to those of the trimmed means discussed in the previous section.

Moreover, Schrader & McKean (1977) have extended this work on robust R-estimation to the general linear model, including an extended discussion of robust analysis of variance. They argue that 'with "good" data, classical analysis of variance offers a valuable tool for discerning structure in complicated situations. For less restrictive distributional assumptions, there are non-parametric alternatives in certain special cases. A serious criticism is that unlike least squares these methods vary with the problem' (Schrader & McKean, 1977, p. 880). They demonstrate the generality of their proposed solution with examples of analysis of covariance with a test of parallelism of regression lines, and an analysis of a two-way layout with interaction term.

Robust estimation of spread

Far less work has been done on robust estimators of spread as substitutes for the standard deviation. The only robust spread estimate in common use is the median absolute deviation, defined as the median of the absolute deviations from the median – known affectionately as MAD. Dividing the MAD by 0.6745 gives an approximately unbiased estimate of σ for normally distributed data. The main uses of the MAD estimate of spread have been as follows:

(1) As a rough but accurate scale estimate in cases where no higher accuracy is required;
(2) As a check for more refined computations;
(3) As a basis for the rejection of outliers (for example, those observations which are more than three times the MAD from the centre of the data); and
(4) As a starting point for iterative calculation of other robust estimators.

Huber (1981) concludes that it is 'crude but simple and safe'.

Intuitive requirements for robust estimators

This section is based largely on analysis offered by Hampel (1974) of the use of the influence function in robust estimation. He presents a list of seven requirements for good robust estimators.

The first is qualitative robustness; the estimator should react little to small perturbations in the data. Second, it should have a high breakdown point – the borderline beyond which the estimator is totally unreliable. Thus the estimator should also be safe in the presence of large contamination. Third, there should be a bound on the maximum relative influence of a fixed amount of contamination – referred to as a low gross error sensitivity. The worst approximate influence which a fixed amount of contamination can have is often infinite, as it is, for example, for the mean and the standard deviation. Hampel suggests that the most important step for a robust estimator is putting a bound on the influence curve (compare for example the unbounded influence curve for the sample mean in Figure 1a with the bounded curve for the median).

The fourth requirement of a good robust estimator is termed low local shift sensitivity. This refers to the worst approximate effect on the estimator of small perturbations in the data, by rounding, grouping of adjacent values or by local inaccuracies in measuring instruments. A good estimator will react smoothly to such perturbations, and the median comes out particularly badly in this respect. The discontinuity in the middle of the influence curve means that as the sample size approaches infinity so the local shift sensitivity of the median approaches infinity.

The fifth requirement is that the estimator should reject observations which are obviously extreme in relation to the bulk of the data. The rejection point of an estimator defines the point outside which the influence curve is zero; all points outside it are rejected. This point is infinity for the mean and all trimmed means (including the median); and is only below infinity for redescending estimators.

Given all this, the estimator should estimate about the right quantity. One implication of this point is that a good estimator will produce sensible answers in the presence of contamination of the kinds described above; and in the absence of such contamination, will produce answers similar to those given by standard methods. Finally, the estimator should have as small a variance as possible under the ideal parametric model.

Three-part redescending M-estimators possess all of these properties as well as high efficiency at the normal distribution (and at others too). In general though, practical convenience may lead to the choice of estimators such as trimmed means and variances which are easy to calculate even though they do not possess all desirable characteristics.

DO ROBUST ESTIMATORS WORK ON REAL DATA?

The title of this section is taken from that of a paper by Stigler (1977) in an official journal of *The Institute of Mathematical Statistics*. The paper is an important and readable account of the application of 11 estimators of location to several different collections of real (and historically very important) data sets from the physical sciences. The estimators included the mean and median ('two ancient and popular favourites without which no study would be complete', p. 1059), several different trimmed means, three M-estimators, an L-estimator similar to the trimean, and several miscellaneous estimators.

Each estimator was applied to each of 24 data sets and their relative performances were assessed. There is something in his results to confirm everyone's prejudices. The best estimators overall were the lightly trimmed means, with the ordinary 0 per cent trimmed mean not far behind. On average, the median did badly: it seems to have been over-protective and therefore much less efficient than the other estimators. The M-estimators did almost as well as those which were much easier to calculate.

The discussion following the presentation of this study was wide-ranging; and the consensus of views was encouraging for robust estimators. Two main conclusions may be drawn from this study. First, 'there is no practical difference between the class of good robust estimators and the arithmetic mean when these are applied to "clean" sets of data' (Andrews, 1977). In general then, robust estimators do no better than the 'ordinary' estimators for clean data. Second, the behaviour of robust estimators is very much more reliable than that of the standard non-robust methods for data which contain substantial noise or outlying values.

ROBUST ESTIMATION OF STANDARD ERRORS

The focus of attention in the second section of this chapter shifts from the choice of a robust estimator to the assessment of the extent of uncertainty or error about an estimate. The rest of this chapter describes three procedures, one very old and two new, which share the same conceptual base: cross-validation, the jackknife and the bootstrap. Efron & Gong (1983) offer the following trailer for these methods: 'they require very little in the way of modelling, assumptions, or analysis, and can be applied in an automatic way to any situation, no matter how complicated' (p. 36). Such properties make these methods very attractive to the applied researcher; though, as ever, care in the application brings rewards in the results.

Leave-one-out cross-validation

Cross-validation refers to the problem of assessing the error rate of a data-based prediction rule. The derivation of such prediction rules is the motivation behind many applications of discriminant analysis to the job of developing a classification rule for assigning future observations to classes where their class membership is unknown. Another example of the same problem is in personnel selection, where weights derived from regression analysis may be used to combine aspects of qualifications, experience and so on to give a prediction of likely success on the job. In each of these examples, the problem is to predict the value of a new observation drawn from an unknown distribution using an estimate derived from existing data.

A key difficulty in assessing the predictive validity of statistical models such as these is what is generally referred to as shrinkage. Any efficient estimation procedure, such as the robust M-estimation methods discussed above, will milk the data dry by using every idiosyncrasy in the data to improve the result. Testing out a model on the same data as that used to generate it is likely to overestimate the performance of the model on new data. Thus the model will almost certainly work better for these data than for any other. 'The apparent degree of fit will be closer than the true fit, on the average' (Mosteller & Tukey, 1977, p. 37). The aim of cross-validation methods is to assess the difference between the apparent fit and the true fit – the extent of over-optimism.

There are three types of procedures which are useful for validating a statistical model (see Montgomery & Peck, 1982, Ch. 10). The first involves careful comparisons with prior experience, substantive theory in a research area, or with the results of simulation studies. Such comparisons are usually done quite informally, though Bayesian methods can sometimes be brought to bear in a formal manner. The second type of procedure is to collect fresh data and directly compare the new data with predictions from the statistical model derived from previous data. This is obviously the most effective method of validating a model; though often it is not practical. The final way is based on data splitting.

The general principle in this form of cross-validation is to divide the data into two sets: an estimation set and a prediction set. The estimation set is used to develop a model; and the prediction set is used to assess the usefulness of the model. Halving the data and doing the check both ways (Mosteller & Tukey, 1977; Stone, 1974) gives what we may call double cross-validation. Such procedures are indeed useful where the number of observations is large since the precision of estimates for $n/2$ is comparable to that for n. However, for very large samples, shrinkage is usually not a big problem, since the extent of shrinkage varies inversely with sample size. The problem is most acute for small samples; and these are the ones where simple double cross-validation is likely to be least effective.

An alternative which may be more palatable is leave-one-out cross-validation, discussed by Mosteller & Tukey (1977), Stone (1974), Snee (1977), and McCarthy (1976). The procedure here is to set aside an individual case, generate an equation for what is left and then derive a predicted value for the set-aside case. Repeating this process for every case gives the best possible idea from the present data of the likely performance of the model with new data.

Jackknifing

Jackknifing is a very similar procedure to leave-one-out cross-validation; indeed some statisticians consider that the term jackknifing should be used for both. The process of subgrouping is the same, but in jackknifing 'pseudovalues' are calculated for each subgroup that is left out and these pseudovalues are used to derive an estimate of the parameter of interest and of the standard error of that estimate.

There are two contributors to uncertainty or error about an estimate – bias and variability – and the jackknife can be useful in relation to both. First of all, it is known that the jackknife removes bias of the order of $1/n$. This led to a number of early applications in cases such as ratio estimation in survey sampling where standard methods give biased estimates (for other examples, see the review by Miller, 1974).

More recently, however, attention has shifted towards the ability of the jack-knife to give workable estimates of variability – the standard error of an estimate. This can be very useful in two sets of circumstances. Sometimes, theoretical derivation of standard errors is difficult or impossible, and the jackknife is the only practical way of assessing confidence limits for an estimate. For example, the jackknife has been used to estimate standard errors for factor loadings and also for the disattenuated correlation coefficient.

However, the greatest benefits are likely to accrue from the use of the jackknife in routine data analytic practice where it is unrealistic to appeal to a standard parametric distribution. Many statistical tests are known to be robust in the sense that they tend to give similar results for distributions other than those for which the test was developed. In these circumstances it is useful to know to what extent a test result is dependent on distribution assumptions. Comparisons of results from standard procedures with those from application of the jackknife can help the analyst to assess the criticality of his or her assumptions.

The jackknife method is completely general; it applies equally to the estimation of means and standard deviations, regression weights, discriminant functions, factor loadings and so on. The steps involved are as follows:

(1) Obtain the estimate $\hat{\theta}$ based on all the data.

(2) Divide the data into a number of equal sized subgroups, say r subgroups each of size s. If there is a single observation in each subgroup ($s=1$), then the number of subgroups is the same as the number of observations ($r=n$).

(3) Recalculate the estimate omitting each subgroup in turn, to give partial estimates $\hat{\theta}_{-i}$. With s observations in each subgroup there are $r-s$ of these partial estimates, each based on $n-s$ observations.

(4) From each partial estimate, calculate a 'pseudovalue'

$$\hat{\theta}^{\star}_{-i}=r\hat{\theta}-(r-s)\ \hat{\theta}_{-i}.$$

(5) The jackknife estimate, $\hat{\theta}^{\star}$, is formed by taking the mean of the pseudovalues. The standard error of the estimate is simply the standard deviation of the pseudovalues, treating these values as if they were independent observations.

(6) In general, a confidence interval for $\hat{\theta}$ may be estimated as

$$\theta^{\star}\pm t/\text{var}\ (\theta^{\star}),$$

where t is the Student's t with $(r-1)$ degrees of freedom for the required level of confidence.

It is clear from the procedure described above that there are strong similarities between the jackknife and the cross-validation method of the previous section. The partial estimates of step 3 above are the same as the estimates formed in leave-one-out cross-validation. In addition, the pseudovalues calculated at step 4 are almost identical to the values of the sample influence function described earlier in this chapter. The jackknife method differs only in the use made of these estimates.

Hinckley (1978) gives the following example which serves to demonstrate the calculations involved in using the jackknife. It also illustrates the way in which the jackknife can fail in a relatively simple situation. The simulated data were generated in the following way. First, he created 19 pairs of data points observations at random from a bivariate normal distribution with a population correlation of 0.95. Then he added a single outlying observation along an axis orthogonal to the main body of the data.

Column 4 of Table 1 shows the partial estimates of the correlation coefficient for each observation, derived by omitting each observation in turn, and column 5 shows their Fisher's z transform. The partial estimates for the first 19 observations (all of them 'good' data) are very similar in value, but none of them near the true value of 0.95. Only the last partial estimate, derived by omitting the single outlying observation, gives a sensible value. The pseudovalues in the last column are formed by the equation

$$\hat{\theta}^{\star}_{-i} = 20\hat{\theta} - 19\hat{\theta}_{-i},$$

and there is clearly something different about the 20th observation. The jackknife estimate is the average of these pseudovalues.

Table 1. Results of the jackknife method for an artificial data set

	Observations		Partial estimates		Pseudo-
i	$X1$	$X2$	Correlation	z-transform	values
1	0.774	0.693	0.768	1.014	1.720
2	−1.325	−0.650	0.781	1.048	1.069
3	0.148	0.547	0.786	1.060	0.852
4	−1.567	−0.915	0.769	1.017	1.661
5	−0.553	−0.256	0.783	1.053	0.989
6	1.017	0.973	0.757	0.988	2.213
7	0.092	0.192	0.781	1.048	1.078
8	−1.211	−1.142	0.759	0.994	2.105
9	−1.264	−1.350	0.754	0.983	2.314
10	1.013	0.960	0.757	0.989	2.197
11	−0.447	−0.320	0.781	1.047	1.094
12	−0.917	−0.764	0.772	1.025	1.517
13	−0.841	−0.778	0.772	1.026	1.487
14	0.428	0.486	0.776	1.035	1.320
15	0.042	−0.223	0.784	1.056	0.927
16	1.017	1.032	0.756	0.986	2.252
17	0.020	−0.516	0.793	1.078	0.498
18	0.423	0.516	0.776	1.036	1.314
19	−0.164	0.129	0.785	1.058	0.883
20	1.000	−1.000	0.943	1.762	−12.491

Table 2. Estimates for data shown in Table 1

	z transform	Correlation coefficient
Standard method	1.05	0.78
Jackknife estimate	0.75	0.64
5 per cent trimmed jackknife	1.40	0.89

The jackknife estimate of the correlation coefficient based on all 20 observations is shown in Table 2, together with the total sample correlation coefficient. Both underestimate the known true value of 0.95 (for 19 of the 20 observations) by a large amount. The jackknife estimate has clearly been affected by the single outlying observation which has a large negative pseudovalue. One solution to this problem suggested by Hinckley is to use a robust estimator rather than the arithmetic mean of the pseudovalues in order to reduce the influence of outlying values. He discusses the use of M-estimates, though for practical work trimmed means are easier to use. Table 2 shows the estimate based on a 5 per cent trimmed mean of the pseudovalues, and this gives a great improvement.

The thing to note is that the jackknife is not a device for correcting outliers. A key assumption in using the jackknife is that all observations are independently, identically sampled from a single unknown distribution. Thus the jackknife can and does fail when outliers are present in the data. In this respect the jackknife differs sharply from the robust estimation procedures described earlier which dealt automatically with outliers by reducing their influence on the sample estimate.

Experience in using the jackknife suggests that variance stabilizing transformations should routinely accompany the jackknife procedure. Transformations are needed to keep jackknife estimates within sensible limits and to prevent distortion of results. Thus inferences about sample variances using the jackknife may produce negative pseudovalues since the jackknife does not know that variances must be positive. Jackknifing log variances is therefore preferred to jackknifing variances. Similarly, Miller (1974) gives an example of jackknifing the product moment correlation where one pseudovalue is above 1. The Fisher z transform of the sample correlation coefficient should replace r itself, as in the worked example. Cressie (1981) gives formal analytic support to these intuitions.

Most discussions of the jackknife assume simple random samples with no built-in structure. This is the basis for deleting only a single observation at a time. Farewell (1978) shows that the grouping of observations which is necessary in order to apply the jackknife method should reflect any pattern or special structure in the data (indeed he argues that only in this way is first-order bias eliminated). Thus, an experimental design may consist of an equal number of observations in each of several groups. To maintain this structure, pseudovalues should be calculated by removing an equal number of observations from each group. Where group sizes are not equal, say where group 1 has 20 observations and group 2 has 10 observations, then the 2:1 ratio in sample sizes should be reflected by removing one observation from group 2 and two from group 1.

Finally, it should be remembered that the jackknife is known to fail in some circumstances. In particular, estimators based on single order statistics do not behave properly under jackknifing. The best known example is the sample median (the middle order statistic), whose influence curve has a discontinuity in the middle (see Figure 1 above). Another case known to be suspect is estimating the maximum (the largest order statistic).

The Bootstrap

Another non-parametric method for attaching standard errors to an estimate is the bootstrap (Efron, 1979, 1981). This method has only recently appeared in the statistical literature and theoretical development is running ahead of practical experience. However, early results are promising and it is clear that the approach underlying the bootstrap is one that social scientists should know about.

In order to estimate the standard error of, for example, a correlation coefficient, a median or a difference between means, it is necessary to know the form of the population distribution from which the sample estimate is drawn. If the form of that population distribution is known then the standard error of an estimate can often be calculated quite simply. For example, the standard error of a Fisher z transformed correlation coefficient is $1/(n-3)$, where n is the sample size, on the assumption that the data are a random sample from a bivariate normal distribution. If this assumption cannot be relied upon then neither can the estimate of standard error based on it.

The aim of the bootstrap is to estimate standard errors without making any assumptions about the form of the population distribution. The principle underlying the bootstrap is the simple one that all the evidence we have about the parent distribution comes from the distribution of the sample data itself. If we take this empirical distribution as an approximation to the unknown parent distribution then we can generate the bootstrap distribution of our estimate by taking repeated samples from the empirical distribution. The standard error of our estimate is then simply the standard deviation of all of the estimates in the bootstrap distribution.

Efron & Gong (1983, p. 37) give a simple example of the bootstrap in action. They report data from 15 classes in American law schools in 1973 (see Table 3). The two variables are average LSAT scores (a national attainment test) and average grade point average (GPA) scores. The Pearson product moment correlation for $n=15$ pairs of points is 0.776.

Applying the bootstrap involves a number of steps. First, choose a sample size for each bootstrap sample; this will usually be the same as the number of observations in the sample data, but either larger or smaller values are possible. In

Table 3. Law school data set from Efron & Gong (1983)

(*a*) Data set

	LSAT	GPA
1	576	3.39
2	635	3.30
3	558	2.81
4	578	3.03
5	666	3.44
6	580	3.07
7	555	3.00
8	661	3.43
9	651	3.36
10	605	3.13
11	653	3.12
12	575	2.74
13	545	2.76
14	572	2.88
15	594	2.96

(*b*) Five bootstrap samples

{2, 7, 7, 9, 3, 9, 2, 9, 4, 5, 7, 2, 4, 7, 14}
{12, 8, 14, 6, 4, 13, 3, 6, 11, 12, 11, 9, 10, 12, 12}
{3, 6, 1, 13, 5, 10, 9, 10, 6, 13, 7, 9, 9, 3, 15}
{13, 13, 6, 2, 14, 10, 1, 3, 2, 5, 2, 13, 10, 2, 4}
{14, 6, 10, 15, 8, 3, 4, 11, 5, 6, 14, 7, 1, 14, 9}

this worked example bootstrap samples of size 15 are drawn – the same size as the data set.

Select observations for inclusion in a bootstrap sample by drawing random numbers in the range 1 to n (in this case 15). Note that this gives sampling with replacement, so that the bootstrap sample may contain an element of the empirical data more than once. Table 3b shows five bootstrap samples, each selected using random number tables. Taking all of the samples together, it may be seen that each observation in the original data appears at least once, and also that every bootstrap sample contains duplicated observations.

The next step is to calculate the parameter of interest, in this case a correlation coefficient, in the usual way from each bootstrap sample. The bootstrap estimate of the standard error of the sample correlation coefficient is simply the standard deviation of the correlation derived from the bootstrap samples. Figure 3, taken from Efron & Gong (1983), shows the histogram of 1000 bootstrap samples for the law school data together with the smooth distribution derived from normal theory. For this example, the bootstrap estimate of the standard error is 0.127 compared with a normal theory estimate of 0.115.

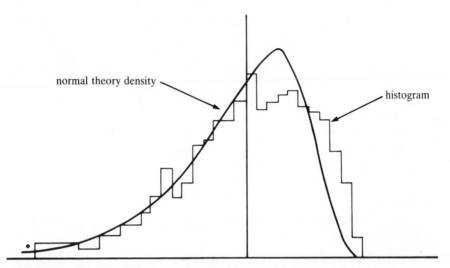

normal theory density

histogram

Figure 3. Histogram of 1000 bootstrap replications, with distribution derived from normal theory (from Efron & Gong, 1983).

There is little guidance yet about how many bootstrap samples need to be drawn for the method to work well. It is likely to vary with quantity to be estimated; though Efron (1981) suggests that generally little is gained by taking more than about 100 bootstrap samples.

Like the methods discussed earlier – cross-validation and the jackknife – the bootstrap assumes independent and identical sampling from a common unknown distribution. In other words, the bootstrap is not a device for correcting observations from a different distribution other than that of the bulk of the data, so that some initial exploratory graphical work is wise. It would also make sense to consider bootstrapping robust estimates such as those discussed in the first half of this chapter rather than their non-robust cousins.

Comparisons between the performance of cross-validation, jackknifing and bootstrapping for estimating the uncertainty of sample estimates shows that they perform about equally well; though, in most cases, the bootstrap does slightly better. One interesting point is that the bootstrap is able to generate correct estimates for the standard error of the sample median, which the jackknife cannot do. This suggests that the bootstrap may be more generally useful than the jackknife, though a great deal more practical experience is clearly required.

CONCLUSIONS

We have covered a great deal of ground in this chapter. The first part described a number of estimators which are robust alternatives to standard estimators, and also recounted several principles which underlie the theory of robust estimation. One recurring theme of this section is that calculating a measure of location, spread or anything else is a choice. Choosing to use an arithmetic mean or a median implies a concern or lack of concern with the influence of each observation on the sample estimate. Robust estimators automatically adjust for outlying observations but they do not thereby absolve the user from thinking hard about his or her data. The second part of the chapter was concerned with deriving standard errors for sample estimates. Combining robust estimators with nonparametric estimates of their standard errors gives a powerful and safe collection of statistical tools for the applied worker.

References

ANDREWS, D.F. (1977). Discussion of Stigler. *Annals of Statistics, 5*, 1055–1098.
ANDREWS, D.F., BICKEL, P.J., HAMPEL, F.R., HUBER, P.J., ROGERS, W.H. & TUKEY, J.W. (1972). *Robust Estimators of Location: Survey and Advances*. Princeton: Princeton University Press.
ATKINSON, A.C. (1982). Regression diagnostics, transformations and constructed variables. *Journal of the Royal Statistical Society, Series B, 44*, 1–36.
BELSLEY, D., KUH, E. & WELSCH, R.E. (1980). *Regression Diagnostics: Identifying Influential Data and Some Sources of Collinearity*. New York: Wiley.
BOX, G.E.P. (1979). Robustness in the strategy of scientific model building. In: R. L. Launer & G. N. Wilkinson (eds) *Robustness in Statistics*. New York: Academic Press.
BOX, G.E.P. (1980). Sampling and Bayes' inference in scientific modelling and robustness. *Journal of the Royal Statistical Society, Series A, 143*, 383–430.
COOK, R.D. (1977). Detection of influential observations in linear regression. *Technometrics, 19*, 15–18.
CRESSIE, N. (1981). Transformations and the jackknife. *Journal of the Royal Statistical Society, Series B, 43*, 177–182.
DEVLIN, S.J., GNANADESIKAN, R. & KETTENRING, J.R. (1975). Robust estimation and outlier detection with correlation coefficients. *Biometrika, 62*, 531–545.
EFRON, B. (1979). Bootstrap methods: another look at the jackknife. *Annals of Statistics, 7*, 1-26.
EFRON, B. (1981). Nonparametric estimates of standard error: the jackknife, the bootstrap and other methods. *Biometrika, 68*, 589–599.
EFRON, E. & GONG, G. (1983). A leisurely look at the bootstrap, the jackknife, and cross-validation. *The American Statistician, 37*, 36–48.
FAREWELL, V. T. (1978). Jackknife estimation with structured data. *Biometrika, 65*, 444–447.
HAMPEL, F. R. (1974). The influence curve and its role in robust estimation. *Journal of the American Statistical Association, 69*, 383–393.
HETTMANSPERGER, T. P. & UTTS, J. M. (1977). Robustness properties for a simple class of rank estimates. *Communications in Statistics – Theory and Methods, A6*, 855–868.
HINCKLEY, D. V. (1978). Improving the jackknife with special reference to correlation estimation. *Biometrika, 65*, 13–21.
HOAGLIN, D.C., MOSTELLER, F. & TUKEY, J.W. (1983). *Understanding Robust and Exploratory Data Analysis*. New York: Wiley.
HOGG, R.V. (1979). An introduction to robust estimation. In: R. L. Launer & G. N. Wilkinson (eds) *Robustness in Statistics*. New York: Academic Press.

HUBER, P.J. (1964). Robust estimation of a location parameter. *Annals of Mathematical Statistics, 35,* 73–101.

HUBER, P.J. (1972). Robust statistics: a review. *Annals of Mathematical Statistics, 43,* 1041–1067.

HUBER, P.J. (1981). *Robust Statistics.* New York: Wiley.

HUYNH, H. (1982). A comparison of four approaches to robust regression. *Psychological Bulletin, 92,* 505–512.

McCARTHY, P.J. (1976). The use of balanced half-sample replication in cross-validation studies. *Journal of the American Statistical Association, 44,* 596–604.

MILLER, R.G. (1974). The jackknife – a review. *Biometrika, 61,* 1–15.

MONTGOMERY, D.C. & PECK, E.A. (1982). *Introduction to Linear Regression Analysis.* New York: Wiley.

MOSTELLER, F. & TUKEY, J.W. (1977). *Data Analysis and Regression.* Reading, Massachusetts: Addison-Wesley.

POLICELLO, G.E. & HETTMANSPERGER, T.P. (1976). Adaptive robust procedures for the one-sample location problem. *Journal of the American Statistical Association, 71,* 624–633.

SCHRADER, R.M. & McKEAN, J.W. (1977). Robust analysis of variance. *Communication in Statistics – Theory and Methods, A6,* 879–894.

SNEE, R.D. (1977). Validation of regression models: methods and examples. *Technometrics, 19,* 415–428.

STIGLER, S.M. (1977). Do robust estimators work with real data? *Annals of Statistics, 5,* 1055–1098.

STONE, M. (1974). Cross-validatory choice and assessment of statistical predictions. *Journal of the Royal Statistical Society, Series B, 36,* 111–147.

THISSEN, D., BAKER, L. & WAINER, H. (1981). Influence-enhanced scatterplots. *Psychological Bulletin, 90,* 179–184.

TUKEY, J.W. (1977). *Exploratory Data Analysis.* Reading, Massachusetts: Addison-Wesley.

VELLEMAN, P.F. & HOAGLIN, D.C. (1981). *Applications, Basics and Computing of Exploratory Data Analysis.* Boston, Massachusetts: Duxbury Press.

VELLEMAN, P.F. & WELSCH, R.E. (1981). Efficient computing of regression diagnostics. *The American Statistician, 35,* 234–242.

3
Identifying Outliers

PATRICIA LOVIE

In the early part of the nineteenth century, an edition of France's *Le Demimonde* might have run the following story.

DON DOCTORS DATA

The academic community was stunned yesterday when it was revealed that Professor A. M. Legendre, the eminent mathematician and astronomer, has admitted publicly to discarding data which appeared to conflict with his predictions.

Commenting on the affair, Professor D. Bernoulli of Basle, who is acknowledged to be an authority on the mathematical combination of astronomical data, today stated that no observations should be rejected solely because they seemed inconsistent with the rest of the data.

Professor Legendre's admission has also attracted criticism from as far afield as Germany, where Herr F. W. Bessel of the Prussian Observatory in Königsberg is reported as saying that all observations should contribute equally to results.

A statement from Professor Legendre's laboratory at the École Normale in Paris is expected later today.

Setting side the obvious liberties taken, not least with dates, reputations and newspapers, Legendre's dilemma – what to do with observations which just do not look right – is still faced by modern experimenters. Nor, incidentally, have attitudes changed much in well over a century: radical Legendrians see no reason to allow a few anomalous observations to spoil a good theory, whilst reactionary Besselites (Bayesians?) scarcely admit to the possibility of 'bad' data.

So, who is right? The answer, of course, is neither and both; it all depends on why the data were collected, how they will be analysed and, fundamentally, why the deviant values arose in the first place.

Many authors refer to any value which appears to the observer to be unrepresentative as an 'outlier'. For example:

> The outliers are values which seem either too large or too small as compared to the rest of the observations (Gumbel, 1960).

44

An outlying observation, or outlier, is one that appears to deviate markedly from the other members of the sample in which it occurs (Grubbs, 1969).

[An outlier would be] an observation which deviates so much from other observations as to arouse suspicions that it was generated by a different mechanism (Hawkins, 1980).

Although these definitions imply only some subjective judgement, the term 'outlier' is often used to mean a value which is discordant on some objective criterion too. To avoid possible confusion, the terms 'outlier' and 'discordant' will be applied only to an observation or set of observations which is judged to be inconsistent with the rest of the sample on objective grounds (following Collett & Lewis, 1976); other observations, or those not yet subjected to such a test, may be 'surprising' or 'deviant', etc.

The presence of an outlier, or a set of outliers, in a sample signals a failure somewhere along the line. The fault may be a mistaken assumption about the data generating mechanism; alternatively, measurement errors or execution errors may have been made in collecting the data. How outliers are generated largely determines how they are dealt with in subsequent data analysis.

Some aberrant observations will be obviously deterministic in origin. For example, only an error in recording (a measurement error) could explain these data on the number of filled teeth in a sample of six (or is it seven?) nine-year-old school children:

$$2 \quad 41 \quad 0 \quad 0 \quad 3 \quad 1.$$

Execution errors too may be of a deterministic nature. Yates (1935), for example, found that human observers selected samples of wheat shoots 'with perhaps a special preference for the very tall shoots'; in other words, the samples obtained were inadvertently biased. Surely even Bessel would have agreed that spurious observations which can be explained in these terms should be rejected outright, or corrected or replaced when this is possible.

How to proceed with outliers which arise from random or otherwise inexplicable sources is less clear cut, mainly because it is uncertain whether these observations are actually 'bad'. Note that surprising values are usually confirmed (or otherwise) as outliers on some objective statistical criterion, where this criterion is a discordancy test based on an assumed initial data generator for the sample (see later sections). Once more, rejection of the offending observation, or set of observations, is in prospect. But such a move should be limited to situations when the initial model is known with certainty.

In fact, the practice of rejection appears to have been widespread amongst eighteenth- and nineteenth-century astronomers (see, for example, Barnett & Lewis, 1978), which is perhaps a little surprising since outliers might have been expected to be of considerable intrinsic interest. However, astronomy appears not to be the only area of science in which rejection has been widely practised. As an instance, the notebooks of the early twentieth-century physicist Millikan indicate that he discarded many observations in his attempts to determine the charge on the electron (Holton, 1981). Presumably, like the astronomers, Millikan was so sure of his theory that he felt justified in rejecting discrepant data and, incidentally, omitting to report the fact in his published work!

Undoubtedly the easiest way of dealing with outliers is to accommodate them by using robust methods in subsequent inference (see Chapter 2 by Jackson). In this way, outliers may be, for example, downgraded (by Winsorizing) or effectively rejected (by trimming). Note that formal outlier tests may not be needed if robust methods for estimation and testing are preferred because, for example, of uncertainty about the underlying model of the data.

However, when it is important to retain a model specific approach, the form of the data generating process should be broadened to one which will incorporate the discordant values. For instance, the whole sample may have arisen from a longer-tailed distribution than was supposed, or from one which was skewed rather than symmetric. Alternatively, it might be reasonable to suppose that two different distributions have generated the 'inlier' and 'outlier' parts of the sample. So what happens to the outliers if the sample has arisen from this mixture? In some situations, the outlier group may be of interest in its own right; for example, a side effect from a drug might show up in only a small number of individuals, but further investigation of such individuals would be essential in addition to pursuing the initial line of study. On the other hand, it may be reasonable to ascribe the outliers to execution error and thus reject them as contaminants (*pace* Bessel!).

The alternative and mixture model approaches to outliers are illustrated in two studies by Box & Tiao (1962, 1968), although, in fact, they were concerned ultimately with estimation. Darwin's data on the differences in heights of cross- and self-fertilized plants (given by Fisher, 1960) were examined on the initial assumption of a normal model $N(\mu, \sigma^2)$. The data are given below in numerical order:

$$
\begin{array}{rrrrr}
-67 & -48 & 6 & 8 & 14 \\
16 & 23 & 24 & 28 & 29 \\
41 & 49 & 56 & 60 & 75.
\end{array}
$$

The values -67 and -48 are surprising. However, these values were not discrepant if the parent population was supposed to be skewed (Box & Tiao, 1962). In an alternative approach in 1968, Box & Tiao assumed that the deviant observations had arisen from a normal distribution with a larger variance than the remainder of the sample.

DETECTING OUTLIERS

Outlier detection is generally thought of as a problem in hypothesis testing but, in fact, the initial stage of the procedure is frequently a subjective judgement about the consistency, or otherwise, of the sample. In Collett & Lewis's (1976) words:

> Any sample might contain an outlier, but only samples judged to contain surprising values can produce detected . . . outliers.

In other words, unless suspicious observations are obviously present, no formal test is likely to be carried out.

As Collett & Lewis (1976) point out, the consequence of such a departure from conventional hypothesis testing practice is that the usual interpretation of the significance level of a formal outlier detection test is no longer valid since Type I (and, for that matter, Type II) error probabilities clearly depend on initial subjective judgements. However, the obtained significance levels *are* meaningful when automatic screening for outliers is a routine part of data analysis.

Subjectivity in outlier detection

The subjective aspect of outlier detection has been largely ignored by statisticians and psychologists alike. Only two studies (Collett & Lewis, 1976; Lovie, 1982) have addressed themselves directly to the perception of outliers. In both investigations, relatively naïve subjects were presented with normal samples containing outliers of varying degrees of discordancy and were asked to decide whether or not the samples contained outliers. The results clearly showed that the perception of inconsistency in a sample was affected, not only by obvious factors such as the degree of discordancy, but also by factors which should have been irrelevant. These included the pattern of the data and method of presentation (Collett & Lewis, 1976) and whether the observation was the upper or lower extreme (Lovie, 1982).

However, most importantly, the judgements were influenced by the spread of the observations. In consequence, too many perfectly acceptable observations are perceived as discordant, particularly when sample variability is high. (But take heart – according to Hawkins (1980), seeing too many outliers is not restricted to statistical novices!)

Simple aids to detecting outliers

It is common practice amongst statisticians to plot data in some suitable form, for example, as stem-and-leaf plots, boxplots, scatterplots or as graphs of residuals (see Chapter 1 by Seheult). Examination of the plotted observations will reveal important features of the data such as location, spread and shape and may also point to outlier candidates.

In addition, there are a few rules of thumb ('quick and exceedingly dirty' methods) which provide simple criteria for judging whether or not the sample contains discordant values. As a general rule, observations more than about three standard deviations from the mean would be considered suspicious. (Note that if the mean and standard deviation are estimated from the sample, the 'outliers' are assumed to be omitted from the calculation.) Similar rules which require less calculation use robust estimators of spread. Possible outliers are any observations more than one and a half times the midspread (interquartile range) beyond the quartiles (easily calculated from a stem-and-leaf plot or a boxplot) or more than three times the median absolute deviation (MAD) from the centre of the data (see Chapter 2 by Jackson).

The last two rules, which rely on robust estimators, are applicable only to samples from symmetric distributions. The rule based on the standard deviation is even more restrictive in expecting at least approximate normality. Unfortunately, there seem to be no equivalent rules of thumb for detecting outliers in skewed distributions or in more complex situations.

Another outlier detection aid is to compute robust estimates routinely alongside the usual least squares estimates: any differences may be due to outliers. This method may be particularly useful in linear regression with bivariate data.

An alternative rule of thumb for linear regression in the multivariate case, suggested by Andrews & Pregibon (1978), compares the residual sums of squares (after least squares fit) with and without the suspected outliers. If dropping these values shrinks the residual sum of squares by a considerable amount, they are probably outliers. They make the further point that only deviant values which substantially reduce the determinant $|X'X|$, where the columns of X correspond to the independent variables, actually matter. Andrews & Pregibon also propose a formal diagnostic test, combining these two ideas, which provides a measure of the collective influence of a set of extreme values.

Formal outlier detection tests

In common with any other statistical test, an outlier detection test chooses between two competing hypotheses; the null, or working, hypothesis, which states the basic data generating model, is retained or rejected on some statistical criterion in favour of an alternative hypothesis which accounts for the presence of outliers. For example, the null hypothesis may be that the sample arises from a normal distribution with a specified mean and variance whilst the alternative hypothesis may be that one or more of the observations come from some other distribution. Both the null and alternative hypotheses must be specified so that percentage points for the test statistic and the performance of the test, respectively, can be determined.

In general, setting up a null hypothesis presents few difficulties since judging an observation, or set of observations, to be suspicious implies some initial knowledge or belief about the underlying model. On the other hand, formulating an appropriate alternative hypothesis is far less straightforward and, as will be seen, little heed is taken of the subjective nature of the initial identification of outlier candidates.

Barnett & Lewis (1978) distinguish five classes of alternative hypothesis, each reflecting a different outlier generating model. Three of these are described below in relation to a random sample $x_1, x_2, \ldots, x_n$ which is assumed to be drawn from a population with distribution F.

(i) Inherent alternative

Under this model, the outliers themselves are of no intrinsic interest but are thought to be symptomatic of an inappropriate data generating model. In other words, the presence of surprising values in a sample may suggest that the inherent variability of the basic model has been underestimated or was of a different form. The null hypothesis

$$H_0: x_i \ (i=1, 2, \ldots, n) \text{ arose from distribution } F$$

is tested against the alternative

$$H_A: x_i \ (i=1, 2, \ldots, n) \text{ arose from distribution } G.$$

F and G may be different distributions, for example, normal and log-normal, or may be distinct members of the same family, for example, normal distributions with different variances.

(ii) Mixture alternative

Under this alternative, the sample is assumed to contain a small proportion of observations from a distribution which is different from the basic model. These contaminating values show themselves as outliers. The hypotheses are:

$$H_0: x_i \ (i=1, 2, \ldots, n) \text{ arose from } F,$$
$$H_A: x_i \ (i=1, 2, \ldots, n) \text{ arose from } (1-\lambda) F + \lambda G,$$

where λ is the (small) proportion of observations coming from distribution G.

As with the inherent alternative hypothesis, F and G may be different distributions or belong to the same family of distributions.

(iii) Slippage alternative

The slippage hypothesis is easily the most common of the outlier generating models. Outliers are accounted for as observations arising from a distribution G, which has the same form as F but with a parameter which has shifted in value. Typically, if F has mean μ and variance of σ^2, then with slippage of location, or of dispersion, respectively, G would have mean $\mu + a \ (a \neq 0)$ or variance $b\sigma^2 \ (b > 1)$.

Hypotheses for the single outlier problem are expressed as:

$$H_0: x_i \ (i=1, 2, \ldots, n) \text{ arose from } F,$$
$$H_A: x_i \ (i \neq j) \text{ arose from } F \text{ and } x_j \text{ arose from } G.$$

It is worth noting that an outlier test under the slippage alternative hypothesis is a special case of a slippage test in which the equality of several populations is assessed against the alternative that one of the populations has 'slipped' (see, for example, Barnett & Lewis, 1978; David, 1981).

A point that needs to be made here is that, unlike the inherent type of alternative hypothesis under which outliers are regarded only as a symptom of an incorrect assumption about the data generating model, the mixture and slippage alternatives actually indicate a small proportion or a small number of contaminating observations. And yet, neither of these alternative hypotheses points to those particular surprising values which motivate embarking on a formal test. For example, the null hypothesis that the data generator is a $N(\mu, \sigma^2)$ distribution is tested only against the (slippage) alternative that one, *unspecified*, member of the sample has arisen from a $N(\mu+a, \sigma^2)$ $(a>0)$ distribution, even though the upper extreme value might be the natural choice. Although a modified form of the slippage hypothesis, known as labelled slippage, denotes the extremes as the only possible candidates, tests under this formulation have not been widely studied. As a consequence, the extreme values are only implicitly identified as outliers in most outlier detection tests.

Measuring test performance

Although the ideal statistical test would be uniformly most powerful, this is a virtually unattainable goal in the outlier detection context. Usually, the best that can be expected is that tests will have properties such as local optimality or invariance to location or scale (dispersion) changes, or will conform to, say, the likelihood ratio principle.

In general, a viable outlier test should exhibit at least one of the above characteristics and have a tractable distributional form for the test statistic under the null hypothesis and, preferably, to allow power calculations, under the alternative hypothesis as well. Interestingly, many outlier tests, which were originally conceived in a somewhat *ad hoc* fashion as a decision rule based on an intuitively reasonable test statistic, have subsequently emerged as, in some senses, the best available tests.

Since globally optimal tests are effectively ruled out, how can the behaviour of the available tests be compared? David & Paulson (1965; see also David, 1981) proposed five performance criteria. Three of these are generally applicable (Barnett & Lewis, 1978; Hawkins, 1980):

P_1: the probability that the test correctly declares an outlier – that is, the power of the test.

P_2: the probability that the test correctly declares an outlier and correctly identifies it as the extreme.

P_3: the probability that the test correctly declares an outlier when the contaminant is the extreme – that is, the conditional power.

It is worth noting that when the distribution of the contaminants is markedly different from that of the 'good' data, the contaminant is increasingly likely to be an extreme value. Thus, the values of all three measures will be similar. A good test, therefore, requires not only that P_1 and P_3 should be high, but also that the difference between P_1 and P_2 should be small.

Although it is sometimes possible to compare the performances of tests using power values that have been obtained analytically or by numerical integration techniques, in many instances simulation methods provide the most feasible solution. For example, Kimber (1979) generated different size gamma samples and adjusted one of the observations in each sample by varying amounts so that it became a single contaminant from a gamma population with a larger scale parameter. He compared several tests by calculating power measures P_1 and P_3 for different sample sizes at fixed significance levels. Dixon (1962) and Tietjen & Moore (1972) have also used simulation methods to compare several outlier tests for normal samples.

However, a graphical method, which avoids the necessity of spelling out the alternative hypothesis, seems to have considerable practical advantages over comparisons based on power considerations. This informal method uses sensitivity contours which are functions showing the effect on the test statistic of additional observations of varying magnitudes. In other words, sensitivity contours are direct analogues of the influence curves for assessing the robustness of estimators which were discussed by Jackson in Chapter 2. Sensitivity contour methods have been used to compare tests for detecting outliers in normal (Prescott, 1976, 1978), exponential (Kimber, 1982; Kimber & Stevens, 1981) and gamma samples (Kimber, 1979, 1983).

Types of test statistic

Test statistics for outliers detection tests fall into two broad categories: 'departure from model' statistics (Hawkins, 1980) and those which assess the separation of the suspicious observation from the remainder of the sample relative to the variability of the sample. The latter will be referred to as 'extreme standardized deviate' statistics.

Departure from model statistics

Since the presence of outliers might be symptomatic of a departure from, say, normality, measures associated with 'goodness of fit' could form the basis of an outlier test. Tests for normality based on skewness and kurtosis measures have been found to be particularly effective in outlier detection, especially in the presence of several outliers (Ferguson, 1961). Another measure which seems to have attracted something of a following is the Shapiro–Wilk W goodness of fit statistic for normal and exponential parent populations (Shapiro & Wilk, 1965, 1972), even though doubts have been expressed about its power as an outlier detector (Tiku, 1975). As alternatives, Hawkins (1980) waxes enthusiastic about test statistics which both focus on the quality of fit in the tails of the distribution and are applicable to a wide range of models. Unfortunately, since tabulated critical values do not seem to be available, tests based on these statistics are of little practical value at present.

Extreme standardized deviate statistics

A bewildering number and variety of test statistics can be included under this label – almost 50 different versions for normal samples alone are listed by Barnett & Lewis (1978). Fortunately, they can be classified under a few broad headings (Barnett & Lewis, 1978; Tietjen & Moore, 1972). Different forms within each class generally reflect the amount of information known about the underlying data generating model or about the number of observations that might be outliers and where they are likely to be located in the ordered sample.

(a) **Deviation/spread statistics.** These are deviations of extreme sample members (either upper or lower) from a measure of location standardized by (that is, divided by) a measure of spread. The mean and standard deviation are the usual measures, although they can be population values, or independent estimates, or internal estimates obtained from the complete or the reduced sample. (Note that the sample can be reduced by excluding any suspicious observations, whether in the upper or lower tails of the sample.)

(b) **Range/spread statistics.** These are ratios of the sample range to some other measure of spread, usually the standard deviation in one of the forms mentioned above.

(c) **Spacing/spread statistics.** Spacing/spread statistics are ratios of the spacings between extreme and neighbouring observations to the range of the whole or the reduced sample, or to another measure of spread, again usually the standard deviation.

(d) **Sums of squares statistics.** These statistics are expressed as ratios of sums of squared deviations for the reduced sample to that of the complete sample, or to the population variance.

(e) **Miscellaneous statistics.** Inevitably, the influence (stranglehold?) of the normal distribution as a general purpose model has shown itself in the outlier field – in the volume of research work and even in this classification scheme: statistics relevant to testing for outliers in other distributions do not always fall so neatly into pigeonholes. One distinct type of statistic, however, is important when the data generating model is from the gamma family of distributions; these statistics are ratios of extreme values to measures of location.

Some problems

Many of the commonly used outlier tests, some of which are even 'best' tests in certain circumstances, have shortcomings. For example, in tests of the range/spread type, the statistic would be of the form

$$(x_{(n)}-x_{(1)})/s,$$

where $x_{(1)}$ and $x_{(n)}$ are the upper and lower extremes of a sample of size n and s is some other measure of spread. All that a significant outcome indicates is that either $x_{(n)}$ or $x_{(1)}$ (or perhaps both) is an outlier.

Two other inherent defects are, however, potentially more serious. Suppose that the upper extreme observation of a sample is judged to be sufficiently surprising to warrant a formal test for discordancy and that a non-significant result is obtained using, say, a deviation/spread statistic

$$(x_{(n)}-\bar{x})/s,$$

where $x_{(n)}$ is the upper extreme and $\bar{x}$ and s are the sample mean and standard deviation, respectively. Now, the non-significant result may have been obtained because $x_{(n)}$ is a perfectly acceptable sample point. Unfortunately, another possibility exists: $x_{(n)}$'s nearest neighbour, or perhaps $x_{(1)}$, might also be an outlier, but be an unidentified candidate. The effect of this missed outlier on the estimates of the mean and standard deviation may well be sufficient to 'mask' the discordancy of $x_{(n)}$. In other words, an outlier test is vulnerable to masking if it fails to detect, say, one outlier when at least two outliers are contained in the sample.

Suppose, for example, that a test for an upper outlier is carried out on the following ordered sample

$$5 \quad 11 \quad 12 \quad 14 \quad 14 \quad 16 \quad 23.$$

The upper extreme 23 may not be declared as an outlier because of the masking effect of the almost equally discrepant lower extreme value. The masking effect for the deviation/spread statistic mentioned above is shown clearly on Prescott's sensitivity contour diagram (Prescott, 1978).

Masking can be a particularly serious problem in test procedures for multiple outliers; both the block and sequential test approaches are susceptible in different ways.

In a sequential procedure one outlier candidate is tested at a time; if this is declared to be an outlier, the next candidate is tested, otherwise the process terminates, and so on. In many sequential procedures the most extreme value is tested first. If this produces a significant result, the discordant value is excluded from the sample and the test is repeated on the reduced sample. The process terminates when a non-significant result is obtained. Clearly, masking could lead to a non-significant result on the first test even if several outliers are contained in the sample.

More recently, an 'inside out' sequential procedure has been suggested by Rosner (1975). Suppose that a sample contains at most k outliers. The values of all k test statistics for the reduced samples are obtained. However, the kth most extreme candidate is tested first. If this is declared discordant, then k outliers must be contained in the sample; if the result is not significant, the $(k-1)$th most extreme value is then tested. The process ends either after k tests (in which case, no discordant values are declared) or when a significant result is obtained. Provided that the chosen value of k is sufficiently large, masking should not occur.

In a block procedure all k possible outliers are examined in a single test, on the basis of which all k observations are declared either to be outliers or to be consistent with the remainder of the sample. Although outliers can be masked if the chosen value of k is too small, and in some circumstances missed if k is too large, block procedures are prone to an additional type of hazard if k is too large. 'Swamping' can occur if the m outliers ($m<k$) are so separated from the rest of the sample that the remaining $k-m$ perfectly reasonable sample members can be carried through as part of the block package, with the result that all k observations are then declared discordant.

As an example, consider the ordered sample

$$7 \quad 8 \quad 11 \quad 12 \quad 18 \quad 53.$$

A block procedure designed to test for two upper outliers, perhaps carried out as part of an automatic screening procedure, might declare both 18 and 53 as outliers even though 18 is not especially surprising.

SOME STATISTICAL TESTS FOR OUTLIERS

The outlier detection tests described in this section are only a handful from a long list of contenders. They have been chosen on the basis of several broad criteria. Firstly, the test must perform reasonably well; some of them will be 'best' tests in certain circumstances, usually against a location slippage alternative hypothesis. The second consideration is that tabulated critical values must be readily accessible either from Barnett & Lewis (1978), denoted by BL, or from source material in major journals.

The third requirement is that computation should be reasonably straightforward. Most of the tests need only a simple hand calculator, but a calculator with mean and standard deviation keys and the facility for deleting observations automatically is a boon. Some calculations, such as those for tests based on measures of skewness and kurtosis, are probably better carried out on a computer (however micro!) if this is available.

The tests are described in relation to sets of real data, although any non-experimentalist reading published reports of empirical work in psychology (or, for that matter, in virtually any other discipline) might be forgiven for believing that discrepant observations are hardly ever encountered!

Fuller descriptions of many of the tests, as well as other versions and approaches for situations not illustrated by the examples, can be found in Barnett & Lewis (1978); reference to the original papers is necessary in some instances. The tests considered will be, in many cases, alternatives but, because test performance can be affected by masking and swamping, tests of different types are sometimes applied in tandem so as to increase the chance of detecting any seriously discordant value.

Testing for outliers in normal samples

The outlier tests illustrated here represent the most general case, that is, when the parameters of the normal distribution, assumed in the null hypothesis, are unknown. However, modified versions of most of these tests can be used when some information is available about either the mean or variance or both. Further tests as well as these modified versions can be found in Barnett & Lewis (1978).

The following notation is adopted: $x_1, x_2, \ldots, x_n$ are n observations; $x_{(1)}, x_{(2)}, \ldots, x_{(n)}$ are n observations in numerical order. The parameters μ and σ^2 are estimated by

$$\bar{x} = \sum_{i=1}^{n} x_i/n \quad \text{and} \quad s^2 = \sum_{i=1}^{n} (x_i - \bar{x})^2/(n-1),$$

respectively. The sum of the squared deviations of the n observations from $\bar{x}$ is

$$S^2 = \sum_{i=1}^{n} (x_i - \bar{x})^2.$$

If $x_{(n)}$ (or $x_{(1)}$) is omitted, the sum of the squared deviations of the remaining $(n-1)$ observations from their own mean is denoted by S_n^2 (or S_1^2). Similarly, when, say, $x_{(n)}$ and $x_{(n-1)}$ are omitted, $S_{n-1,n}^2$ denotes the corresponding reduced sum of squares.

Note that the symmetry of the normal distribution means that tests for upper outliers need only slight modifications to become tests for lower outliers.

Example 1

The following data are average reaction times (to the nearest millisecond) of the same six subjects under two (of six) conditions in a memory experiment carried out as an undergraduate laboratory practical.

Subject	Condition	
	I	II
S1	1288	2681
S2	864	1249
S3	828	887
S4	820	746
S5	629	616
S6	312	382

It is intended that the data from all six conditions should be subjected to an analysis of variance (ANOVA), but in view of S1's long reaction times can the normality (and homogeneity of variances) assumptions be met? In other words, assuming that no errors have been made in obtaining or recording S1's readings, are 1288 and 2681 outliers under a null hypothesis that the sample was drawn from a normal population?

Two tests for a single outlier based on extreme standardized deviate statistics will be considered first. A suitable deviation/spread test statistic is

$$T_1 = \frac{x_{(n)} - \bar{x}}{s}.$$

The null hypothesis of all n observations arising from a normal distribution $N(\mu, \sigma^2)$ is rejected if T_1 is greater than the tabulated critical value in BL, Table VIIa, or Grubbs & Beck (1972), Table I; $x_{(n)}$ is then declared to be an outlier.

For Condition I, the mean and standard deviation of the six observations are 790.17 and 319.45, respectively, and $T_1 = (1288 - 790.17)/319.45 = 1.56$. The mean and standard deviation for Condition II are 1093.50 and 829.70 and $T_1 = (2681 - 1093.50)/829.70 = 1.91$. Comparing these observed values of T_1 with the critical value for $n=6$ and $\alpha=0.05$ of 1.82 leads to the conclusion that $x_{(n)} = 2681$ is an outlier.

An alternative to T_1 is the spacing/spread statistic

$$T_2 = \frac{x_{(n)} - x_{(n-1)}}{x_{(n)} - x_{(1)}}.$$

The observation $x_{(n)}$ is declared discordant if T_2 exceeds the tabulated critical value in BL, Table XIIIa, or Dixon (1950), Table I.

For Condition I, $T_2 = (1288 - 864)/(1288 - 312) = 0.434$ and for Condition II $T_2 = (2681 - 1249)/(2681 - 382) = 0.623$. The critical value for $n=6$ and $\alpha=0.05$ is 0.560 so, as with T_1, only 2681 is an outlier.

Two departure from model statistics, which actually test a sample for normality but implicitly test either $x_{(n)}$ or $x_{(1)}$ for discordancy, are measures of sample skewness and kurtosis. The sample skewness is

$$T_3 = \frac{n^{1/2} \sum_{i=1}^{n} (x_i - \bar{x})^3}{(S^2)^{3/2}}.$$

If the absolute value of T_3 exceeds the tabulated critical value in BL, Table XIVa, or, for $n \geq 25$, Pearson & Hartley (1966), Table 34B, $x_{(n)}$ or $x_{(1)}$ is an outlier depending upon whether T_3 is positive or negative.

For Condition I, $T_3 = 6^{1/2}(10349340.10)/(510228.83)^{3/2} = 0.07$ and for Condition II, $T_3 = 6^{1/2}(3.484682 \times 10^9)/(3441973.10)^{3/2} = 1.34$. The critical value for $n=6$ and $\alpha=0.05$ is approximately 1.0 and T_3 is positive for both conditions, so once again only 2681 is declared to be an outlier.

The kurtosis statistic

$$T_4 = \frac{n \sum_{i=1}^{n} (x_i - \bar{x})^4}{(S^2)^2}$$

tests whichever of $x_{(n)}$ and $x_{(1)}$ is further from $\bar{x}$ (that is, tests whichever corresponds to the larger residual); $x_{(n)}$ (or $x_{(1)}$) is declared discordant if T_4 is greater than the tabulated critical value in *BL*, Table XIV*b* (with useful supplementary tables for small samples in Table I of d'Agostino & Tietjen, 1971) or, for $n \geqslant 50$, in Pearson & Hartley (1966), Table 34C.

For Condition I, $T_4 = 6(1.14408718 \times 10^{11})/(510228.83)^2 = 2.64$ and for Condition II, $T_4 = 6(6.67643058 \times 10^{12})/(3441973.10)^2 = 3.38$. The approximate critical value for $n = 6$ and $\alpha = 0.05$ is 3.23, indicating a departure from normality for Condition II due to the discordant upper extreme value 2681.

Example 2

The Darwin data on the differences in heights (in eighths of an inch) of cross- and self-fertilized plants, quoted by Box & Tiao (1968) and mentioned earlier, illustrate well the problems of testing for several possible outliers. Of the 15 observations (in order of magnitude)

$$\begin{array}{ccccc} -67 & -48 & 6 & 8 & 14 \\ 16 & 23 & 24 & 28 & 29 \\ 41 & 49 & 56 & 60 & 75 \end{array}$$

-67 and -48 are sufficiently surprising, under a null hypothesis of normality, to warrant formal discordancy testing.

The two suspected outliers will be examined using both block and sequential procedures; two block tests which are many outlier versions of T_1 and T_2 of Example 1 will be considered first. (Note that the test statistics have been modified in the obvious way to test for lower outliers.)

Block tests. The deviation/spread statistic

$$T_5 = \frac{k\bar{x} - (x_{(1)} + \ldots + x_{(k)})}{s}$$

tests for k lower outliers $x_{(1)}, \ldots, x_{(k)}$. Values of T_5 greater than the tabulated critical value in *BL*, Table IX*a* (for $k = 2, 3$ and 4), lead to rejection of the null hypothesis of all n observations arising from a normal distribution $N(\mu, \sigma^2)$ and $x_{(1)}, \ldots, x_{(k)}$ are declared to be outliers.

The mean and standard deviation of the 15 observations are 20.93 and 37.74, respectively, and for $k = 2$, $T_5 = \{2(20.93) - (-67 - 48)\}/37.74 = 4.16$. The tabulated critical value for $n = 15$, $k = 2$ and $\alpha = 0.05$ is approximately 3.74, so both $x_{(1)} = -67$ and $x_{(2)} = -48$ are discordant.

The spacing/spread statistic

$$T_6 = \frac{x_{(3)} - x_{(1)}}{x_{(n)} - x_{(1)}}$$

tests for two lower outliers. (Note too that if T_6 is used to test for a single outlier

$x_{(1)}$, the risk of masking by $x_{(2)}$ is avoided.) The null hypothesis is rejected if T_6 exceeds the tabulated critical value in *BL*, Table XIIIe or Dixon (1950), Table IV. Since $T_6=(6+67)/(75+67)=0.51$ is greater than the critical value for $n=15$ and $\alpha=0.05$ of approximately 0.43, both values again are taken to be outliers.

A third block procedure uses a sum of squares statistic

$$T_7=\frac{S^2_{1,2,\ldots,k}}{S^2},$$

where $S^2_{1,2,\ldots,k}$ is the sum of the squared deviations from the mean in the reduced sample (that is, with $x_{(1)}, x_{(2)}, \ldots, x_{(k)}$ deleted) to test for k lower outliers. The null hypothesis is rejected if T_7 is smaller than the tabulated critical value in *BL*, Table IXb (for $k=2$, 3, and 4) or Grubbs & Beck (1972), Table II (for $k=2$), and Tietjen & Moore (1972), Table I (for $k=3$ and 4 and additionally for values of k up to 10). For $k=2$, $T_7=S^2_{1,2}/S^2=5568.00/19944.93=0.279$, which is less than the critical value for $n=15$, $k=2$ and $\alpha=0.05$ of approximately 0.381, so -67 and -48 are declared discordant.

Choosing k. The maximum number of possible outliers, k, can be estimated by procedures such as that suggested by Jain & Pingel (1982), but is usually chosen to be the number of surprising values. In less clear-cut cases, a rule of thumb due to Tietjen & Moore (1972) sets the number of, say, lower outlier candidates as the number of observations to the left of the largest gap between successive observations below the mean. With the present data, for example, the largest gap is between $x_{(2)}$ and $x_{(3)}$, so k is estimated to be two. The importance of selecting an appropriate value of k is illustrated when the data are tested for a maximum of $k=1$ and $k=3$ outliers.

When $k=1$, T_5 and T_6 are merely the lower outlier forms of T_1 and T_2, say, $T_1^{\star}$ and $T_2^{\star}$. Now $T_1^{\star}=(\bar{x}-x_{(1)})/s=(20.93+67)/37.74=2.33$, which is smaller than the critical value for $n=15$ and $\alpha=0.05$ of 2.41 (*BL*, Table VII), so -67 is not an outlier. Similarly, $T_2^{\star}=(x_{(2)}-x_{(1)})/(x_{(n)}-x_{(1)})=(-47+67)/(75+67)=0.134$ is smaller than the appropriate critical value of approximately 0.339 (*BL*, Table XIIIa), which leads to the same conclusion that -67 is not discordant. In other words, the discordancy of $x_{(1)}=-67$ has been masked by the influence of its neighbour $x_{(2)}=-48$.

Suppose that the maximum number of outliers is thought to be three. Now, T_5 will test $x_{(1)}, x_{(2)}$ and $x_{(3)}$, and comparing

$$T_5=\frac{3(20.93)-(-67\;-48\;+6)}{37.74}=4.55$$

with the critical value for $n=15$, $k=3$ and $\alpha=0.05$ of approximately 4.71 (*BL*, Table IXa) leads to the conclusion that no outliers are present. In this case, the discordancy of $x_{(1)}$ and $x_{(2)}$ has been masked by testing the completely unremarkable value 6.

By way of contrast, $T_7=S_{1,2,3}^2/S^2=4778.25/19944.93=0.240$ is smaller than the critical value of approximately 0.275 for $n=15$, $k=3$ and $\alpha=0.05$ (*BL*, Table IXb). Since all three lower extreme values are declared discordant swamping has occurred. In fact, $x_{(3)}=6$ is not even the observation with the next largest residual (absolute deviation from the mean) after -67 and -48, so there are clearly problems in blindly testing for an unreasonable number of outliers.

Swamping can occur, however, even in a modified version of T_7 which tests the k observations with the k largest residuals, irrespective of whether they are upper or lower values. For example, a test for the three most extreme observations -67, -48 and 75 yields $T_7=S_{1,2,n}^2/S^2=3657.00/19944.93=0.183$. Since T_7 is smaller than the critical value for $n=15$, $k=3$ and $\alpha=0.05$ of 0.206 (*BL*, Table XV; or Tietjen & Moore (1972, Table II)) all three observations are declared discordant. A later test will indicate, however, that $x_{(15)}=75$ has been carried through on the backs of $x_{(1)}=-67$ and $x_{(2)}=-48$.

Sequential tests. The 'outside-in' sequential procedure uses a single outlier test to examine the most extreme observation first. If this observation is proved to be an outlier, the next most extreme value (usually that with the next largest residual) is then tested using the reduced sample. The procedure terminates when a non-significant result is obtained.

In addition to the obvious problem of the overall size of the significance level when a test is repeated several times, the 'outside-in' procedure will often fail to detect even an obvious outlier at the first hurdle because of masking; this is, of course, exactly what happened in the $k=1$ case with $T_1^\star$ and $T_2^\star$.

The skewness and kurtosis statistics, T_3 and T_4, are often applied sequentially in the 'outside-in' fashion.

For the present data, $T_3=15^{1/2}(-721332.56)/(19944.93)^{3/2}=-0.99$. Since $|T_3|$ is greater than the critical value for $n=15$ and $\alpha=0.05$ of 0.80 (*BL*, Table XIVa) and T_3 is negative, $x_{(1)}=-67$ is an outlier. Deleting $x_{(1)}$ and repeating the procedure leads to $T_3=14^{1/2}(-264781.09)/(11660.36)^{3/2}=-0.79$, which is smaller than the approximate critical value of 0.82 (for $n=14$ and $\alpha=0.05$). Since T_3 is negative, the observation tested is $x_{(2)}=-48$, but it is not discordant.

Perhaps even more surprisingly, $T_4=15(95614681.50)/19944.93=3.61$ tests $x_{(1)}$ (the critical value for $n=15$ and $\alpha=0.05$ is 4.1 (*BL*, Table XIVb)) but fails to declare it discordant.

The skewness and kurtosis statistics are, of course, tests for normality and, in fact, are sensitive to different kinds of non-normality. Sensitivity contours (Prescott, 1976) show clearly that T_3 is a suitable statistic in the asymmetric case (that is, when the outliers are on the same side), whereas T_4 is appropriate in the presence of both upper and lower outliers. On balance, however, neither of these measures seems particularly satisfactory for repeated use.

The alternative, 'inside-out', sequential procedure tests the kth most extreme observation first. If this gives a non-significant result, the $(k-1)$th most extreme is examined. The process ends either when all k values have been tested (and none are found to be outliers), or when a significant result is obtained (and the observation under test and any values more extreme are declared discordant).

On the face of it, the 'inside-out' procedure appears to have the disadvantages of needing to select k and of the increasing significance level associated with using single outlier tests consecutively. In fact, the choice of k is less important than in block tests where either all or none of the k values examined are confirmed as outliers. The significance level problem has been overcome by obtaining critical values from the joint distribution of the set of k test statistics (under the null hypothesis), thus giving an overall significance level for all k tests.

Some tabulated values are available for the many outlier equivalents of the deviation/spread statistic T_1 (Rosner, 1975) and the single outlier version of T_7 (Prescott, 1979). A further statistic is similar to T_1 but uses the trimmed mean and standard deviation, that is, the mean and standard deviation calculated from the $n-2k$ observations remaining after trimming k (the assumed maximum number of outliers) from each end of the sample (Rosner, 1977).

The k deviation/spread statistics are $T_{1,1}, T_{1,2}, \ldots, T_{1,k}$, where

$$T_{1,j} = \frac{|x^{(j)} - \bar{x}_j|}{s_j},$$

$x^{(j)}$ is the observation farthest from the mean $\bar{x}_j$, and $\bar{x}_j$ and s_j are calculated from the $n-j+1$ observations remaining after deleting the $j-1$ most extreme at each step. $T_{1,k}, T_{1,k-1}, \ldots, T_{1,1}$ are compared in turn with critical values in Rosner (1975), Table 9 (for $k=2$ only). A value of $T_{1,j}$ greater than the critical value leads to the conclusion that $x^{(j)}$ and observations more extreme are outliers.

In the first instance, the possibility of a maximum of two outliers is considered. $T_{1,1} = |-67 - 20.93|/37.74 = 2.33$ and $T_{1,2} = |-48 - 27.21|/29.95 = 2.51$, and since $T_{1,2}$ is larger than the critical value for $n=15$, $k=2$ and $\alpha=0.05$ of 22.65, both -67 and -48 are confirmed as discordant. Note that although critical values are given for all k test statistics, in practice it is unnecessary to compare the remaining $T_{1,j}$ once a significant result is obtained.

The k sums of squared deviations statistics are $T_{7,1}, T_{7,2}, \ldots, T_{7,k}$, where

$$T_{7,j} = \frac{S_j^2}{S_{j-1}^2}$$

and S_j^2 is calculated from the $n-j$ observations remaining after deleting the j most extreme at each step. The j most extreme values are outliers if $T_{7,j}$ is smaller than the critical value from Prescott (1979), Tables 1 and 2, for $k=2$ and $k=3$, respectively.

Deleting the value with the largest residual, -67, gives

$$T_{7,1} = \frac{11660.36}{19944.93} = 0.585.$$

The next largest residual corresponds to -48, so

$$T_{7,2} = \frac{5568.00}{11660.93} = 0.477.$$

Since $T_{7,2}$ is less than 0.520, the critical value for $n=15$, $k=2$ and $\alpha=0.05$, both -67 and -48 are outliers.

Finally, the k trimmed deviation/spread statistics are $T_{8,1}, T_{8,2}, \ldots, T_{8,k}$, where

$$T_{8,j} = \frac{|x^{(j)} - a|}{b},$$

$x^{(j)}$ is, as before, the observation with the jth largest residual, but this time from the trimmed mean a,

$$a = \frac{\sum\limits_{i=k+1}^{n-k} x_i}{n-2k} \quad \text{and} \quad b = \left\{ \frac{\sum\limits_{i=k+1}^{n-k} (x_i - a)^2}{n-2k-1} \right\}^{1/2}$$

As usual, the j most extreme observations are outliers if $T_{8,j}$ exceeds the critical value from Rosner (1977), Tables, 1, 2 and 3 for $k=2$, 3 and 4, respectively. Note that although the T_8 procedure is slightly less powerful (in terms of the proportion of correct detections) than the T_1 many outlier procedure, the computation is particularly simple.

For $k=2$, -67, -48, 60 and 75 are trimmed off the sample. The trimmed mean and standard deviation are 26.73 and 16.25, $T_{8,1} = |-67-26.73|/16.25 = 5.77$ and $T_{8,2} = |-48-26.73|/16.25 = 4.60$ (-48 is still the observation with the second largest residual). $T_{8,2}$ is greater than the appropriate critical value of 4.31 (for $n=15$, $k=2$ and $\alpha=0.05$), so both -48 and -67 are outliers.

Suppose now that the three observations with the largest residuals $x_{(1)} = -67$, $x_{(2)} = -48$ and $x_{(15)} = 75$, are to be tested for discordancy. The only available tabulated critical values for samples of size 15 and $k=3$ are for the many outlier sums of squares statistic, T_7. These are given by Prescott (1979), Table 2, who also uses the Darwin data as an example.

The three values of the test statistics are $T_{7,1} = 0.585$ and $T_{7,2} = 0.477$ (as before), and $T_{7,3} = 3657.00/5568.00 = 0.657$. The critical values for $n=15$, $k=3$ and $\alpha=0.05$ corresponding to $T_{7,3}, T_{7,2}$ and $T_{7,1}$ are 0.505, 0.495 and 0.445. Since $T_{7,3}$ is greater than 0.505, but $T_{7,2}$ is smaller than 0.495, -67 and -48 are discordant. It is worth adding that only -67 and -48 are declared discordant if all three observations are tested using the single outlier statistic T_1 in the 'inside-out' procedure. The consequences of overestimating k, therefore, seem to be less serious than with block tests although, of course, outliers will still be missed if k is too small. In fact, the masking effect is sometimes seen even with this sequential procedure if, say, the $(n-1)$th largest observation is relatively close to $x_{(n)}$, but not necessarily discordant, or if there is an undetected lower outlier candidate.

The final point concerns the repeated use of single outlier tests. At present, tables of critical values cover only a very restricted range of many outlier tests and situations. Where no suitable tables exist, however, a single outlier test, applied according to the 'inside-out' sequential procedure will give a fairly rough-and-ready test for up to *k* outliers, provided that the significance level at each stage is reasonably low.

Testing for outliers in gamma samples

Compared with the normal case, the problem of outliers in gamma samples has received relatively little attention. And yet, the gamma distribution is of considerable practical importance as a pragmatic model for skewed data as well as being the natural model in lifetesting and whenever a Poisson process is appropriate, for example, in monitoring events over time, such as in supermarket queueing behaviour or in operant conditioning schedules.

The gamma distribution with scale and shape parameters λ and r, respectively, is denoted by $\Gamma(r, \lambda)$. The exponential distribution is a special case of the gamma distribution where $r=1$, so any outlier test for a gamma sample can be applied to exponential samples. In fact, many of the tests in this section are only suitable for exponential samples, usually because of the availability of tabulated critical values.

All the tests for the gamma case assume that the origin of the distribution is known; if the origin is not at zero, the test statistics can be modified in the obvious way (the equivalent procedure to rescaling the data). Knowledge of the origin is not always necessary for exponential samples. In all the tests, the scale parameter is assumed to be unknown: some tests for gamma samples allow an unknown shape parameter too.

The notation generally follows that of the normal case. Test statistics for upper outliers usually need only the obvious modifications for the lower outlier case, but the asymmetry of the gamma distribution often means that separate tables are required. A particular difficulty in examining lower outliers from gamma samples is that lower values are not always recorded to a sufficient degree of accuracy.

Further tests, as well as various versions of those presented here, are considered in Barnett & Lewis (1978), Kimber (1979, 1982, 1983) and Kimber & Stevens (1981).

Example 3

The following data are the intervals (to the nearest hundredth of a second) between reversals of a Necker cube for two subjects. They were obtained as part of a pilot study to examine Restle's (1961) claim that inter-reversal times follow a gamma distribution with shape parameter *r* depending on the complexity of the reversible figure.

The 22 observations for each subject are (in order of magnitude):

S1	10	11	11	11	13	16	16	17
	23	23	24	29	30	38	43	47
	53	57	78	96	168	385		

S2	14	40	47	47	51	52	56	66
	68	71	72	72	87	90	90	105
	153	177	178	360	575	687		

Sample moments suggest that an exponential model is a reasonable fit to the data in each case, provided that $x_{(22)}=385$ is omitted from S1's times and $x_{(21)}=575$ and $x_{(22)}=687$ from S2's. Are these observations outliers under the null hypothesis that both samples arose from exponential distributions, that is, gamma distributions with shape parameter $r=1$?

Note that, for simplicity, it is assumed that reversals can take place virtually simultaneously and that reaction times are negligible, relative to the accuracy of the timing equipment. The assumed origin of the distribution, therefore, is at zero rather than at some point corresponding to a minimum time between logged reversals.

Tests for single outliers. Tests on the single outlier candidate $x_{(22)}=385$ in the data for S1 will be considered first.

Since the spread of a gamma distribution can be measured by the sample mean (or by the sample sum) as well as the standard deviation, a suitable deviation/spread statistic for a single upper outlier is

$$T_9 = \frac{x_{(n)}}{\sum_{i=1}^{n} x_i}.$$

The null hypothesis of all n observations arising from a gamma distribution $\Gamma(r, \lambda)$, with known r, is rejected, and $x_{(n)}$ is declared discordant, if T_9 exceeds the critical value in BL, Table I, or in Eisenhart *et al.* (1947), Tables 15.1 and 15.2.

The corresponding test statistic T_9^* for a lower outlier has $x_{(1)}$ instead of $x_{(n)}$ as its numerator. If T_9^* is smaller than the critical value in BL, Table II, $x_{(1)}$ is an outlier.

For S1's data, $T_9=385/1199=0.3211$. Since T_9 is larger than the critical value for $n=22$, $r=1$ and $\alpha=0.05$ of approximately 0.2529, $x_{(22)}=385$ is declared discordant in relation to the exponential model.

A spacing/spread statistic for exponential samples which does not assume a zero origin for the distribution is

$$T_{10} = \frac{x_{(n)}-x_{(n-1)}}{x_{(n)}-x_{(1)}}.$$

$x_{(n)}$ is an outlier if T_{10} exceeds the critical value in BL, Table III (for $n \leqslant 21$). In the corresponding lower outlier test using T_{10}^* (with the obvious change in notation),

$x_{(1)}$ is discordant if T_{10}^* exceeds the critical value in *BL*, Table V (for $n \leqslant 20$). Since $T_{10} = (385 - 168)/(385 - 10) = 0.579$ and the critical value (for $n = 21$ and $\alpha = 0.05$) is 0.567, $x_{(22)} = 385$ is an outlier on this test too.

Some recent tests for outliers in samples from gamma distributions with unknown shape parameter are due to Kimber (1979, 1983). These tests are particularly suitable for bell-shaped gamma data, that is, when $r > 1$; however, they will be applied to the present, assumed exponential, data to illustrate the methods.

A test statistic for an upper outlier in a gamma sample, which is broadly of the deviation/spread type is

$$T_{11} = \frac{D_{(n)}}{\ln (\bar{x}/\tilde{x})},$$

where

$$D_{(n)} = -\ln (x_{(n)}/\tilde{x}) - (n-1) \ln \{(n - x_{(n)}/\tilde{x})/(n-1)\}$$

and

$$\tilde{x} = \left(\prod_{i=1}^{n} x_i \right)^{1/n},$$

the sample geometric mean. The value of the statistic $\{(n-1)/n\}T_{11}^{1/2}$ is compared with the critical values in *BL*, Table VII*a*, or Grubbs & Beck (1972), Table I. (Note that these are the tables for the normal test using T_1.) $D_{(n)}$ is replaced by $D_{(1)}$ to test for a single lower outlier.

For subject 1's data, $\bar{x} = 54.5$, $\tilde{x} = 31.5257$ so $T_{11} = 5.2010/0.5474 = 9.5013$. Since $(21/22) (9.5013)^{1/2} = 2.942$ is greater than the critical value for $n = 22$ and $\alpha = 0.05$ of 2.603, $x_{(22)} = 385$ is declared discordant, as before.

In an alternative approach, outlier tests for normal samples are applied to suitably transformed gamma data. Either square rooting or cube rooting will transform gamma samples to normality, but the cube root method is preferred if computation presents no practical problems.

Denoting the transformed observations as $v_i = x_i^{1/3}$ $(i = 1, 2, \ldots, n)$, $\bar{v}$ and s_v are the sample mean and standard deviation, respectively, of the v_i and $v_{(1)}, v_{(2)}, \ldots, v_{(n)}$ are the n ordered observations. Then

$$T_{12} = \frac{v_{(n)} - \bar{v}}{s_v}$$

is just the deviation/spread statistic T_1 and the upper outlier $v_{(n)}$ (or, with the obvious modification to T_{12}, $v_{(1)}$) is tested in the usual way.

The mean and standard deviation of the transformed sample are 3.302 and 1.235. $T_{12} = (7.275 - 3.302)/1.235 = 3.217$ which is greater than the critical value of 2.603 (as for T_{11}) and leads to the same conclusion.

A test which examines either the upper or lower outlier, $v_{(n)}$ or $v_{(1)}$, depending on which is the more extreme is the departure from model statistic based on the measure of kurtosis (see T_4):

$$T_{13} = \frac{n \sum_{i=1}^{n} (v - \bar{v})^4}{(S_v^2)^2} = 5.94$$

which exceeds the critical value of approximately 4.17 for $n=22$ and $\alpha=0.05$ (*BL*, Table XIV*b*, or d'Agostino & Tietjen (1972), Table I), so the most extreme value $x_{(22)}=385$ is discordant. Note that T_{13} can be applied consecutively if more than one outlier is suspected.

Tests for multiple outliers. Turning now to S2's data, the obvious outlier candidates are $x_{(21)}=575$ and $x_{(22)}=687$. A block test and a sequential test which are the many outlier equivalents of T_9 are considered first.

The deviation/spread statistic

$$T_{14} = \frac{x_{(n-k+1)} + x_{(n-k+2)} + \cdots + x_{(n)}}{\sum_{i=1}^{n} x_i}$$

will test for k upper outliers in a sample from an exponential distribution with zero origin. The null hypothesis is rejected if T_{14} exceeds the critical value given in Kimber & Stevens (1981), Table I (for $k=2$). At present, no tables seem to be available for the case of k lower outliers.

Now, for $k=2$, $T_{14}=(575+687)/3158=0.400$ and the critical value for $n=22$ and $\alpha=0.05$ is 0.391, so both $x_{(21)}=575$ and $x_{(22)}=687$ are declared discordant. Note that single outlier tests on $x_{(22)}$, for example, those based on either T_9 or T_{10}, will fail to detect 687 as an outlier due to masking by $x_{(21)}$.

An 'inside-out' sequential test for a maximum of k upper outliers in an exponential sample is based on the k deviation/spread statistics $T_{9,1}, T_{9,2}, \ldots, T_{9,k}$, where

$$T_{9,j} = \frac{x_{(n-j+1)}}{\sum_{i=1}^{n-j+1} x_{(i)}},$$

that is, T_9 calculated after the $j-1$ largest observations have been deleted. $T_{9,k}$, $T_{9,k-1}, \ldots, T_{9,n}$ are compared in turn with the critical values in Kimber (1982), Tables, 1, 2 and 3, for $k=2$, 3 and 4. A value of $T_{9,j}$ exceeding the critical value leads to $x_{(n-j+1)}$ and all larger values being declared as outliers.

For testing up to k lower outliers, the corresponding k statistics are $T^\star_{9,1}$, $T^\star_{9,2}$, ..., $T^\star_{9,k}$, where

$$T^\star_{9,j}=T_{9,n-j}=\frac{x_{(j+1)}}{\sum\limits_{i=1}^{j+1}x_{(i)}}.$$

If $T^\star_{9,j}$ is greater than the critical values in Kimber (1982), Table 4 (for $k=2$, 3 and 4), $x_{(j)}$ and all smaller observations are discordant. Note that, in effect, lower outlier candidates are tested by their influence on the denominator.

For a maximum of two upper outliers, $T_{9,1}=687/3158=0.218$ and $T_{9,2}=575/2471=0.233$. Since the critical values for $n=22$, $k=2$ and $\alpha=0.05$ for $T_{9,2}$ and $T_{9,1}$ are 0.222 and 0.273, respectively and $T_{9,2}$ is greater than 0.222, both $x_{(21)}$ and $x_{(22)}$ are declared discordant, as before.

Suppose now that the three largest observations $x_{(20)}=360$, $x_{(21)}=575$ and $x_{(22)}=687$ are to be tested. $T_{9,1}=0.218$ and $T_{9,2}=0.233$, as above, and $T_{9,3}=360/1896=0.190$ with critical values (for $n=22$, $k=3$ and $\alpha=0.05$) 0.291, 0.235 and 0.216, respectively, so no observations are now outliers; choosing a suitable value of k is clearly important.

The final tests are two block tests for gamma samples where the origin of the distribution is at zero, but the shape parameter is unknown. Like the single sample tests for this case, neither test is entirely satisfactory for exponential data (or, in fact, for $r\leqslant1$ generally).

The first test is the many outlier version of T_{11}. To test for k upper outliers

$$T_{15}=\frac{D_{(n),(n-1),\dots,(n-k+1)}}{\ln(\tilde{x}/\bar{x})},$$

where

$$D_{(n),(n-1),\dots,(n-k+1)}=-\sum_{j=0}^{k-1}\ln(x_{(n-j)}/\bar{x})-(n-k)\ln\left[\left\{n-\sum_{j=0}^{k-1}(x_{(n-j)}/\bar{x})\right\}\bigg/(n-k)\right].$$

The value of the statistic $(1-T_{15}/n)$ is compared with critical values given in BL, Table IXb; Grubbs & Beck (1972), Table II (for $k=2$); or Tietjen & Moore (1972), Table I (for $k=3$ and 4). (Note that these are the tables for the block test for normal samples using T_7.) Values of the statistic smaller than the critical value are significant. $D_{(n),(n-1),\dots,(n-k+1)}$ is replaced by $D_{(1),(2),\dots,(k)}$ in testing for k lower outliers.

For subject 2's data, with outlier candidates 687 and 575, $\bar{x}=143.5455$, $\tilde{x}=91.8460$, so $T_{15}=5.3442/0.4465=11.9690$ and $(1-T_{15}/22)=0.4560$ which is smaller than the critical value of 0.5107 (for $n=22$, $k=2$ and $\alpha=0.05$); both 687 and 575 are declared as outliers, as before.

In contrast to the results obtained from the sequential exponential test on the three upper values 360, 575 and 687, the block test for $k=3$, using T_{15}, leads to the conclusion that all three observations are outliers. In other words, there appears to be a risk of swamping with T_{15}. A further problem noted by Kimber (1983) is that the presence of a lower outlier may mask upper discordant values.

The second block test for k upper (or lower) outliers in a gamma sample is, in fact, the normal test based on the sums of squared deviations statistic T_7 (for upper outliers) applied to the transformed data. The statistic is

$$T_{16} = \frac{S^2_{n,\,n-1,..,n-k+1}(v)}{S^2(v)},$$

where $S^2_{n,\,n-1,\,\ldots,\,n-k+1}(v)$ and $S^2(v)$ are the sums of squared deviations of the v_i from the appropriate mean. Values of T_{16} are compared directly with the same critical values as for T_{15}.

Transforming the observations for subject 2's data by $v_i = x_i^{1/3}$ ($i = 1, 2, \ldots, 22$) and testing the two values $x_{(21)}$ and $x_{(22)}$, $T_{16} = 19.1108/51.8342 = 0.3687$ which is smaller than the critical value of 0.5107 (as for the corresponding test with T_{15}), so both 687 and 575 are discordant. The swamping phenomenon also leads to the three largest observations being declared as outliers in a $k=3$ test using T_{16}.

Testing for outliers in other distributions and situations

Samples from Pareto distributions and from extreme-value distributions, such as the Weibull, can be transformed easily to allow outlier tests for normal samples to be applied. Similarly, simple transformations to normality make normal tests suitable for testing discordancy in Poisson, binomial and log-normal distributions.

Details of these procedures, as well as some specific tests for outliers in Poisson, binomial and uniform samples are given by Barnett & Lewis (1978).

Outliers, of course, are not confined to the single univariate samples considered in this chapter; outliers arise and need to be detected in multivariate data and also in structured situations such as designed experiments and time series (for overviews, see Barnett & Lewis, 1978; Hawkins, 1980; Beckman & Cook, 1983). Many of the concepts and general principles about the nature of outliers and how they should be tested are common to both simple and complex situations: implementing them in the latter case is a different matter. But that's a story for another day!

Acknowledgements

It will be obvious, not least from the number of times Barnett and Lewis's book *Outliers in Statistical Data** has been cited, that the chapter has drawn heavily on this comprehensive review of the widely scattered outlier literature. This debt is hereby acknowledged.

* A second edition (1984), containing much of the more recent material, has appeared since this chapter was written.

References

ANDREWS, D.F. & PREGIBON, D. (1978). Finding the outliers that matter. *Journal of the Royal Statistical Society, Series B, 40*, 85–93.

BARNETT, V. & LEWIS, T. (1978). *Outliers in Statistical Data.* Chichester: Wiley.

BECKMAN, R.J. & COOK, R.D. (1983). Outlier ...s. *Technometrics, 25*, 119–149.

BOX, G.E.P. & TIAO, G.C. (1962). A further look at robustness via Bayes' theorem. *Biometrika, 49*, 419–432.

BOX, G.E.P. & TIAO, G.C. (1968). A Bayesian approach to some outlier problems. *Biometrika, 55*, 119–129.

COLLETT, D. & LEWIS, T. (1976). The subjective nature of outlier rejection procedures. *Applied Statistics, 25*, 228–237.

D'AGOSTINO, R.B. & TIETJEN, G.L. (1971). Simulation probability points for b_2 for small samples. *Biometrika, 58*, 669–672.

DAVID, H.A. (1981). *Order Statistics* (2nd ed.). Chichester: Wiley.

DAVID, H.A. & PAULSON, A.S. (1965). The performance of several tests for outliers. *Biometrika, 52*, 429–436.

DIXON, W.J. (1950). Analysis of extreme values. *Annals of Mathematical Statistics, 21*, 488–506.

DIXON, W.J. (1962). Rejection of observations. In: A. E. Sarhan & B. G. Greenberg (eds) *Contributions to Order Statistics*, 299–342. New York: Wiley.

EISENHART, C., HASTAY, M.W. & WALLIS, W.A. (eds) (1947). *Selected Techniques of Statistical Analysis.* New York: McGraw-Hill.

FERGUSON, T.S. (1961). On the rejection of outliers. *Proceedings of the Fourth Berkeley Symposium on Mathematical Statistics and Probability, 1*, 253–287.

FISHER, R.A. (1960). *The Design of Experiments* (7th ed.). Edinburgh: Oliver and Boyd.

GRUBBS, F.E. (1969). Procedures for detecting outlying observations in samples. *Technometrics, 11*, 1–21.

GRUBBS, F.E. & BECK, G. (1972). Extension of sample sizes and percentage points for significance tests of outlying observations. *Technometrics, 14*, 847–854.

GUMBEL, E.J. (1960). Discussion of 'Rejection of outliers' by Anscombe, F. J. *Technometrics, 2*, 157–166.

HAWKINS, D.M. (1980). *Identification of Outliers.* London: Chapman and Hall.

HOLTON, G. (1981). Thematic presuppositions and the direction of scientific advance. In: F. A. Heath (ed.) *Scientific Explanation.* Oxford: Oxford University Press.

JAIN, R.B. & PINGEL, L.A. (1982). A unified approach for estimation and detection of outliers. *Communications in Statistics, 11*, 2953–2976.

KIMBER, A.C. (1979). Tests for a single outlier in a gamma sample with unknown shape and scale parameters. *Applied Statistics, 28*, 243–250.

KIMBER, A.C. (1982). Tests for many outliers in an exponential sample. *Applied Statistics, 31*, 263–271.

KIMBER, A.C. (1983). Discordancy testing in gamma samples with both parameters unknown. *Applied Statistics, 32*, 304–310.

KIMBER, A.C. & STEVENS, H.J. (1981). The null distribution of a test for two upper outliers in an exponential sample. *Applied Statistics, 30*, 153–157.

LOVIE, P. (1982). *Some studies in intuitive statistics: estimation and inference in normal populations.* Unpublished Ph.D. Thesis, University of Liverpool.

PEARSON, E.S. & HARTLEY, H.O. (eds) (1966). *Biometrika Tables for Statisticians, Volume 1* (3rd ed.). London: Cambridge University Press.

PRESCOTT, P. (1976). Comparison of tests for normality using stylised sensitivity surfaces. *Biometrika, 63*, 285–289.

PRESCOTT, P. (1978). Examination of the behaviour of tests for outliers when more than one outlier is present. *Applied Statistics, 27,* 10–25.
PRESCOTT, P. (1979). Critical values for a sequential test for many outliers. *Applied Statistics, 28,* 36–39.
RESTLE, F. (1961). *Psychology of Judgment and Choice.* New York: Wiley.
ROSNER, B. (1975). On the detection of many outliers. *Technometrics, 17,* 221–227.
ROSNER, B. (1977). Percentage points for the RST many outlier procedure. *Technometrics, 19,* 307–312.
SHAPIRO, S.S. & WILK, M.B. (1965). An analysis of variance test for normality (complete samples). *Biometrika, 52,* 591–611.
SHAPIRO, S.S. & WILK, M.B. (1972). An analysis of variance test for the exponential distribution (complete samples). *Technometrics, 14,* 355–370.
TIETJEN, G.L. & MOORE, R.H. (1972). Some Grubbs-type statistics for the detection of several outliers. *Technometrics, 14,* 583–597.
TIKU, M.L. (1975). A new statistic for testing suspected outliers. *Communications in Statistics, 4,* 737–752.
YATES, F. (1935). Some examples of biased sampling. *Annals of Eugenics, 6,* 202–213.

4

Cross-classified Data

GRAHAM J. G. UPTON

This chapter is concerned with data which consist of *counts*. In the social sciences, these counts are most likely to be direct counts of people or of attributes pertaining to people, such as their attitudes to various situations, their sex, their health, and so forth. We shall be specifically concerned with situations in which *information has been collected on at least two variables simultaneously*. For example, information might be collected on a random sample of hospital patients in order to study the efficiency of some particular treatment for a disease. The information might reasonably be expected to include the following three variables:

A: Sex (A_1=male, A_2=female)
B: Treatment (B_1=given treatment, B_2=not given treatment)
C: Outcome (C_1=patient recovers, C_2=patient dies).

In this case, each of the three variables is a dichotomy, so there are $2^3=8$ possible categories to which a patient might belong. Suppose that our sample size is n and that f_{ijk} ($i=1, 2; j=1, 2; k=1, 2$) is the observed number of patients in the sample having sex i, treatment j and outcome k. Our interest focuses on the relation between the response variable C, and the factor variables, A and B: in other words on the manner in which recovery is affected by the patient's sex and by the treatment received.

The analysis of cross-classifications involving continuous measurements has been well understood for half a century, following the work by Sir R. A. Fisher and others on the analysis of agricultural experiments, but it is only in the last decade that a corresponding method of analysis for discrete data has been ironed out. The pioneering papers were those of Leo Goodman in various statistics and sociology journals. Goodman continues to publish profusely and the subject is still developing its techniques. Nevertheless the massive tome of Bishop *et al.* (1975), which includes many examples from a wide range of subject areas, is likely to remain the standard reference work for some time to come. A much shorter, simplified version of this book, has been produced by Fienberg (1980), while a still simpler – but regrettably more expensive – alternative is provided by Upton (1978). The introductory book by Everitt (1977) is a revised version of the popular but dated earlier work by A. E. Maxwell. Everitt, however, pays rather little attention to the new methods. All these books are more or less mathematical;

for readers who find mathematics impenetrable, but want to know about the new methods, the book by Gilbert (1981), which is 'equation-free', should prove ideal. An excellent recent introductory account is given by Swafford (1980).

In this chapter I shall attempt to convey some impression of the flavour and the immense possibilities of the new approach. To anticipate what comes, the essence of the models that we shall consider is that they permit *the simultaneous assessment of all possible associations* between the variables. They are therefore a far cry from our previous reliance on studying variables two at a time. The emphasis of the chapter will be placed on the more recent developments in contingency table analysis which postdate the books listed in the previous paragraph.

THE 2×2 TABLE

Although we shall be principally concerned with multiway tables, I shall start with the 'simple' 2×2 table, both to introduce the notation and also because of the misunderstandings that surround this commonly encountered table. Table 1 illustrates the notation: there are two variables, A and B, with 'cell' probabilities $\{p_{ij}\}$, for which the observed cell frequencies are $\{f_{ij}\}$ and $\Sigma f_{ij} = n$. We use the zero suffix to denote a total, so that $f_{i0} = f_{i1} + f_{i2}$, etc.

Table 1. Notation for the 2×2 table

Theoretical probabilities			Observed frequencies			Expected estimated frequencies		
B_1	B_2		B_1	B_2		B_1	B_2	
A_1 $\;p_{11}$	p_{12}	p_{10}	A_1 $\;f_{11}$	f_{12}	f_{10}	A_1 $\;e_{11}$	e_{12}	e_{10}
A_2 $\;p_{21}$	p_{22}	p_{20}	A_2 $\;f_{21}$	f_{22}	f_{20}	A_2 $\;e_{21}$	e_{22}	e_{20}
p_{01}	p_{02}	1	f_{01}	f_{02}	n	e_{01}	e_{02}	n

The expected frequency for cell (i, j) is the total frequency, n, multiplied by the cell probability, p_{ij}. However, we do not usually know the individual values of the $\{p_{ij}\}$, although we may hypothesize one or more relations that interconnect these values. We call these relations our 'model'. The specification of a model enables us to construct estimates, $\{e_{ij}\}$, of the expected cell frequencies. It is usual to refer to these quantities simply as 'expected' frequencies with the adjective 'estimated' being suppressed.

Conventionally the first subscript always refers to the category of variable A, the second to the category of variable B, and so on. To fix this notation consider a hypothetical study of the psychic powers of a medium, in which a card is taken from a pack of playing cards by an investigator. The medium is required to state whether the card is red or black. If we let variable A be the true colour of the card and variable B the colour stated by the medium, with black being category 1 in each case, then f_{12} will be the number of occasions on which a black card was stated by the medium to be red.

The fundamental question that concerns us, when analysing a 2×2 table is: 'Why are the numbers not all the same?' Quite how we answer this depends upon how the data were collected. For example, in the case of the medium there are at least three distinct situations, as illustrated below.

(i) The medium is *told* that there will be a sequence of 10 cards of which 6 will be black and 4 will be red.

(ii) The investigators choose 6 black cards and 4 red cards but *do not tell* the medium.

(iii) The investigators select 10 cards at random.

The differences in the situations lie in which of the marginal totals of the 2×2 table have been fixed by the experiment. In case (i), assuming that the medium is rational, we have $f_{10}=f_{01}=6$, $f_{20}=f_{02}=4$. In case (ii) we have only that $f_{10}=6$, $f_{20}=4$, while in case (iii) we only know that $n=10$.

In case (i), knowledge of f_{11} enables us to deduce the remaining three cell frequencies, because of our knowledge of the marginal totals. For example, the limiting values for f_{11} are 6 (all correct) and 2. The appropriate test is the well-known 'exact' test of Fisher (1970). An approximation to the exact test which is very useful for large values of n is based upon the fact that the statistic

$$X_y^2=n(|f_{11}f_{22}-f_{12}f_{21}|-n/2)^2/f_{10}f_{20}f_{01}f_{02} \tag{1}$$

has an approximate χ_1^2 distribution (Yates, 1934).

The case (ii) is better known as the 2×2 binomial or comparative trial, in which we are primarily interested in whether or not there is a difference between the column proportions of the two rows: that is, does

$$p_{11}/p_{10}=p_{21}/p_{20}?$$

Simple algebraic manipulation reveals that this is equivalent to the comparison of p_{11}/p_{01} with p_{12}/p_{02}. If equality does hold then it is easy to show that

$$\alpha=p_{11}p_{22}/p_{12}p_{21}=1. \tag{2}$$

The parameter α was first introduced by Yule (1900) and is variously termed the cross-product ratio or odds ratio, the latter term arising from the rearrangement

$$\alpha=(p_{11}/p_{12})/(p_{21}/p_{22}), \tag{3}$$

which is the ratio of the odds on column 1 rather than column 2, given row 1, to the odds on column 1 rather than column 2, given row 2.

If the null hypothesis that $\alpha=1$ is correct then the estimated expected cell frequencies are given by

$$e_{ij}=f_{i0}f_{0j}/n. \tag{4}$$

Provided that all the expected frequencies are large, useful test statistics are provided by

$$X^2= \sum_{\text{all cells}} (f-e)^2/e, \tag{5}$$

the familiar Pearson goodness-of-fit statistic and

$$Y^2=2 \sum_{\text{all cells}} f \ln (f/e), \tag{6}$$

the likelihood-ratio statistic. Under the null hypothesis, both these statistics have an approximate chi-squared distribution with one degree of freedom. These statistics are widely used in a huge variety of situations. In the case of the 2×2 table we can rewrite X^2 as

$$X^2=n(f_{11}f_{22}-f_{21}f_{12})^2/f_{10}f_{20}f_{01}f_{02}. \tag{7}$$

In recent studies of the 2×2 comparative trial both Upton (1982) and Rhoades & Overall (1982) have concluded that a more accurate test is provided by $X_u^2=(n-1)X^2/n$, but see also Yates (1984).

In case (iii) interest centres upon whether the two classificatory variables are independent or whether they are associated. If they are independent then we again have $\alpha=1$ and the expected cell frequencies are again given by equation (4). For large n, the X^2 and Y^2 tests given by equations (5) and (6) should be used to test the hypothesis of independence. For very small n (such that a large proportion of the $\{e_{ij}\}$ are less than 1), the chi-squared approximation breaks down. Lawal & Upton (1980, 1984) have suggested an alternative approximation and Lawal (1980) gives tables of the percentage points of X^2 for use with small expectations.

THE 2×2×2 TABLE

We return now to the example given at the beginning, where there were three dichotomous variables A, B and C corresponding to sex, treatment and outcome, respectively. Table 2 presents some fictitious data to add colour to the discussion.

Extending our previous notation in a natural fashion, we have, for example, $f_{111}=40, f_{110}=120, f_{100}=300$ and $n=600$. Similarly the theoretical probabilities are denoted by $\{p_{ijk}\}, \{p_{i00}\}$ and so forth, with

$$p_{i00}=\sum_j \sum_k p_{ijk}.$$

Table 2. Hypothetical frequencies for a $2\times2\times2$ table

	A_1				A_2		
	B_1	B_2			B_1	B_2	
C_1	40	100	140	C_1	100	10	110
C_2	80	80	160	C_2	60	30	90
	120	180	300		160	40	200

As with the 2×2 table there are alternative sampling schemes. For the present we shall assume that sampling is conducted under the equivalent of scheme (iii) with only n being fixed. As before, out interest centres on the extent to which the three variables A, B and C are associated – we shall place more emphasis on the response variable C subsequently. Under the hypothesis of complete mutual independence, the cell probabilities $\{p_{ijk}\}$ are interrelated by the equation

$$p_{ijk}=p_{i00}\cdot p_{0j0}\cdot p_{00k},\tag{8}$$

so that the estimated expected cell frequencies under this model are given by

$$e_{ijk}=f_{i00}\cdot f_{0j0}\cdot f_{00k}/n^2,\tag{9}$$

which is the analogue of equation (4). For the data of Table 2 we have $f_{100}=300$, $f_{200}=200, f_{101}=280, f_{020}=220, f_{001}=250$ and $f_{002}=250$ so that the expected frequencies corresponding to independence are those shown in Table 3.

Comparison of the observed frequencies of Table 2 with the fitted frequencies of Table 3 suggests that the independence model provides a poor explanation of the data. This is confirmed by the goodness-of-fit statistics X^2 and Y^2. Using

Table 3. Estimated expected frequencies under independence

	A_1				A_2		
	B_1	B_2			B_1	B_2	
C_1	84	66	150	C_1	56	44	100
C_2	84	66	150	C_2	56	44	100
	168	132	300		112	88	200

equations (5) and (6) we obtain $X^2 = 109$ and $Y^2 = 118$, both of which are vastly greater than the upper 0.1 per cent point of the χ^2_4 distribution – it is evident that complete mutual independence between the variables is *not* a reasonable explanation of the data.

Table 4. Table 2 collapsed over variable A

	B_1	B_2
C_1	140	110
C_2	140	110

The danger of collapsing a table

Suppose, in the previous example, we were to ignore variable A and that we consequently pooled the data. We would obtain the collapsed table shown as Table 4. In this table, recovery appears to be a 50:50 chance independent of whether the patient has been treated. We know that this is not really the case: from Table 2 we can see that 62.5 per cent of those female patients that are treated will recover, while only 25 per cent of untreated females recover. For males the recovery rate is greater amongst those who are untreated.

If we calculate the value of the cross-product ratio, α, for the male patients, we get $\alpha = 40 \times 80 / 100 \times 80 = 0.4$, which is less than 1 and indicates a negative association between recovery and treatment amongst males. On the other hand, for females, $\alpha = 100 \times 30 / 10 \times 60 = 5$, a strong positive association. If we use regression lines with negative and positive slopes then we can show what is happening using the graphical analogy pictured in Figure 1. The key is that, in the combined situation, we are incorrectly treating two distinct populations as though they were a single population.

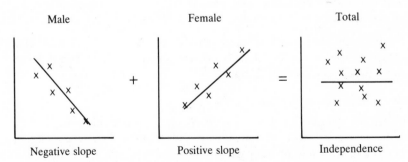

Figure 1. Regression analogy of the combining of two separate populations.

It is obvious that by suitably positioning the separate regression lines we can achieve any number of weird composite results. Similarly, pooling separate populations can lead to any outcome for the composite table. Table 5 shows, as an example, the inverse situation to the previous data set, where two tables showing independence combine to produce a table showing a strong association.

Table 5. Collapsing a table to obtain a false association

	A_1					A_2					A		
	B_1	B_2				B_1	B_2				B_1	B_2	
C_1	5	25	30		C_1	150	30	180		C_1	155	55	210
C_2	15	75	90	+	C_2	50	10	60	=	C_2	65	85	150
	20	100	120			200	40	240			220	140	360
	$\alpha=1$					$\alpha=1$					$\alpha=3.68$		

The sources of variation in a $2\times2\times2$ table

A $2\times2\times2$ table contains eight cell frequencies which, in general, will require us to make eight separate statements ($f_{111}=40, ..., f_{222}=30$) in order to specify the table.

Obviously, there is an infinite number of ways in which we could convey this information and, while listing the eight cell frequencies may be the simplest way, it is not necessarily the most helpful. An alternative breakdown would be couched in terms of the following characteristics:

1. An overall mean.
2. The relative 'popularity' of A_1 and A_2.
3. The relative 'popularity' of B_1 and B_2.
4. The relative 'popularity' of C_1 and C_2.
5. The interaction (association) between A and B.
6. The interaction (association) between A and C.
7. The interaction (association) between B and C.
8. The three-variable interaction between A, B and C.

The independence model presumes that there are no interactions so that the last four items in this list are all zero – this explains why there were 4 degrees of freedom for the goodness-of-fit tests.

Odds, odds-ratios and ratios of odds-ratios

Consider the data on the males (A_1) in Table 2. We found that the odds on recovery were 2:1 against for treated males and 5:4 on for untreated males. These odds are a natural way of comparing the sizes of each pair of numbers – they amount to a division of one number by the other. If we pursue this idea and divide one ratio by the other we get α, the odds-ratio. For males, as we noted earlier, this is $(1/2)/(5/4)=0.4$, while for females it is equal to 5.

Notice that the value of α – which is measuring association between B and C – is dependent upon the category of A. This is what we mean by a *three-variable interaction*. We can quantify the importance of such an interaction by considering the ratio of the odds-ratios: $0.4/5=0.08$.

Table 6. A rearrangement of Table 2

	B_1				B_2		
	A_1	A_2			A_1	A_2	
C_1	40	100	140	C_1	100	10	110
C_2	80	60	140	C_2	80	30	110
	120	160	280		180	40	220

Table 6 illustrates that, as we would hope and expect, the value of this 'super ratio' is independent of the order in which we do our sums. The values of the odds-ratios for the association between A and C are 0.3 for B_1 and 3.75 for B_2, giving the ratio of odds-ratios as $0.3/3.75=0.08$ as before.

A GENERAL MODEL

From the foregoing discussion it is evident that, for the $2\times2\times2$ table, we seek a model involving eight terms. Such a model was suggested by Goodman (1970) and is given as equation (10).

$$p_{ijk}=\eta \ \tau_i^A \tau_j^B \tau_k^C \tau_{ij}^{AB} \tau_{jk}^{BC} \tau_{ijk}^{ABC} \qquad (i, j, k=1, 2) \qquad (10)$$

In this multiplicative model, η represents the 'average' probability, while τ_x^X represents a multiplying factor reflecting the relative abundance ($\tau>1$) or scarcity ($\tau<1$) of category x of variable X. Similarly, τ_{xy}^{XY} represents the abundance or scarcity of the combination $X=x$ and $Y=y$ as opposed to the value that would be expected for this combination under the model of independence. Finally τ_{xyz}^{XYZ} represents the influence of the three-variable interaction over and beyond those of the other terms in the model.

In order to restrict the model to exactly eight parameters, one corresponding to each of the eight characteristics noted earlier (and in the same order), it is necessary to impose some arbitrary side conditions. One set is

$$1=\prod_i \tau_i^A= \ldots =\prod_i \tau_{ij}^{AB}=\prod_j \tau_{ij}^{AB}= \ldots =\prod_k \tau_{ijk}^{ABC}, \qquad (11)$$

where the Π sign implies the product over the suffix concerned. Incidentally, the 'average' referred to for the definition of η is actually the geometric mean of the individual $\{p_{ijk}\}$.

If one or more of the τ parameters is equal to 1 then the model is correspondingly simplified. For example, the independence model – no associations – is simply

$$p_{ijk}=\eta \ \tau_i^A \tau_j^B \tau_k^C \tag{12}$$

and involves just four of the eight parameters.

To estimate the parameters from a set of data it is necessary to solve a set of equations too complex to include in this short description. However, in practice this tedious hard work is performed by computer. If we invoke the model given by equation (10) as a description of the data of Table 2, we obtain the results

$$\hat{\eta}=68.07, \quad \hat{\tau}_1^A=1.05, \quad \hat{\tau}_1^B=0.97, \quad \hat{\tau}_1^C=1.17,$$

$$\hat{\tau}_{11}^{AB}=0.82, \quad \hat{\tau}_{11}^{AC}=0.76, \quad \hat{\tau}_{11}^{BC}=0.82, \quad \hat{\tau}_{111}^{ABC}=0.97,$$

where the 'hats' on top of the parameters indicate that these are maximum likelihood estimates.

Using the constraints (11) we also have, for example, that $\hat{\tau}_2^A=1/\hat{\tau}_1^A=1/1.05$, so that

$$f_{111}=68.07\times1.05\times0.97\times1.17\times0.82\times0.76\times0.82\times0.97=40.2\approx40,$$

and

$$f_{213}=\frac{68.07\times0.97\times0.76\times0.97}{1.05\times0.82\times1.17\times0.82}=58.9\approx60.$$

The deviations from exact equality in these two equations are entirely due to the round-off errors consequent upon truncating the parameter estimates to just two decimal places.

We have, therefore, substituted the eight parameter estimates for the original eight observations, whilst retaining all the information provided by those observations. We must now consider how we should interpret these parameter estimates. We begin with $\hat{\tau}_1^C$, since the variable C (recovers/dies) is the variable of prime interest. The ratio of $\hat{\tau}_1^C$ to $\hat{\tau}_2^C$ represents the estimated odds on recovery as opposed to death and is quantified as 1.17 to $1/1.17$ or as 1.17^2 to 1: in other words we can say that the odds on a patient, chosen at random, recovering rather than dying are estimated at about 4:3.

These odds of 4:3 change as we obtain more information about the patient. Thus, if we know that the patient is male (that is category 1 of variable A) then the odds become

$$1.17\times0.76 \text{ to } 1/(1.17\times0.76)$$

or about 4:5, whereas, if we know that the patient has not been treated (category 2 of variable B) then the odds become

$$1.17/0.82 \text{ to } 0.82/1.17$$

or about 2:1. The decision as to whether to multiply or divide is based on the category suffices and on the following result that arises from the constraints in equation (11):

$$\tau_{11}^{YZ} = \tau_{22}^{YZ} = 1/\tau_{12}^{YZ} = 1/\tau_{21}^{YZ}. \tag{13}$$

The result (13) is only relevant to the case of dichotomous variables.

A transformation to give a linear model

While it may be easiest to interpret models such as those given by equations (10) and (12) in their multiplicative form, those familiar with regression or analysis of variance techniques will find a multiplicative model rather unusual, since the general least squares theory applies to models that describe linear combinations of parameter values.

It is, however, a simple matter to transform the multiplicative τ-model into a linear λ-model – we simply take logarithms. If we write

$$v_{ijk} = \ln(p_{ijk}), \mu = \ln(\eta), \lambda_i^A = \ln(\tau_i^A)$$

and so on, then model (10) becomes

$$v_{ijk} = \mu + \lambda_i^A + \lambda_j^B + \lambda_k^C + \lambda_{ij}^{AB} + \lambda_{ik}^{AC} + \lambda_{jk}^{BC} + \lambda_{ijk}^{ABC}. \tag{14}$$

This model is the analogue, for discrete data, of the general model for a three-way crossed-classification for continuous data. The differences are that the underlying distribution here is Poisson or multinomial, not normal, and that the parameters of interest here are the interaction parameters as opposed to the 'main effect' parameters.

Since the model consists of a linear combination of logarithms, we refer to it as a *log-linear model*. The particular model (14) is the *saturated* model for a three-way cross-classification because it includes *all* the possible effects and interactions. For the $2 \times 2 \times 2$ table we have eight parameters that entirely explain the eight observations: the fit is perfect.

For the independence model (equation (12) or below),

$$v_{ijk} = \mu + \lambda_i^A + \lambda_j^B + \lambda_k^C,$$

the fit is far from perfect, but the model is very much simpler. We have to strike a balance between simplicity and goodness-of-fit. Our task is to select the *most parsimonious log-linear model that provides an adequate explanation of the data*. In other words we shall attempt to set as many as possible of the λ-parameters equal to 0. However, we do not have a completely free choice as to which λ-parameters are set to zero because of the hierarchy principle described below.

THE HIERARCHY PRINCIPLE

Suppose that we discover that a complex three-variable association exists interlinking the variables X, Y and Z. This means, for example, that the two-variable association between X and Y is dependent upon the category of variable Z. Now it may happen that the 'average' value of the XY association (measured by the λ^{XY} parameter) is equal to zero – but this must be a numerical accident, since it cannot make sense to claim that there is *no* association between X and Y when one has acknowledged an association between X, Y and Z!

The upshot of this argument is that, if we decide to include λ^{XYZ} in the model, then we must automatically also include λ^X, λ^Y, λ^Z, λ^{XY}, λ^{YZ} and λ^{XZ} – all the λ parameters whose indices are subsets of XYZ.

There is an equivalent algebraic restriction that ensures that the hierarchy principle is observed. This restriction arises because the maximum likelihood estimation of a particular λ-parameter guarantees that the corresponding fitted marginal totals will be exactly equal to the observed marginal totals. As an example, consider the model for a three-way cross-classification that includes λ_{ij}^{AB}. The marginal total corresponding to λ_{ij}^{AB} is the total over all the remaining variables, which is simply the total over C in this case and is the marginal total that we denote by f_{ij0}. Maximum likelihood estimation requires that

$$e_{ij0} = f_{ij0}. \tag{16}$$

If we sum both sides of equation (16) over all possible categories of variable B, we get

$$e_{i10} + e_{i20} + \ldots = f_{i10} + f_{i20} + \ldots,$$

that is,

$$e_{i00} = f_{i00}, \tag{17}$$

which is precisely the restriction that is imposed when λ_i^A appears in the model. Similarly, if we were to sum over the categories of variable A we would get $e_{0j0} = f_{0j0}$, indicating that λ_j^B must be in the model.

One advantage of the hierarchy principle is that we can write our models in a more 'snappy' form. We do not need to write out the entire right-hand side of equation (14) since the term with index ABC guarantees the presence of all the other terms. We can go a stage further and dispense with the λ and with its indices, simply writing the saturated model (equation (14)) as the model ABC.

For unsaturated models it is necessary to identify the most complex associations that are not implicit through the hierarchy principle. For example, model (15) – independence – becomes $A/B/C$. As a more complicated example, consider the 5-variable unsaturated model:

$$v_{ijklm} = \mu + \lambda_i^A + \lambda_j^B + \lambda_k^C + \lambda_l^D + \lambda_m^E + \lambda_{ij}^{AB} + \lambda_{ik}^{AC} + \lambda_{jk}^{BC} + \lambda_{kl}^{CD} + \lambda_{ijk}^{ABC}.$$

In the compressed shorthand notation this is just $ABC/CD/E$.

UNSATURATED MODELS

Our aim is to find a simple explanation of the data. We may be approaching this problem from one of two viewpoints, depending on the nature of the problem. The easier situation occurs when we have one or more models of definite interest that have been suggested on some theoretical grounds. The more complex situation occurs when we have no prior expectations concerning the structure of the data. With five classificatory variables there are thousands of alternative unsaturated models and the grounds for a choice of a 'best' model must be somewhat arbitrary, though we can usually restrict the choice somewhat from the outset because of the distinction between factor variables and response variables.

Table 7. A rearrangement of Table 2

A category		1		2	
B category		1	2	1	2
C category	1	40	100	100	10
	2	80	80	60	30
Total		120	180	160	40

In Table 7 the original $2 \times 2 \times 2$ table has been represented as a $(2 \times 2) \times 2$ table to emphasize that what interests us is the difference between the relative proportions of the categories of *C within* each column, rather than between the columns. The fact that there are 180 observations of one *AB* category combination, but only 40 on another category combination may be important, but is only of secondary importance in the present analysis. In other words, the inequality of the factor marginal totals is irrelevant to our analysis – we can happily regard 120, 180, 160 and 40 as fixed totals that our model must reproduce. 'Fixed totals' implies inclusion of the relevant parameter in the model. Consequently, *all models should include the all-factor interaction.*

With this restriction, together with that imposed by the hierarchy principle, we see that the only possibly interesting models for our $(2 \times 2) \times 2$ table are, using the shorthand form:

AB

AB/C

AB/AC

AB/BC

AB/AC/BC

ABC

Before we consider possible strategies for the selection of a 'best' model, we first consider the problem of obtaining the estimated expected frequencies corresponding to our unsaturated model.

Fitting an unsaturated model

A number of alternative methods exist, the simplest being that described below which was due originally to Deming & Stephan (1940). The algorithm exploits the identity between observed and fitted marginal totals that was illustrated by equations (16) and (17). For the model AB/AC the algorithm would have just four stages:

Stage 1: Form a working $2 \times 2 \times 2$ table with all cell frequencies, $\{W_{ijk}\}$, equal to 1.

Stage 2: Calculate the AB marginal totals for the working table, $\{W_{ij0}\}$, and for the original data, $\{f_{ij0}\}$. Multiply the working frequency, W_{ijk}, by f_{ij0}/W_{ij0} to obtain a revised working frequency $W^{\star}_{ijk}$.

Stage 3: Calculate the AC marginal totals for the revised working table, $\{W^{\star}_{i0k}\}$ and for the original data, $\{f_{i0k}\}$. Multiply the revised working frequency, $W^{\star}_{ijk}$, by $f_{i0k}/W^{\star}_{i0k}$.

Stage 4: Repeat stages 2 and 3 until the fitted marginal totals are as close as is desired to the corresponding totals for the original data.

This routine is certain to converge, though it usually requires more than the single complete cycle that is illustrated in Table 8. For more complex models convergence will not be immediate, though it is rare that more than a dozen cycles are required to give convergence to two decimal places in the fitted totals. If there are very large cell frequencies or if the table is incomplete (see below), then more cycles may be required.

The simplicity of the algorithm is evident: no more than simple multiplication is required, so that the computations are very fast and there is no need to implement more complex routines in an effort to achieve faster convergence.

It is a fairly easy matter to write one's own computer program to implement the algorithm for any special case, but there is a published FORTRAN version of the algorithm due to Lustbader & Stodola (1981) which is easy to use, although it does not supply parameter estimates but only the final values of the $\{W_{ijk}\}$ which are our $\{e_{ijk}\}$. Parameter estimates may be obtained by calculating the odds and odds-ratios for the fitted table, or by an analysis of that table using ordinary least squares.

Most readers, however, will probably have access to one of the specialist computer packages. In the latest version of the package BMDP4, there is an excellent fleet of subroutines for handling contingency tables. Tables may also be analysed using GENSTAT or GLIM, whilst there are many specialist programs constructed for contingency table analysis. These include ECTA, CTAB and MULTIQUAL, and there are probably at least a dozen others in addition. My advice would be to use the BMDP routines if available, or the GLIM package (but only if the reader is already a GLIM devotee). If there are no packages available, then I would recommend the purchase of ECTA (at a very reasonable price) from

Table 8. Fitting the model AB/AC to the data of Table 2 using the Deming–Stephan algorithm

Stage 1. $\{W_{ijk}\}$:

	A_1			A_2	
	B_1	B_2		B_1	B_2
C_1	1	1	C_1	1	1
C_2	1	1	C_2	1	1

Stage 2. $\{W_{ij0}\}$:

	A_1	A_2
B_1	2	2
B_2	2	2

$\{f_{ij0}\}$:

	A_1	A_2
B_1	120	160
B_2	180	40

$\{f_{i0k}/W_{i0k}\}$:

	A_1	A_2
B_1	60	80
B_2	90	20

Revised working table $\{W_{ijk}\}$:

	A_1			A_2	
	B_1	B_2		B_1	B_2
C_1	60	90	C_1	80	20
C_2	60	90	C_2	80	20
	120	180		160	40

Stage 3. $\{W_{i0k}\}$:

	A_1	A_2
C_1	150	100
C_2	150	100

$\{f_{i0k}\}$:

	A_1	A_2
C_1	140	110
C_2	160	90

$\{f_{i0k}/W_{i0k}\}$:

	A_1	A_2
C_1	0.9$\dot{3}$	1.1
C_2	1.0$\dot{6}$	0.9

Revised working table $\{W_{ijk}\}$

	A_1			A_2		
	B_1	B_2		B_1	B_2	
C_1	56	84	140	88	22	110
C_2	64	96	160	72	18	90

the computing service at the University of Chicago. The advantages of ECTA are its small size and price. It remains my favourite, but we have an improved version at Essex which is more 'user-friendly' than the current Chicago version which is somewhat primitive. However, for copyright reasons our version is not, unfortunately, available.

STRATEGIES FOR MODEL SELECTION

In general, when dealing with a multi-dimensional contingency table, there will be huge numbers of alternative models available and some selection strategy will be essential. The problems that arise are exactly equivalent to those that arise in multiple regression analyses and we shall adopt similar tactics.

A reasonable definition of a 'best' model would be 'the simplest model that provides a tolerable fit to the data' (this is the principle of parsimony). Of course it is up to us to specify what we mean by 'tolerable', and we might, nevertheless, prefer a more complex model, if that complex model were either more easily interpreted or was suggested by some theory or led to a significant improvement in fit as compared to the simplest model.

There are at least four selection strategies that appear in the literature, although in practice one tends to hit the data with every statistical tool in sight! These strategies are:

1. All models.
2. Single-model stepwise selection.
3. Screening.
4. Multi-model stepwise selection.

In the case of our example there are only six models of interest, so that it is perfectly feasible to fit each in turn and to examine their fit to the data in a very thorough fashion. Fitting all possible models will not usually be feasible, however, even given the speed of the Deming–Stephan algorithm, which can provide the fitted values for a single model within a few seconds using a mainframe computer.

One possibility is to proceed in a stepwise fashion through the tree of models. Using single steps, at each stage one new effect or interaction is added to the model so that a chain of models is constructed that links the simplest model of interest to the saturated model. This procedure is illustrated, for our simple case, in Figure 2, with the dotted lines indicating those parts of the tree that are not 'visited'. Examples of trees of specialized models are given in Bishop *et al.* (1975), Ch. 9). A worked example of the numerical side of the procedure is given by Upton (1978, Ch. 7). This single-step procedure is a little tedious, but reasonably thorough, though there can be no guarantee that the 'best' model will be found. An improvement, illustrated in Upton (1978), allows for an erratic course through the tree, in that forward moves may alternate with backward moves (which eliminate parameters that have become redundant).

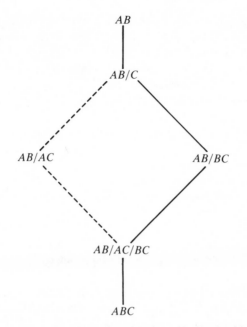

Figure 2. The tree of models for a $(2\times2)\times2$ table.

The importance of a parameter depends upon which other parameters are included in the model. For example, there might appear to be a direct association between variables X and Y because of the association of both X and Y with some other variable Z. In the context of linear regression, an oft-quoted example of this situation is concerned with the apparent strong correlation between the consumption of rum in Havana and the number of ministers of religion at that locality. Of course this 'nonsense' correlation is due to both rum consumption and the size of the church being dependent upon the size of the population!

Brown (1976) has suggested a screening procedure which attempts to discover, in an efficient manner, approximate upper and lower bounds for the importance of a parameter. An illustration of the worth of his procedure is provided by Upton (1981).

We postpone discussion of the multi-model stepwise selection procedure until after we have established a general procedure for evaluating the difference between rival models.

THE COMPARISON OF ALTERNATIVE MODELS

Consider two models M_1 and M_2 with degrees of freedom d_1 and d_2 (calculated automatically by our computer program). Suppose that these models lead to values of the likelihood ratio statistic Y^2 (equation (6)) of Y_1^2 and Y_2^2. We suppose that model M_1 is the simpler of the two models and that model M_2 contains all the parameters included in model M_1 plus some extra set of parameters, S. We must have $d_2 < d_1$ and $Y_2^2 < Y_1^2$, because of the extra complexity of model M_2.

The worth of the extra parameters in model M_2 is given a value by calculating $Y_1^2 - Y_2^2$. If this difference is very much greater than $d_1 - d_2$ then we conclude that the extra parameters were worthwhile. To specify how much greater we utilize the result that, if the extra parameters have true values equal to 0 then $Y_1^2 - Y_2^2$ will be an observation from a χ^2 distribution with $d_1 - d_2$ degrees of freedom. The comparison of models differing by a single parameter forms the basis of Brown's (1976) screening procedure. The question remains as to which models we should choose and at what significance level we should perform our tests. We have already seen that the abundance of alternative models creates an embarrassment of choice and we now consider the problems involved in the selection of an appropriate significance level.

Suppose that the parameters in the set S really can be set to zero and suppose that we compare the observed value of $Y_1^2 - Y_2^2$ with the upper 100 α per cent point of the χ^2 distribution with $d_2 - d_1$ degrees of freedom. By the nature of random variation there is a chance of 100 α per cent that we shall (incorrectly) conclude that we have a 'significantly' large value for the difference. Of course α will be small so that this is not a great worry. However, there are many models that might be compared. If we make each comparison at the 100 α per cent level, then the chance that not one of m comparisons proves 'significant' – when, in truth, none are significant – is only 100 $(1-\alpha)^m$ per cent. As an example, when $m = 30$ and $\alpha = 0.01$ the probability of a falsely 'significant' result is 26 per cent. An indication of the critical nature of the choice of value for α is given by retaining $m = 30$ and setting $\alpha = 0.05$ when the global error rate rises from 26 to 79 per cent. A formalization of the problem is embodied in the multi-model stepwise selection procedure.

Of course one should not confuse *statistical* significance with *real* significance. A value may appear 'significant' (statistically) just by chance: it is up to the researcher to incorporate common sense into the analysis and not to feel over-constrained by the particular statistical machinery.

Multi-model stepwise selection procedure

This procedure was developed by Aitkin (1979, 1980) and is based on his earlier (1974) simultaneous testing procedure for the analogous multiple regression situation. The procedure addresses the problems of maintaining a reasonable overall error rate and of restricting the number of models that need to be tested.

The first stage of Aitkin's method involves the fitting of the simplest model of possible interest (in the previous example this would be AB or AB/C). The object of fitting this model is to determine m, the maximum number of parameters that might be set to zero. The value of m is simply the degrees of freedom of that simplest model and is calculated automatically by any of the computer routines previously mentioned.

Using this value of m, we next ensure a reasonable global error rate by selecting a value for α such that $1-(1-\alpha)^m$ is not less than 0.5. If the goodness-of-fit value for the simplest model happens to be less than the upper $1-(1-\alpha)^m$ value of a chi-squared distribution with m degrees of freedom then this simplest model provides a satisfactory fit. This is an unlikely situation in practice and we normally proceed to the second stage.

Suppose that there are v variables and that the model M_k, which has d_k degrees of freedom and a goodness-of-fit value of Y_k^2, is the model including the all-factor interaction together with all k-variable interactions. The second stage of Aitkin's procedure consists of fitting the successive models $M_{v-1}, M_{v-2}, \ldots$ The fit of each model is examined in turn and this succession of models is terminated as soon as a model, M_k say, is discovered for which $Y_k^2 > C_k$, where C_k is the upper $1-(1-\alpha)^{d_k}$ point of the chi-squared distribution with d_k degrees of freedom. Note that, in Aitkin's procedure, in order to preserve the global error rate, the test statistic is Y_k^2 rather than the difference $Y_k^2 - Y_{k+1}^2$ suggested in the previous section.

The third stage amounts to an investigation of the reasons why model M_{k+1} was satisfactory while model M_k was unsatisfactory. The cause is plainly that at least one of the $(k+1)$-variable interactions is of significance. An *ad hoc* investigation now takes place (possibly utilizing the results from Brown's (1976) screening procedure) to ascertain the simplest model lying between the models M_{k+1} and M_k which has a goodness-of-fit value less than C_k. If there is no such model then the simplest reasonable model is the model M_{k+1}.

Assuming that a final model has not yet been obtained we now arrive at stage 4 of Aitkin's procedure. This stage is really a repeat of the previous two stages, but with any multi-variable interactions that have been found to be of importance being retained in all subsequent models. The critical values for comparison are, however, unaffected by the extra parameters and remain those that would have been appropriate for the models M_{v-1}, M_{v-2}, etc.

The procedure terminates when no simpler model can be discovered which provides an adequate explanation of the data. The reader will be relieved to learn that the method is easier to use than to describe!

A feature of this procedure is that the significance levels will not usually be the familiar 'tidy' 5 or 1 per cent levels, but will be determined by the value of the awkward formula $1-(1-\alpha)^{d_k}$. Published tables of upper-tail significance points for chi-squared distributions are therefore of little use but, fortunately, there is a comparatively simple approximation due to Hoaglin (1977):

$$c_k = [\sqrt{k} + 2\sqrt{-\log_{10}\{1-(1-\alpha)^{d_k}\}} - 7/6]^2. \tag{18}$$

Example

Sissons (1981) reports a study of how helping behaviour by individuals is related to the sex and race of the person requiring help. In a very neat experiment, eight similarly dressed Sussex University students approached people with a 5p coin in hand and said: 'Excuse me, do you have change for 5p?' The eight students consisted of four males and four females with two of each sex being English and two being Asian. All the students spoke English fluently. Those requested for change were all English and walking alone in a shopping precinct. Information was recorded on age, sex, and social class of each respondent together with the helpfulness or otherwise of that respondent. For the present we discount the age and social class of the respondent and consider the four variables:

A: helpfulness of respondent: help given or refused
B: race of requester: English or Asian
C: sex of requester: male or female
D: sex of respondent: male or female

Variable A is the single response variable. Variables B and C had their category frequencies fixed by the design of the experiment. Variable D has category frequencies fixed by chance. Since the interrelations between B, C and D are all fixed by chance or design these are of no concern to us and we concentrate on the associations between A and the other variables. In addition, we are not really concerned with any imbalance in the categories of A. So the simplest model of interest is the model BCD/A. The data are given in Table 9.

Table 9. A cross-classification of helpfulness by race and sex

| | Respondents | | | |
| | Male | | Female | |
Requester	Gave help	Refused help	Gave help	Refused help
English				
Male	20	4	21	5
Female	23	0	24	3
Asian				
Male	9	15	21	5
Female	25	2	17	11

We shall analyse the table using Aitkin's multi-model stepwise selection procedure in order to cut down on the number of models tested. The model BCD/A has 7 degrees of freedom. Thus $m=7$. Trying $\alpha=0.05$ we find $1-(1-\alpha)^7=30$ per cent which is conveniently less than Aitkin's upper bound of 50 per cent.

Commencing stage 2 of the procedure, we fit the model $M_3=BCD/ABC/ABD/ACD$ for which $Y_3^2=0.08$ and $d_3=1$. The critical value is 3.84 which is the upper $100\{1-(1-\alpha)^1\}$ per cent point of a chi-squared distribution with 1 degree of freedom. Since $0.08 \ll 3.84$ we conclude that there is no 4-variable association present in the data. We next fit the model $M_2 = BDC/AB/AC/AD$ for which $Y_2^2 = 22.66$ and $d_2 = 4$. The critical value $C_2 = 6.13$ is the $100\{1-(1-\alpha)^4\}$ per cent point of a chi-squared distribution with 4 degrees of freedom. Since $22.66 \geqslant 6.13$ we conclude that there is at least one important 3-variable association, and stage 2 is concluded.

Table 10. The models fitted to Table 9

	Model	d.f.	Y^2
M_1:	BCD/A	7	40.87
M_3:	$BCD/ABC/ABD/ACD$	1	0.08
M_2:	$BCD/AB/AC/AD$	4	22.66
	$BCD/ACD/AB$	3	5.88
	BCD/ACD	4	19.64

In stage 3 we seek to identify the important 3-variable association. Contemplation of the parameter estimates for the earlier model M_3 suggested that ACD is the only important association. This proves to be the case, since the new model $BCD/ACD/AB$ has a Y^2 value of 5.88 which is less than $C_2 = 6.13$ and therefore provides an adequate fit to the data.

Given that both BCD and ACD must be included in all subsequent models, the only possible simplification is the omission of AB from the model. The critical value is now $C_1 = 8.38$, the upper $100\{1-(1-\alpha)^7\}$ point of a chi-squared distribution with 7 degrees of freedom. Since the value of Y^2 for this model (BCD/ACD) is $19.64 \geqslant 8.38$, we conclude that the simplest satisfactory model is $BCD/ACD/AB$. The five models (out of a possible total of 18 models) tested are listed in Table 10.

The relevant (multiplicative form) parameter estimates for the model $BCD/ACD/AB$ are (omitting the tau and the suffices):

$$A = 2.310, \quad AB = 1.414, \quad AC = 0.724, \quad AD = 1.150, \quad ACD = 0.659.$$

Interpreted into English these say that:

1. The odds on a helpful rather than an unhelpful response are 2.310 to 1/2.310 or about 11:2.

2. These odds change to 2.310×1.414 to $1/(2.310 \times 1.414)$ or about 11:1, if the requester is English, but $2.310/1.414$ to $1.414/2.310$ or about 5:2 if the requester is Asian.

3. The odds change to 2.310×0.724 to $1/(2.310 \times 0.724)$ or about 11:4, if the requester is male but to $2.310/0.724$ to $0.724/2.310$ or about 10:1 if the requester is female.

4. These odds change to 2.310×1.150 to 1/(2.310/1.150) or about 7:1 if the respondent is male, but to 2.310/1.150 to 1.150/2.310 or about 4:1 if the respondent is female.

5. If the requester is known to be both English and female then the odds become $(2.310 \times 1.414/0.724)^2$ to 1 or about 20:1, with corresponding modifications to the other categories.

In summary, the response is most dependent upon the race of the requester, but is also affected by both the sex of the requester and the sex of the respondent. In addition there is a much greater effect (since $1/0.659 > 1/0.724 > 1.414 > 1.150$) due to the interaction of the sexes of the requester and the respondent: requests by a (young) person of the opposite sex are much more likely to be productive than are requests by a person of the same sex. Even in these gay times we should not be too surprised! Table 11 shows the data collapsed over race and represented as the percentage of helpful responses. Of course the collapsing of the table somewhat distorts the picture, but it does, I think, help to clarify matters.

Table 11. Percentage helpful (collapsed over race)

		Respondent Male	Female
Requester	Male	60	81
	Female	96	75

SPECIALIZED MODELS

In this short chapter I have concentrated on the general log-linear model without reference to any special circumstances that affect the data. Naturally special cases demand special treatment.

One obvious case that arises occurs when the count in a cell is zero not by chance but because it is certain to be zero. For example, suppose that patients are asked five questions and interest centres on the subgroups giving at least one negative reply – patients giving five positive replies are 'normal'. The resulting contingency table of 2^5 table (yes/no for five questions) with one impossible cell (+++++).

In this simple case one degree of freedom is lost from every model fitted to the data (because there is one cell missing). Fitting models is as simple as for the complete tables; we simply commence the fitting (Deming–Stephan) algorithm with a zero in the (+++++) cell and ones elsewhere. No amount of multiplication will then alter that zero. With lots of impossible cells the calculation of degrees of freedom becomes complicated: see Bishop *et al.* (1975).

With dichotomous variables the nature of the variables is largely irrelevant, but the nature becomes relevant when working with polytomies. Suppose, for example, that a variable is measured on the five-point ordinal scale: 'strongly agree', 'agree', 'neutral', 'disagree', 'strongly disagree'. We would want to take account of the ordering of these categories in our analysis. Various specialized models have been suggested and details are to be found in McCullagh (1980) and Goodman (1979*a*, *b*; 1981*a*, *b*).

A final class of models of particular interest are those for panel data follow-up studies where the classificatory variables are the same as each other except that they are displaced in time. We expect most observations in these square tables to lie on the main diagonal. Specialized models have been suggested by Goodman (1972) and Upton & Sarlvik (1981).

References

AITKIN, M.A. (1974). Simultaneous inference and the choice of variable subsets in multiple regression. *Technometrics, 16*, 221–227.

AITKIN, M.A. (1979). A simultaneous test procedure for contingency table models. *Applied Statistics, 28*, 233–242.

AITKIN, M.A. (1980). A note on the selection of log-linear models. *Biometrics, 36*, 173–178.

BISHOP, Y.M.M., FIENBERG, S.E. & HOLLAND, P.W. (1975). *Discrete Multivariate Analysis: Theory and Practice.* Cambridge, Massachusetts: MIT Press.

BROWN, M.B. (1976). Screening effects in multidimensional contingency tables. *Applied Statistics, 25*, 37–46.

DEMING, W.E. & STEPHAN, F.F. (1940). On a least squares adjustment of a sampled frequency table when the expected marginal totals are known. *Annals of Mathematical Statistics, 11*, 427–444.

EVERITT, B.S. (1977). *The Analysis of Contingency Tables.* London: Chapman-Hall.

FIENBERG, S.E. (1980). *The Analysis of Cross-classified Categorical Data* (2nd ed.). Cambridge, Massachusetts: MIT Press.

FISHER, R.A. (1970 [1925]). *Statistical Methods for Research Workers* (14th ed.). New York: Hafner.

GILBERT, G.N. (1981). *Modelling Society.* London: Allen and Unwin.

GOODMAN, L.A. (1970). The multivariate analysis of qualitative data: interactions amongst multiple classifications. *Journal of the American Statistical Association, 65*, 226–256.

GOODMAN, L.A. (1972). Some multiplicative models for the analysis of cross-classified data. In: L. Lecarn (ed.) *Proc. Sixth Berkeley Symposium on Mathematical Statistics and Probability*, Vol 1, 649–696. Berkeley: University of California Press.

GOODMAN, L.A. (1979*a*). Multiplicative models for the analysis of occupational mobility tables and other kinds of cross-classification tables. *American Journal of Sociology, 84*, 804–819.

GOODMAN, L.A. (1979*b*). Simple models for the analysis of association in cross-classifications having ordered categories. *Journal of the American Statistical Association, 74*, 537–552.

GOODMAN, L.A. (1981*a*). Association models and the bivariate normal for contingency tables with ordered categories. *Biometrika, 68*, 347–355.

GOODMAN, L.A. (1981*b*). Association models and canonical correlation in the analysis of cross-classifications having ordered categories. *Journal of the American Statistical Association, 76,* 320–334.

HOAGLIN, D. (1977). Exploring a table of percentage points of χ^2. *Journal of the American Statistical Association, 72,* 508–515.

LAWAL, H.B. (1980). Tables of percentage points of Pearson's goodness-of-fit test statistic for use with small expectations. *Applied Statistics, 29,* 292–298.

LAWAL, H.B. & UPTON, G.J.G. (1980). An approximation to the distribution of the χ^2 goodness-of-fit statistic for use with small expectations. *Biometrika, 67,* 447–454.

LAWAL, H.B. & UPTON, G.J.G. (1984). On the use of χ^2 as a test of independence in contingency tables with small cell expectations. *Australian Journal of Statistics, 26,* 75–85.

LUSTBADER, E.D. & STODOLA, R.K. (1981). Partial and marginal association in multidimensional contingency tables. *Applied Statistics, 30,* 97–105.

McCULLAGH, P. (1980). Regression models for ordinal data. *Journal of the Royal Statistical Society, Series B, 42,* 109–142.

RHOADES, H.M. & OVERALL, J.E. (1982). A sample size correction for Pearson chi-square in 2×2 contingency tables. *Psychological Bulletin, 91,* 418–423.

SISSONS, M. (1981). Race, sex and helping behaviour. *British Journal of Social Psychology, 20,* 285–292.

SWAFFORD, M. (1980). Three parametric techniques for contingency table analysis: a nontechnical commentary. *American Sociological Review, 45,* 664–690.

UPTON, G.J.G. (1978). *The Analysis of Cross-tabulated Data.* Chichester: Wiley.

UPTON, G.J.G. (1981). Log-linear models, screening and regional industrial surveys. *Regional Studies, 15,* 33–45.

UPTON, G.J.G. (1982). A comparison of alternative tests for the 2×2 comparative trial. *Journal of the Royal Statistical Society, Series A, 145,* 86–105.

UPTON, G.J.G. & SARLVIK, B.H. (1981). A loyalty-distance model for voting change. *Journal of the Royal Statistical Society, Series A, 144,* 247–259.

YATES, F. (1934). Contingency tables involving small numbers and the χ^2 test. *Journal of the Royal Statistical Society Supplement, 1,* 217–235.

YATES, F. (1984). Tests of significance for 2×2 tables. *Journal of the Royal Statistical Society, Series A, 147.*

YULE, G.V. (1900). On the association of attributes in statistics. *Philosophical Transactions of the Royal Society, London, Series A, 194,* 257–319.

5
Analysing Data from Longitudinal Comparative Studies

IAN PLEWIS

Psychologists commonly collect data from the same subjects over time. Sometimes subjects are sampled from or are assigned to different groups, and measurements are taken at frequent and regular intervals – every minute or every day, say – and these studies are then referred to as 'repeated measures studies' or 'repeated measures experiments'. Often, the aim of studies with this design is to measure the effects of practice or fatigue (or both) on the performance of a task. In other studies involving repeated measurement, data are collected much less frequently, for example, every year. These studies are often known as 'longitudinal studies'. There are several reasons for using a longitudinal design. Researchers, particularly in developmental psychology, frequently use it to study the way in which psychological variables change with age and how these relationships vary between individuals. Such studies often have a long time span – the ages of childhood, even the whole life cycle – and have been strongly influenced by the classic longitudinal studies of children's growth (for example, Tanner, 1961). Another reason for doing longitudinal studies is to measure the effects of social and educational interventions, and to compare randomly and non-randomly formed groups over time. It is this type of longitudinal, comparative study which is the major focus of this chapter.

There are three kinds of longitudinal comparative study. The first, and rarest, is an *experiment*: subjects are randomly assigned to treatment and control groups and measured on two or more occasions. However, the interval between measurements is often sufficiently wide for subjects to be lost from the study. It is not unusual for those who leave the experimental group to have characteristics which differ from those leaving the control group and, if this is so, then it would be more realistic to regard the study as a *quasi-experiment*. The formation of the groups in a quasi-experiment is not completely determined by a random procedure and there is usually a pretreatment measure either of the outcome variable or of a variable closely related to it. The third type of longitudinal comparative study is the *observational* study. The groups in observational studies are less easily labelled 'treatment' or 'control' and there is no deliberate attempt to obtain 'pretreatment' measures for all the subjects. This is particularly true when the groups are defined by background variables such as social class and marital status. It could be argued that quasi-experiments might, in some sense, have been experiments whereas this is not true of observational studies – in other words, the differences between the groups in an observational study are much more fundamental. The distinction between observational studies and quasi-experiments also has implications for analysis. In certain circumstances, the measurement of group differences will be the only requirement of an observational study, whereas the rationale of quasi-experiments (and experiments) is the causal explanation of group differences.

There is reasonable agreement among statisticians about appropriate methods for the analysis of repeated measures experiments. These are merely outlined in the next section, and readers may wish to supplement this by looking at the textbooks referred to there. However, these methods are often not well suited to the analysis of studies which compare groups over a long period of time, for reasons which are explained and illustrated later. The final section of the chapter looks at other issues in the design and analysis of comparative studies. Each section is augmented by analyses of a real data set. These data come from one of the Educational Priority Area (EPA) intervention studies carried out in the early 1970s. This study consisted of three groups of children with data collected on five occasions over four years. The children were originally assigned at random to the three groups, but losses from the study were not random and so the study is better treated as a quasi-experiment; further details can be found in Smith & James (1975).

ANALYSING REPEATED MEASURES EXPERIMENTS

Consider a fairly typical psychological experiment consisting of K groups each with independent samples of n subjects. Suppose that each of the Kn subjects are measured on T equally spaced occasions and that the dependent variable is measured on an interval scale. The experimenter wants to know whether there are any overall differences between the groups and between occasions (the 'main' effects) and whether one group changes more than another (the interaction between group and occasion or time). It is often the interaction which is of most interest.

Experiments of this type are commonly analysed using the method given by, for example, Winer (1971, Ch. 7). The variance is partitioned into 'between subjects' and 'within subjects' components and there are therefore two error terms. The first of these, the 'between subjects' term, is used to test for differences between the groups and the other, the 'within subjects' term, is used to test the effect of time and the interaction between group and time. The resulting analysis of variance (ANOVA) table looks like Table 1.

However, the F tests for the two 'within subjects' effects are only valid if, in addition to the usual assumptions needed for ANOVA, the within-group variances of the dependent variable are constant across occasions and if the

Table 1. ANOVA table for repeated measures experiment

Source of variation	d.f.	Mean square	F
Between subjects			
Group	$K-1$	a	a/b
Error 1	$K(n-1)$	b	
Within subjects			
Time	$T-1$	c	c/e
Group time	$(K-1)(T-1)$	d	d/e
Error 2	$K(n-1)(T-1)$	e	

correlations between measures are constant for all pairs of occasions. The second of these two conditions is rarely satisfied; much more likely is a pattern of decreasing correlations as the time between measurements increases. One solution to this problem, given by Winer, is to adjust the degrees of freedom for the F tests so instead of the F test for the time effect having $(T-1)$ and $K(n-1)(T-1)$ d.f., it has 1 and $K(n-1)$ while the test for the interaction is changed to have $(K-1)$ and $K(n-1)$ d.f. However, this adjustment will often result in tests which are too 'conservative' in the sense that the true significance level will be lower than the nominal level.

Using multivariate analysis of variance (MANOVA)

A more satisfactory solution is to change from a univariate to a multivariate mode of analysis and so to treat the T measures on the dependent variable as a multivariate set (Bock, 1975). This approach to testing the 'within subjects' effects assumes that the samples from the groups come from K multivariate normal distributions each having the same variance–covariance matrix. But it does not impose any conditions on the pattern of within-group correlations between occasions. A slight disadvantage of the multivariate (MANOVA) approach is that there are a number of significance tests to choose from for the within subjects effects (the test for the group effect is unaffected by the switch to a multivariate analysis). Work by Olson (1974) suggests that the Pillai–Bartlett test is most robust when the distributional assumptions mentioned above are not satisfied and so it is perhaps the test to choose.

If the groups are measured on just two occasions $(T=2)$ then a multivariate analysis is unnecessary and a simple one-way analysis of variance of the differences between the two occasions will test the group–time interaction. For just two groups $(K=2)$, this reduces to a t-test of whether the relative change,

$$\text{RC} = (\bar{x}_{22} - \bar{x}_{21}) - (\bar{x}_{12} - \bar{x}_{11}), \tag{1}$$

is zero, where $\bar{x}_{ij}$ is the mean of the dependent variable for group i at occasion j.

Both the univariate and the multivariate tests of the group–time interaction test only whether the time curves for the groups are parallel but they do not give any information about the form of the curves. For example, do straight lines with different slopes account for the variation in the dependent variable over the T occasions or is the relationship curvilinear for one group but not for another? This extra information can be obtained by partitioning a statistically significant interaction into components, using either orthogonal or ordinary polynomials to describe the relationship with time. Orthogonal polynomials are convenient for assessing the shape of the relationship (whether it is linear, quadratic, cubic, etc.) but the coefficients from ordinary polynomials are easier to interpret.

Often, the variation over time can be adequately modelled with just a straight line. In this case, the interaction can be characterized by the following equation:

$$x = \gamma + \delta_i\, t, \tag{2}$$

where x is the dependent variable, t is time and $\delta_i\,(i=1, 2, \ldots, K)$ gives the slope of the straight line relating x to t for group i. If there were no group–time interaction, then δ_i would not vary from group to group and, if there were no time effect, then $\delta_i = 0$. The constant term, γ, would vary from group to group if there is a group effect.

An example

Let us turn now to the study data mentioned at the beginning, and let us suppose for now that it is reasonable to treat it as an experiment. The children in the study were tested with the English Picture Vocabulary Test (EPVT) on each of five occasions. The preschool version of the test was used for the first two occasions and version 1 for occasions 3, 4 and 5, and both raw and standardized test scores were available for analysis. It would not be sensible to apply an ANOVA-type model to all the raw scores because the scale changes and this change of scale would also make an analysis of the standard scores rather difficult to interpret. However, 19 children were given both versions of the test at occasion 2 and the relationship between the raw scores on the two versions can be characterized well by:

$$EPVT_1 = -3.73 + 0.50\ EPVT_{ps} \tag{3}$$

with a multiple correlation of 0.74. Assuming that equation (3) applies to all the sample both at occasion 2 and at occasion 1, it is possible to estimate a raw score on version 1 of the test whenever the preschool version was used. Some of the estimated values are negative but as the scale is arbitrary, this does not matter. Table 2 gives the occasion means and standard deviations for the three groups, a control group (C) and two experimental groups $(E1$ and $E2)$. Separate intervention strategies were developed for the two experimental groups, and an obvious question to ask of these data is whether the experimental groups changed more, or 'grew' faster, than the control group over time.

Table 2. Raw scores on EPVT 1: means and standard deviations

Group	Time				
	1	2	3	4	5
C	4.3	6.9	12.3	17.2	19.9
(*n*=15)	(4.2)	(5.2)	(6.2)	(6.6)	(7.3)
*E*1	1.2	6.4	10.4	16.3	21.5
(*n*=15)	(1.1)	(3.8)	(4.0)	(5.2)	(4.3)
*E*2	0.3	4.5	11.8	15.9	21.4
(*n*=15)	(2.5)	(3.6)	(3.6)	(5.9)	(4.1)

There are no significant differences between the groups when averaged over the five occasions ($F=0.47$, d.f.$=2, 42, p>0.6$). The within-subjects effects were analysed by transforming the dependent variables to orthogonal polynomials and then using MANOVA. The main effect of time is highly significant ($F=187.0$, d.f.$=4, 39, p<0.001$) but there is also a significant group–time interaction with the Pillai–Bartlett test giving an F statistic of 2.69 with 8 and 80 d.f. ($p<0.02$). It is clear from the univariate test statistics that nearly all the group–time interaction is accounted for by the linear orthogonal polynomial and so the analysis was carried out again using an ordinary linear transformation (see Goldstein, 1979*a*, Appendix 4.1, for details). The resulting coefficients, δ_i in equation (2), were 0.36 for the control group and 0.45 and 0.47 for the two experimental groups (see Figure 1). One would therefore conclude from this analysis that the experimental groups show a similar growth pattern in the abilities measured by the EPVT over the four years of the study and one which is indeed different from the control group.

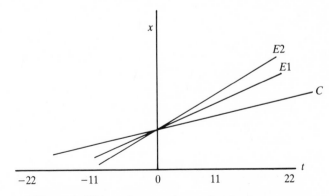

Figure 1. EPA study: growth rates for the three groups

It has not been possible to go into some of the statistically more complex aspects of this method of analysis. Interested readers are referred to Goldstein (1979a), Guire & Kowalski (1979) and Bock (1979) for these. However, this method is not well suited to these data, as we shall see in the next section.

CONDITIONAL AND UNCONDITIONAL MODELS FOR CHANGE

The previous section has discussed briefly methods which are used both for the analysis of repeated measures experiments and for studies of growth. Models which use these methods for measuring relative change are referred to as 'unconditional' or 'time-related' models by Goldstein (1979a) and can be contrasted with the 'conditional' or regression approach discussed in this section. Unconditional models make assumptions which tend to make them unsuitable for the analysis of many longitudinal comparative studies. Let us assume, for the rest of this chapter, that all comparative studies are non-randomized studies. However, it is worth bearing in mind that, even for longitudinal experiments, the unconditional model is often not ideal because it assumes that the same variable is measured on each occasion.

The simplest conditional model for two groups measured on two occasions is

$$y = \alpha + \beta_0 d + \beta_1 x + \varepsilon, \tag{4}$$

where y is the measure at the second occasion, x is the measure at the first occasion, d is a 'dummy variable' taking two values (0 and 1) corresponding to the two groups (control and treatment, respectively, in quasi-experiments), ε is an error term and β_0 is the measure of relative change. This model assumes that the relation between y and x can be characterized adequately by a straight line and that the line has the same slope, β_1, in the two groups (Figure 2). Equation (4) is a simple regression or analysis of covariance model and the least squares estimate of relative change is

$$\hat{\beta}_0 = (\bar{y}_2 - \bar{y}_1) - \hat{\beta}_1 (\bar{x}_2 - \bar{x}_1), \tag{5}$$

where $\bar{y}_2$ is the mean of y for group 2, etc.

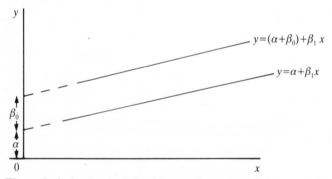

Figure 2. A simple conditional (regression) model for two groups

It is important to realize that the measure of relative change given in equation (5) is conceptually quite different from the measure given in equation (1) even though, when $\beta_1 = 1$, the values are identical. In equation (5), $\hat{\beta}_0$ is the difference between the groups at the second occasion for *fixed* values of the measure at the first occasion; it is this conditioning on first occasion measures which is absent from equation (1) and which is particularly important when discussing possible causal interpretations of β_0, as we shall see.

Comparing the unconditional and conditional approaches

A major problem with the unconditional approach to the analysis of data from comparative studies is that the results about relative change can be altered by simple transformations of the scale. This is most easily illustrated by considering the popular 'pre-test post-test' or 'non-equivalent control group' design (Cook & Campbell, 1979) with two groups measured on just two occasions. Suppose the group–time means are as follows:

	Group		
Time	1	2	
1	A	$A+c$	$b, c>0$
2	$A+b$	$A+b+c$	

As they stand, these data show that there has been no relative change, each group having gained b units. Suppose, however, that the pooled within-group (or population) standard deviation at time 1 is s_1 while at time 2 it is ks_1. Standardizing the measures at each time to give constant variance over time and then using an unconditional model gives a relative change of

$$\left(\frac{A+b}{ks_1} - \frac{A}{s_1}\right) - \left(\frac{A+b+c}{ks_1} - \frac{A+c}{s_1}\right) = \frac{c(k-1)}{ks_1}, \tag{6}$$

which is >0 or <0 depending on whether $k>1$ or $k<1$ respectively. Similarly, 'positive' change can be transformed to 'negative' change if $k<1$ and *vice versa* for $k>1$. This general point is relevant both to situations where the variances of the pre- and post-tests are not equal and to situations where the measures are standardized to have equal variances at all ages (for example, IQ) but where the variance of the latent trait (that is, intelligence) may not be constant.

Goldstein (1979a) points out that there is no relative change in the mean heights of boys and girls between the ages of four and eight using an unstandardized unconditional model, but that the gap narrows if height is standardized to have equal variance at four and eight. Kenny (1975) discusses a similar phenomenon which is postulated to occur with some psychological variables and is known as 'fan spread', that is, increasing raw differences between groups and increasing variance over time. The results for the EPA data are not substantially altered when a variance-stabilizing transformation is applied although the Pillai–Bartlett F statistic for the group–time interaction goes up to 3.71 ($p<0.001$). Nevertheless, the correlation between the individual linear coefficients for the two scales is only 0.87.

It may be most useful to work with the untransformed scale for variables with a fixed and widely accepted scale such as height. But it is not at all clear, in the absence of theoretical guidelines, which criteria should be used to decide between unstandardized and standardized unconditional models for those variables with arbitrary scales which are common in the social sciences. Kenny recommends the use of standardized differences for fan spread situations but he does not really justify this choice nor does he consider the alternative of a conditional model, for which the conclusions are unchanged by these changes of scale.

Conditional models are more logical than time-related or unconditional models because they take account of the direction of time. It would be possible to change equation (4) round so that x is the dependent variable and y the explanatory variable. However, the estimate of relative change would not, in general, be the same, whereas RC in equation (1) is symmetric with respect to time.

It is the non-randomized or non-experimental aspect of most longitudinal comparative studies which provides the conditional approach with its greatest strength, especially when the aim of the study is to *explain* rather than just to *describe* change. It only makes sense to try to talk about the causal explanation of relative change for groups which are either equal at the outset (as in experiments) or are 'made equal' statistically. There is nothing in the unconditional model's comparison of net changes which implies this kind of equality, whereas the notion of analysing time 2 scores for fixed scores at time 1 does at least begin to tackle this problem.

In essence, a conditional analysis attempts to answer the question: had the groups been alike at time 1 on *all* the variables which influence outcome, then what would the difference have been between the groups at time 2 (this being, of course, the relative change)? However, it is only when the attempt to eliminate all the important initial differences between the groups is successful that there is a possibility of giving a valid causal interpretation to the observed change. Thus, instead of equation (4), it may be necessary to estimate a more complicated regression model:

$$y=\alpha+\beta_0 d+\sum_{i=1}^{k}\beta_i x_i+\varepsilon, \qquad (7)$$

where the x_i represent the variables which account for initial differences between the groups and where each x_i makes an independent contribution to the explanation of the variance of the measure at occasion 2. The estimate of relative change, $\hat{\beta}_0$, from equation (7) will not, in general, be the same as the one given in equation (5).

It will often be unwise to suppose that all the initial differences between non-randomly constructed groups can be accounted for by differences in the measure at occasion 1. For example, Goldstein (1979*b*) shows, by using data from the National Child Development Study, that, not only were there social class differences in reading and arithmetic for children aged seven, but also, for fixed 7-year scores, there were further social class differences at 11 years. This has implications for educational quasi-experiments of a compensatory nature, where social class is often associated with treatment and treatment is spread over, say, a school year. Goldstein's result suggests that social class would be correlated with the pre-test and have a partial correlation with the post-test after controlling for the pre-test. In this case, any model for British data which did not include a social class term would lead to estimated 'treatment effects' which would be biased downwards because of this tendency for working-class children to drop further behind in the population.

If equation (7) contains *all* the variables which separate the two groups initially and which are related to outcome, then $\hat{\beta}_0$ will be an unbiased estimate of the treatment effect. However, it is rarely possible both to know and to measure these variables and so the results from comparisons of non-randomly formed groups will usually be more equivocal than those from experiments. Certainly, an accurate estimate of the causal effect, $\hat{\beta}_0$, can be obtained only if there is extensive pre-treatment measurement, a clear understanding of how the groups were formed, careful model specification and detailed analysis. On the other hand, it would perhaps be wrong to be too pessimistic. There is a tendency to devalue findings from non-randomized studies by invoking unknown 'third variables' (or 'regression to the mean' or 'Lord's paradox' – Lord, 1967), and it would be better to see analysis of this type in the context of ongoing research which is often trying, in various ways, to find answers to important but difficult questions. As our knowledge of the underlying models for both the determination of outcomes and of assignment to groups increases, so will it be possible to reduce bias. (Plewis, 1985, gives a more detailed discussion of model specification for this type of longitudinal comparative study, and a useful book by Anderson *et al.*, 1980, also discusses these issues, but with a medical orientation.)

Extensions to more than two occasions

It is reasonably straightforward to extend the ideas represented by equations (4), (5) and (7) to studies with measurements taken at more than two occasions. For three occasions, there could be two equations:

$$y_2 = \alpha_0 + \beta_0 d + \beta_1 y_1 + \varepsilon_1, \tag{8}$$

$$y_3 = \alpha_1 + \gamma_0 d + \gamma_1 y_1 + \gamma_2 y_2 + \varepsilon_2, \tag{9}$$

with equation (8) equivalent to equation (4). In some circumstances, another version of equation (9) might be preferred, that is,

$$y_3 = \alpha_2 + \theta_0 d + \theta_1 y_1 + \varepsilon_3. \tag{10}$$

Equations (8) and (9) (or 10) can usually be estimated separately using ordinary least squares.

Expectations about the sign and size of γ_0 and θ_0 will depend very much on the study design. For quasi-experiments with just a treatment and a control group, with the treatment withdrawn at the second occasion and with a positive initial treatment effect, β_0, the γ_0 might be zero. This would show that the effect of the treatment had been maintained. A positive value of γ_0 would show that the treatment had a further effect after its withdrawal, which could be thought of as a kind of 'sleeper' effect. If γ_0 is negative then one would conclude that at least some of the effect washes out as soon as the treatment is withdrawn; if y_3 is regressed against y_1 only and θ_0 is zero then all the effect washes out.

When conditional models are estimated from the EPA data, conclusions emerge which are rather different from those presented in the previous section. Four equations were estimated using the standard scores (Table 3), the first relating y_2 to y_1, d_1 and d_2 (that is, equation (8) but with two dummy variables because there are three groups) and the other three relating y_t to y_{t-1}, y_{t-2}, d_1 and d_2 ($t = 3, 4, 5$). Even though the treatments were in operation only between occasions 1 and 2, there was no evidence of any difference between the groups at occasion 2 after controlling for y_1 ($F = 0.66$, d.f. $= 2, 41, p > 0.5$). However, in the year after the treatment was withdrawn, there is some evidence of an effect ($F = 3.70$, d.f. $= 2, 40, p < 0.04$) with all this effect concentrated in the second experimental group which gained 7.3 points more than the control group. There is again no evidence for a group effect from the other two equations ($F = 0.17$, d.f. $= 2, 40$, $p > 0.8$ and $F = 2.11$, d.f. $= 2, 40, p > 0.13$ respectively). Both y_{t-1} and y_{t-2} make statistically significant contributions to the explanation of y_t when $t = 4$ and 5 but not when $t = 3$ and other terms in y_{t-k} could, in theory, have been included. (Residual plots show that non-linear terms in y_{t-k} are not needed.)

An alternative approach is to relate y_t to y_1, d_1 and d_2 for $t = 2, 3, 4, 5$ (that is,

Table 3. EPVT standard scores: means and standard deviations

Group	Occasion				
	1	2	3	4	5
C	97.8	95.0	98.6	97.6	91.1
	(11.4)	(12.3)	(14.8)	(13.0)	(12.8)
E1	92.8	95.8	98.9	98.9	96.1
	(8.8)	(10.5)	(10.8)	(9.3)	(9.0)
E2	88.4	90.6	100.9	97.0	95.5
	(10.2)	(11.0)	(9.8)	(11.4)	(7.0)

equation (10)). Again, no convincing pattern emerges, with a group effect only when $t=5$, which is not easy to explain.

A prudent person would conclude that there is little evidence for treatment effects from these analyses and certainly no evidence for an effect of the treatment applied to the first experimental group. This is in sharp contrast to the results from the unconditional analyses which provide apparently unequivocal evidence for faster growth in the two experimental groups. Of course, the conditional analyses are limited by the fact that they take no account of other variables; nevertheless, the differences between the two analyses are striking and arise because, as Tables 2 and 3 show, there are substantial differences between the group means on the pre-test.

Some statistical problems

The regression approach does, I believe, represent the most suitable way of analysing the majority of longitudinal comparative studies at present. Nevertheless, there are alternative approaches which are discussed in the next section and there are some potential statistical problems. Some of these problems are common to all users of linear regression models – questions of linearity, homoscedasticity and outliers, for example – and these are discussed in a number of texts (for example, Draper & Smith, 1981; Weisberg, 1980); and in the September, 1982, issue of *Biometrics*, which has a number of articles on analysis of covariance. However, others are particular to comparative studies. For example, estimates of β_0, γ_0 and θ_0 in equations (4), (7), (8), (9) and (10) will contain a considerable degree of uncertainty if there is little or no overlap between the groups on the explanatory variables and this should always be checked by plotting the data before any analysis. It is also important to check, by plotting or in the analysis, or both, that the relationship between the dependent and explanatory variables is the same for both (all) groups as it was in the EPA study; if it is not then the interpretation of the coefficients of d (β_0, γ_0, θ_0) can become problematic. Cochran & Rubin (1973) discuss ways of dealing with non-parallel regressions, sometimes known as 'group-covariate interactions'.

However, perhaps the most serious problem with conditional models arises when the explanatory variables are measured with error as they so often are. This problem can crop up whenever linear regression is used but it can be particularly awkward in longitudinal comparative studies, and its effect can be such as to change the sign of an estimated treatment effect. Given a simple model like equation (4), with x measured with error, then it is easy to demonstrate that the least squares estimates of β_1 and so of β_0 are biased. But, given a knowledge of the reliability (ϱ) of x then an unbiased estimate of β_0 is

$$\hat{\beta}_0 = (\bar{y}_2 - \bar{y}_1) - \frac{\hat{\beta}_1}{\varrho}(\bar{x}_2 - \bar{x}_1). \tag{11}$$

If $\hat{\beta}_1$ – the pooled within-groups regression coefficient of y on x – is not corrected, then, for $\bar{x}_2 > \bar{x}_1$ and $\hat{\beta}_1 > 0$, the true relative change or treatment effect is over-estimated, while for $\bar{x}_1 > \bar{x}_2$, it is under-estimated.

The correction procedure given above is simple but it has several limitations. Often prior information on reliabilities or error variances (σ_u^2) is unavailable. Reliabilities and error variances of some standardized educational and psychological tests are given in the manuals for these tests but they are often based on small, non-probability samples and so may not apply to the population under study. It is often argued that, although reliabilities are population specific, error variances are not, but even if reasonable estimates of σ_u^2 are available, they may be subject to considerable sampling error and this sampling error should be incorporated into any correction procedure.

A second problem with the simple method is that it does not extend easily to situations where there is more than one unreliable explanatory variable. It also assumes that the measurement errors of the dependent variable and any explanatory variable are uncorrelated and this will not always be reasonable. For example, if y and x are both obtained by the same interviewer in a survey or by the same psychological tester, this could introduce correlated measurement error. There is always the chance that the measurement errors of explanatory variables will be correlated, particularly as these variables will often have been measured at the same time and so might contain similar 'transitory' errors.

Although several correction methods have been suggested to deal with some of the limitations outlined above, perhaps the two most useful are those associated with Fuller (Degracie & Fuller, 1972; Warren *et al.*, 1974; Fuller & Hidiroglou, 1978; Fuller, 1980) and those based on the theoretical work of Jöreskog (1970) and further developed by Sörbom (1976, 1978). The latter are often referred to as the LISREL approach after the computer program of that name. Only the briefest introduction to these methods can be given here and readers interested in more details are referred to the articles cited above, to Goldstein (1979*b*) and to Plewis (1985).

The methods developed by Fuller and his colleagues extend the simple model in several ways. They can deal with more than one explanatory variable and with a mixture of perfectly and imperfectly measured explanatory variables. Also, they allow for correlated measurement error both between the explanatory variables and between the dependent variable and any of the explanatory variables. If the measurement errors are estimated rather than known, then the variances of the corrected regression coefficients are inflated to take account of this. The feature of Jöreskog's (and Sörbom's) methods is that they do not require prior knowledge about reliabilities or error variances but instead assume that there are at least two measures or indicators of each of the underlying variables which are then combined to provide estimates of error variances and covariances for the sample. The method can also handle known error variances but cannot incorporate sampling errors of error variances into the estimated variances of the regression coefficients in the way that Fuller's methods are able to do.

It was not possible to do a complete analysis of the effects of measurement error on the conditional models for the EPA data. However, a limited application of Fuller's methods was possible and it showed that there was a tendency for the magnitudes of the treatment effects to be greater after correction although the overall conclusions from the conditional models were unchanged. There is no need to take account of the effects of measurement error on the unconditional model because the explanatory variables, group and time, are error-free.

ALTERNATIVE METHODS OF ANALYSIS

There is a sizeable literature on the analysis of longitudinal comparative studies containing articles which propose supposedly improved methods and others which are critical of the more established techniques. Conditional models have received their fair share of criticism but much of this has been directed against the simplest analysis of covariance model, equation (4). However, extended versions of this model, particularly if they are corrected for measurement error, do make many of the criticisms redundant. Nevertheless, it would be a mistake to suppose that other methods have no value and so this section gives a brief description of one of the popular alternatives and two of the more promising suggestions.

Matching

Perhaps the most popular alternative to regression is to select matched samples, when an attempt is made at the design stage to obtain samples which are equivalent on all relevant pre-treatment variables. The treatment effect, or the relative change over two occasions, is then estimated as the difference between the group means at post-test, that is, $\bar{y}_2 - \bar{y}_1$. Various methods of constructing matched samples have been suggested. With just one continuous matching variable, Cochran & Rubin (1973) describe (a) 'paired caliper' matching where, for each individual, $|x_2 - x_1| < \alpha$, where α is predetermined and small, (b) 'nearest available' matching in which, for a fixed treatment group sample, a computer algorithm is used to select an equal number from a large reservoir of control elements to give pairs similar in value on x, and (c) 'mean' matching, which focuses solely on making $\bar{x}_2 = \bar{x}_1$. However, to match on just one variable, even if that variable is a relevant and perfectly reliable pre-test measure of the outcome variable, suffers from the same disadvantage of potential bias as does regression adjustment with one explanatory variable. In other words, some kind of multivariate matching procedure is often needed and one method is discussed by Rubin (1976).

What are the relative merits of matching and regression adjustment? The omission of relevant explanatory variables from a regression model is equivalent to ignoring relevant matching variables in the design and neither method can completely deal with one of the fundamental problems of comparing groups not formed by randomization. A serious drawback of paired caliper matching, particularly if the matching criterion employed is tight, is that the group samples are often no longer random samples of their populations and this restricts the inferences that can be made. Also, this kind of matching can result in a serious diminution of sample size, especially when there are more than two groups. For example, it was only possible to create 9 (out of a possible 15) matched triplets from the EPA data even though the criterion used, $|x_i - x_j| \leqslant 5$ ($i, j = 1, 2, 3, i \neq j$), was rather loose. The unmatched children were those with either particularly high or particularly low pre-test scores. To some extent, this problem can be avoided by retaining all the sample elements in the treatment groups and finding matches from a larger control group reservoir as in nearest available matching. A particular disadvantage of mean matching is that it assumes an underlying linear relationship between y and x.

It would appear unnecessary, for any form of matching, to see whether the relation between the dependent and explanatory variables is the same for all groups. But this is not the case and $\bar{y}_2 - \bar{y}_1$ will estimate the average treatment effect only for the treatment population if the regressions are not parallel. Another disadvantage is that it is not possible to take account of changes in background variables used for matching whereas these changes can be specified in a regression model. Also, analyses which extend beyond two occasions (as given earlier) are very difficult for samples matched only at the first occasion unless they are supplemented by regression models.

Matching on an observed pre-treatment variable which contains errors of measurement leads to just the same kind of biases as occur in regression adjustment. However, it could be argued that such a practice carries even more dangers because there is no need to write down a statistical model for a matched design and, without one, there is no possibility of adjusting for reliability in the analysis. This is perhaps the most serious disadvantage of matching.

Value-added analysis

Dissatisfied with regression adjustment and motivated by the need for a dynamic rather than a static approach to estimating the effects of educational intervention, Bryk & Weisberg (1976) propose a technique called 'value-added analysis'. Essentially, this assumes an underlying developmental process which can be adequately modelled and measures a treatment effect by the difference between the observed mean post-test score and the predicted mean had there been no intervention, only maturation (see Figure 3). A control group is not necessary for this analysis although it could be used to provide a check on the model, in that the mean value-added, $\bar{V}$, should be zero for the control group; $\bar{V}$ will not be zero if an extraneous event occurs at the same time as the intervention.

The EPA data for occasions 1 and 2 can be used to show one way of doing value-added analysis. This time the raw scores for the pre-school version of the EPVT were used, so the scores of those children tested only with version 1 at the second

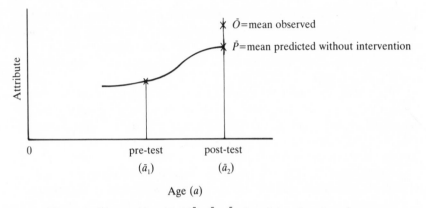

Figure 3. Mean value-added $\bar{V}=\bar{O}-\bar{P}$ when P is a function of age.

occasion were transformed, as follows:

$$\text{EPVT}_{ps}=15.7 + 1.02 \text{ EPVT}_1. \tag{12}$$

The developmental process can be modelled by looking at the relationship between the test scores at occasion 1 and age at occasion 1 (a_1). This could be done more precisely by including data from another, similar study to give an overall sample size of 98 with ages varying between 36 and 54 months. Straight lines with different intercepts for the different groups but a common slope, or growth rate, of 0.49 accounted for 26 per cent of the variance of the pre-test (see Table 4).

Table 4. EPA data: value-added analysis

Group	Predictive equation	Predicted mean	Observed mean	Value-added (SD)
C	$y=-7.8+0.49\ a_1$	20.3	21.8	1.5
				(3.3)
E1	$y=-12.8+0.49\ a_1$	13.6	20.3	6.7
				(2.7)
E2	$y=-13.9+0.49\ a_1$	13.5	17.0	3.5
				(2.5)

There was no evidence that more complicated functions of age would improve the fit.

It could be argued that the pre-test differences between the groups shown in Tables 2 and 3 arose because their mean growth rates were different but this is only weakly supported for these data (the null hypothesis of equal slopes is rejected only at the 0.09 level). An alternative explanation, which finds more support, is that growth on the underlying variable measured by the test did not, on average, start at the same time in each group so that groups behind on the pre-test started developing later. However, this is speculative because data were not available for very young children.

Table 4 gives the results of substituting the mean age at occasion 2 for each group into the predictive equation based on the pre-test ('predicted mean'). It shows that neither C nor $E2$ have 'value-added' which differs significantly from zero, but $E1$ does appear to have made significantly more progress than expected. The standard errors for the predicted values, and thus for the value-added, are only approximate, being calculated from the standard theory for the variability of predictions made from regression equations (see Weisberg, 1980), together with the assumption that all the observations within a group at occasion 2 were made at the same time, that is at the mean age.

It is not possible to make a direct comparison with the results from the conditional model for occasions 1 and 2, corrected for measurement error, because standard scores were used there. However, if the two sets of results are expressed in standard deviation units, then the magnitudes of the treatment effects are similar to the value-added. The value-added for $E1$ is estimated more precisely than the treatment effect mainly because it was possible to estimate the model for the developmental process on a larger sample than was available for the conditional model.

Although the idea of value-added analysis is an attractive one, particularly for developmental psychologists, the method has serious drawbacks and limitations as it stands. It could only be used where the notion of an age-related process is theoretically sensible and also where the measures exist to model it satisfactorily – most standardized test scores would not be suitable. The method assumes a reasonable range of ages at pre-test and, crucially, it assumes that it is reasonable to extrapolate the estimated line or curve to age at post-test. It is reasonable for the EPA data up to occasion 2, but it would not be wise to go beyond this and so the method is not really suitable for studies which collect data on several occasions after an intervention. Another problem with the method is that it models developmental (or longitudinal) processes from cross-sectional data collected at the first occasion and this can be dangerous if there are 'cohort' effects – effects due to date or season of birth – as well as age effects. There are some similarities between the value-added approach and the time-related models discussed earlier, but the former can take account of pre-test differences. However, the growth rates from MANOVA are estimated from longitudinal data.

Ideas from econometrics

A second promising approach to the estimation of treatment effects can be found in the econometric literature. Here an attempt is made separately to model the process determining the outcome and the process determining assignment to groups (self-selection). There are therefore two equations:

$$y=\alpha+\beta_0 d+\sum_{i=1}^{k}\beta_i x_i+\varepsilon_1 \tag{13}$$

for the outcome, which is the same as equation (7), and

$$t=\sum_{i=1}^{k}\gamma_i x_i+\varepsilon_2 \tag{14}$$

for assignment, such that $d=1$ when $t>0$ and $d=0$ when $t<0$.

In addition, because it is possible that there are unmeasured variables influencing both selection and outcome, it is assumed that ε_1 and ε_2 are correlated. Thus, equations (13) and (14) form a simultaneous equation system and must be estimated jointly. One method of doing this is given by Heckman (1979) and elaborated by Barnow *et al.* (1980). They assume that ε_1 and ε_2 come from a bivariate normal distribution and then estimate γ_1 in equation (14) using maximum likelihood probit analysis (Finney, 1971). The $\hat{\gamma}_i x_i$ are then used to estimate the probability, p, that an individual would be in the treatment group (i.e. the probability that $d=1$) for the particular values of x_i. A revised version of equation (13),

$$y=\alpha+\sum_{i=1}^{k}\beta_i\ x_i+\delta_p+\varepsilon_3, \tag{15}$$

is then estimated using ordinary least squares to give an unbiased esimate, $\hat{\delta}$, of the treatment effect.

The advantage of the method is that, *providing* ε_1 and ε_2 are uncorrelated with the x_i, and *providing* the x_i are measured without error, then it can produce unbiased estimates of the treatment effect which none of the other methods can do. However, the estimates may not be very precise, particularly when there is only one explanatory variable as in the EPA study. The correlation between p and x in equation (15) is likely to be high because there is a strong, albeit non-linear, relationship between t and x_i in equation (14) and a high correlation inevitably leads to regression coefficients with large standard errors. The situation could be eased if data on several explanatory variables were available, especially if some of these variables influenced assignment and others influenced outcome, because the correlation between p and x_i in equation (15) would then be reduced. On the other hand, if a number of explanatory variables have been measured, then the bias in $\hat{\beta}_0$ when equation (7) (or (13)) is estimated on its own may well be unimportant.

This method, and others like it, have not yet been used extensively on real data and there is still little evidence about the performance of the methods when compared with bias-correcting procedures using multiple regression. Extensions to more than two groups and more than two occasions may not always be straightforward. Nevertheless, the idea of separating models for assignment from models for outcome is a sensible one.

CONCLUDING REMARKS

This chapter presents a number of ways of analysing data from longitudinal comparative studies. Readers unfamiliar with these studies may be disappointed to find that, when applied to the EPA study, the different methods give different results. Thus, there is strong evidence from the unconditional model that the experimental groups made more progress during the study than the control group, but no firm evidence of any relative change when the conditional approach is used. Yet this is not a contradiction: the two approaches are providing answers to different questions. The unconditional approach gives some descriptive, although not easily interpreted, information about change in the three groups, but this information cannot be given the causal interpretation that is needed when quasi-experiments are analysed. The results from fitting the conditional models are more convincing from a causal point of view, but they are far from unequivocal without further details about initial differences between the groups. The results from the value-added analysis are a little different from the conditional models but cannot, unfortunately, be extended beyond the second occasion. Researchers faced with studies of this type might consider a three-pronged attack on the data, spearheaded by a conditional (that is, a multiple regression) analysis but backed up, when appropriate, by value-added analysis and econometric techniques. They would do well to avoid matching.

Analysing data from comparative studies is not always easy and inevitably some aspects, particularly the problems created by measurement error, have not been considered in detail here while others have been omitted altogether. For example, it has been assumed throughout that interval scale measures of the outcome are available but psychologists often have to work with categorical outcomes. The distinction between conditional and unconditional models applies for all types of data and the two approaches are contrasted for dichotomous and for ordered and unordered polytomous data in Plewis (1981).

Another omitted topic is one which affects practically all longitudinal comparative studies – the problem of missing data. One way of dealing with this is to analyse only those cases with complete data and that was the tactic used in this chapter with the EPA data. However, it is not entirely satisfactory because the sub-sample with complete data will often have different characteristics from the sub-sample with missing data. Beale & Little (1975) describe one method of adjusting for missing data and others are based on the so-called EM algorithm presented by Dempster *et al.* (1977). Another approach is to try and model the sample attrition in essentially the same way as self-selection is modelled. Hausman & Wise (1979) give an example of this. These methods are likely to be used much more extensively in the next few years as computer programs become more accessible.

Nearly all the analysis in this chapter was carried out using the Statistical Analysis System (SAS) package. This is somewhat more flexible than the more widely used Statistical Package for the Social Sciences (SPSS) and a wider variety of time-related models can be estimated by using the powerful matrix procedures built in the package. However, specialist programs are needed to correct for measurement error: Fuller's methods are incorporated into SUPER CARP (Hidiroglou *et al.*, 1980) and Jöreskog's into LISREL (Jöreskog & Sörbom, 1981).

Acknowledgements

I would like to thank George Smith for letting me have the EPA data, and colleagues at the Thomas Coram Research Unit for comments on an earlier draft of this chapter. Some of the work for this chapter was done while I held an SSRC Fellowship in the Department of Statistics and Computing at the Institute of Education.

A more detailed account of this work by this author can be found in *Analysing Change* (1985) and appears here by kind permission of John Wiley & Sons Ltd.

References

ANDERSON, S., AUQUIER, A., HAUCK, W.W., OAKES, D., VANDAELE, W. & WEISBERG, H.I. (1980). *Statistical Methods for Comparative Studies*. New York: John Wiley & Sons.

BARNOW, B.S., CAIN, G.G. & GOLDBERGER, A.S. (1980). Issues in the analysis of selectivity bias. In: E. W. Stromsdorfer & G. Farkas (eds), *Evaluation Studies Review Annual*, Volume 5. Beverley Hills: Sage.

BEALE, E.M.L. & LITTLE, R.J.A. (1975). Missing values in multivariate analysis. *Journal of the Royal Statistical Society, Series B, 37*, 129–145.

BOCK, R.D. (1975). *Multivariate Statistical Methods in Behavioral Research*. New York: McGraw-Hill.

BOCK, R.D. (1979). Univariate and multivariate analysis of variance of time-structured data. In: J. R. Nesselroade & P. B. Baltes (eds), *Longitudinal Research in the Study of Behavior and Development*. New York: Academic Press.

BRYK, A.S. & WEISBERG, H.I. (1976). Value-added analysis: a dynamic approach to the estimation of treatment effects. *Journal of Educational Statistics, 1*, 127–155.

COCHRAN, W.G. & RUBIN, D.B. (1973). Controlling bias in observational studies: a review. *Sankhya, A, 35*, 417–446.

COOK, T.D. & CAMPBELL, D.T. (1979). *Quasi-Experimentation*. Chicago: Rand McNally.

DEGRACIE, J.S. & FULLER, W.A. (1972). Estimation of the slope and analysis of covariance when the concomitant variable is measured with error. *Journal of the American Statistical Association, 67*, 930–937.

DEMPSTER, A.P., LAIRD, N.M. & RUBIN, D.B. (1977). Maximum likelihood from incomplete data via the EM algorithm (with Discussion). *Journal of the Royal Statistical Society, Series B, 39*, 1–38.

DRAPER, N. & SMITH, H. (1981). *Applied Regression Analysis*, 2nd ed. New York: John Wiley & Sons.

FINNEY, D.J. (1971). *Probit Analysis*, 3rd ed. Cambridge: University Press.

FULLER, W.A. (1980). Properties of some estimators for the errors-in-variables model. *Annals of Statistics*, 8, 407–422.

FULLER, W.A. & HIDIROGLOU, M.A. (1978). Regression estimation after correction for attenuation. *Journal of the American Statistical Association*, 73, 99–104.

GOLDSTEIN, H. (1979a). *The Design and Analysis of Longitudinal Studies*. London: Academic Press.

GOLDSTEIN, H. (1979b). Some models for analysing longitudinal data on educational attainment (with Discussion). *Journal of the Royal Statistical Society, Series A*, 142, 407–442.

GUIRE, K.E. & KOWALSKI, C.J. (1979). Mathematical description and representation of developmental change functions on the intra- and interindividual levels. In: J. R. Nesselroade & P. B. Baltes (eds), *Longitudinal Research in the Study of Behavior and Development*. New York: Academic Press.

HAUSMAN, J.A. & WISE, D.A. (1979). Attrition bias in experimental and panel data: the Gary income maintenance experiment. *Econometrica*, 47, 455–473.

HECKMAN, J.J. (1979). Sample selection bias as a specification error. *Econometrica*, 47, 153–161.

HIDIROGLOU, M.A., FULLER, W.A. & HICKMAN, R.T. (1980). *SUPER CARP* 6th ed. Statistical Laboratory, Iowa State University.

JÖRESKOG, K.G. (1970). A general method for analysis of covariance structures. *Biometrika*, 57, 239–251.

JÖRESKOG, K.G. & SÖRBOM, D. (1981) LISREL V – analysis of linear structural relationships by maximum likelihood and least squares methods. Research Report 81–8, University of Uppsala.

KENNY, D.A. (1975). A quasi-experimental approach to assessing treatment effects in the nonequivalent control group design. *Psychological Bulletin*, 82, 345–362.

LORD, F.M. (1967). A paradox in the interpretation of group comparisons. *Psychological Bulletin*, 68, 304–305.

OLSON, C.L. (1974). Comparative robustness of six tests in multivariate analysis of variance. *Journal of the American Statistical Association*, 69, 849–908.

PLEWIS, I. (1981). A comparison of approaches to the analysis of longitudinal categoric data. *British Journal of Mathematical and Statistical Psychology*, 34, 118–123.

PLEWIS, I. (1985). *Analysing Change*. Chichester: John Wiley & Sons.

RUBIN, D.B. (1976). Multivariate matching methods that are equal percent bias reducing. I: Some examples. *Biometrics*, 32, 109–120.

SMITH, G. & JAMES, T. (1975). The effects of pre-school education: some American and British evidence. *Oxford Review of Education*, 1, 223–240.

SÖRBOM, D. (1976). A statistical model for the measurement of change in true scores. In: de D. N. M. Gruijter, L. J. Th. van der Kamp, & H. F. Crombag (eds), *Advances in Psychological and Educational Measurement*. New York: John Wiley & Sons.

SORBOM, D. (1978). An alternative to the methodology for analysis of covariance. *Psychometrika*, 43, 381–396.

TANNER, J.M. (1961). *Growth at Adolescence*, 2nd ed. Oxford: Basil Blackwell.

WARREN, R.D., WHITE, J.K. & FULLER, W.A. (1974). An errors-in-variables analysis of managerial role performance. *Journal of the American Statistical Association*, 69, 886–893.

WEISBERG, S. (1980). *Applied Linear Regression*. New York: John Wiley & Sons.

WINER, B.J. (1971). *Statistical Principles in Experimental Design*, 2nd ed. New York: McGraw-Hill.

6
Finite Mixture Distributions as Models for Group Structure

BRIAN S. EVERITT

Consider taking a random sample of people living in London and recording for each member of the sample their height. What might be a sensible model for the distribution of this variable in the population? First we have to allow for our sample containing both males and females, and it is well known that, on average, males are taller than females. Within each sex it might be reasonable to assume that height is normally distributed with a particular mean and variance. Such considerations lead naturally to the following density function for height:

$$f \text{ (height)} = pN(\mu_f, \sigma_f) + (1-p) N(\mu_m, \sigma_m),$$ (1)

where p is the proportion of females in the population and, since we assume that the population consists only of males or females, $1-p$ is the proportion of males; μ_f, σ_f and μ_m, σ_m are, respectively, the mean and standard deviation of height for females and males. Such a density function is an example from a class of density functions known as *finite mixtures*, the general definition of which is given in the next section. For this particular example the major concern would be to use the sample of recorded heights to estimate the five parameters of the density function namely, p, μ_f, σ_f, μ_m and σ_m. Of course, if we had been sensible enough to record the sex of each member of the sample, estimation of these quantities would have been straightforward; in this case this could have been done very simply, even allowing for the eccentricities of dress in London! In other areas, however, sexing of species is more difficult and estimation of the parameters must be made from the unlabelled sample.

In the example described above, the existence of two 'types' or 'classes' of people in the data is known *a priori*, and the density function given by (1) becomes a natural choice. However, such a density function may also prove extremely useful in investigations where the purpose is to examine and explore the data for the possible existence of groups, since it may be used as a model for the presence of two groups and perhaps tested against a single normal distribution, this acting as a model for the data consisting of a single homogeneous set of observations. For example, in psychiatry there has long been controversy over whether or not the depressive disorders consist of two subtypes. A number of studies, for example,

113

Kiloh & Garside (1963) and Pilowsky *et al.* (1969), indicate the existence of two subtypes of depression, whilst others, for example, Kendell (1969) and Kendell & Gourlay (1970) argue for the existence of only a single type. In many such studies variation in symptomatology has been expressed by a score on a linear discriminant function found from the analysis of a number of items measured for patients diagnosed originally as neurotic or psychotic depression. The distribution of such scores has been used to make inferences about the structure of depression, usually in an informal manner. However, the frequency distribution of discriminant function scores could be investigated more formally by fitting a mixture density of the form given in (1); if the mixture provided a significantly better fit than a single normal distribution the implication would be that the data did consist of two groups.

The density function given in (1) provides a useful model for the existence of *two* groups in the data provided this is *univariate* and the variable is *continuous*. In later sections mixture densities will be introduced which may act as models for more than two groups, more than a single variable, and for categorical data. In the next section, however, we discuss finite mixtures in general and the problems of estimating their parameters.

ESTIMATING THE PARAMETERS OF FINITE MIXTURE DISTRIBUTIONS

The general form of a finite mixture density function is as follows:

$$f(\mathbf{x};\,\Theta)=\sum_{i=1}^{c}p_i\,h(\mathbf{x};\,\theta_i), \tag{2}$$

$$0<p_i<1:\ \sum_{i=1}^{c}p_i=1$$

where $\mathbf{x}$ is a d-dimensional random vector (in the previous section we considered only the case $d=1$), c is the number of groups in the data (in the previous section, $c=2$), $h(\mathbf{x};\,\theta_i)$ is the density function of $\mathbf{x}$ in the ith group and θ_i is a vector of parameters for this density function (in the previous section we considered only the case where h was a normal density, so that $\theta_i'=(\mu_i,\,\sigma_i))$: $\Theta=(\theta_1 \ldots \theta_c)$ is simply a matrix containing *all* the parameters of the mixture.

If we assume for the moment that c is known *a priori*, the estimation problem becomes that of determining estimates for the elements of Θ, and for the mixing proportions, $p_1,\ldots,p_{c-1}$. Many methods have been devised and used for estimating the parameters of finite mixture distributions, ranging from Pearson's (1894) method of moments, through formal maximum likelihood approaches, to informal graphical techniques. All of these are described in detail in Everitt & Hand (1981). Here we shall concentrate on the method of maximum likelihood. (The question of determining the appropriate value of c will be taken up in the final section.)

Maximum likelihood estimation

The maximum likelihood method for estimating the parameters of statistical distributions possesses a number of desirable statistical properties. For example, under very general conditions the estimators obtained by the method are consistent (they converge in probability to the true parameter values) and they are asymptotically normally distributed.

Let's begin by assuming that we have sampled n observations from a population in which the distribution of a random vector, $\mathbf{x}$, is described by (2); let these observations be represented as $\mathbf{x}_1, \mathbf{x}_2, \ldots \mathbf{x}_n$. The joint probability density of these observations is

$$\mathscr{L}(\mathbf{x}_1 \ldots \mathbf{x}_n; \Theta) = \prod_{i=1}^{n} f(\mathbf{x}_i; \Theta). \tag{3}$$

Now instead of regarding $\mathscr{L}$ as a function of the $\mathbf{x}_i$ we can regard it as a function of Θ. It is then called the *likelihood function* – it measures the relative likelihood that different Θ will have given rise to the observations. The method of maximum likelihood tries to find that particular Θ, say Θ_0, which maximizes $\mathscr{L}$; that is, that Θ_0 such that the observations, $\mathbf{x}_1 \ldots \mathbf{x}_n$ are more likely to have come from $f(\mathbf{x}; \Theta_0)$ than from $f(\mathbf{x}; \Theta)$ for any other value of Θ.

The maximization can be handled in the traditional way of differentiating $\mathscr{L}$ with respect to the elements of Θ and equating the derivatives to zero to give the *normal equations*. (In some cases it is simpler to work with $\ln \mathscr{L}$ since this has its maxima at the same parameter values as (3), but often the subsequent algebra becomes simpler.) The details of this procedure are given in Everitt & Hand (1981), but it is important to note that for most mixture distributions the normal equations are not explicitly solvable for the parameters, and so iterative techniques have to be adopted. One of these will be described in detail in a later section.

MIXTURES WITH NORMAL COMPONENTS

The mixture density given by (1) involves two univariate, normal components. It is useful as a model for the existence of two groups in *univariate* data where the single variable is measured on a continuous, interval scale. The extension to a model for more than two groups is simple, that is,

$$f(x) = \sum_{i=1}^{c} p_i N(\mu_i, \sigma_i), \tag{4}$$

where c is the number of groups assumed. Here there is a total of $3c - 1$ parameters to estimate.

If the investigator wishes to consider such a model for a set of *multivariate* data, the obvious extension to (4) is to let the component densities be multivariate normal with a particular mean vector, μ_i, and a particular variance–covariance matrix, Σ_i, that is,

$$f(\mathbf{x})=\sum_{i=1}^{c}p_i\ \text{MVN}\ (\mathbf{x};\mu_i,\Sigma_i).\tag{5}$$

Now there are $c-1$ mixing proportions, cd means, and $cd(d+1)/2$ variances and covariances to estimate.

The estimation of the parameters in mixture densities involving normal components has been considered by a large number of authors; the earliest was Pearson (1894), who tackled the problem of estimating the five parameters of the two component normal mixture given by (1) by the method of moments. The numerical solution of the resulting system of equations was however formidable, as it involved finding the roots of a ninth-degree polynomial. Various attempts were made to simplify the procedure, notably by Charlier (1906). Hald (1952), Harding (1949) and Cassie (1954) introduced a number of graphical methods for estimating the parameters in two-component normal mixtures, and Rao (1948) first considered the method of maximum likelihood; it is the latter that we shall concentrate on here.

Estimating the parameters of finite mixtures of normal densities by maximum likelihood

The log of the likelihood function for the mixture density given by (5) is

$$L=\ln\ \mathscr{L}=\sum_{i=1}^{n}\ln\ \left\{\sum_{k=1}^{c}p_k\ \text{MVN}\ (\mathbf{x}_i;\mu_k,\Sigma_k)\right\}.\tag{6}$$

The maximum likelihood equations are obtained by equating the first partial derivatives of (6) with respect to the p_k, the elements of each matrix, Σ_k, and those of each vector, μ_k to zero. Details of this procedure are given in Everitt & Hand (1981, Ch. 2), where it is shown that, by introducing the posterior probability that observation $\mathbf{x}_i$ arises from the kth component of the mixture, that is,

$$P(k\,|\,\mathbf{x}_i)=\frac{p_k\text{MVN}\ (\mathbf{x}_i;\mu_k,\Sigma_k)}{f(\mathbf{x}_i)}\tag{7}$$

(from Bayes theorem), the maximum likelihood equations can be written in the following form

$$\hat{p}_k=\frac{1}{n}\sum_{i=1}^{n}\hat{P}(k\,|\,\mathbf{x}_i),\qquad k=1,\ldots,c-1,\tag{8}$$

$$\bar{\mu}_k=\frac{1}{n\hat{p}_k}\sum_{i=1}^{n}\mathbf{x}_i\ \hat{P}(k\,|\,\mathbf{x}_i),\qquad k=1,\ldots,c,\tag{9}$$

$$\hat{\Sigma}_k = \frac{1}{n\hat{p}_k} \sum_{i=1}^{n} \hat{P}(k \mid \mathbf{x}_i) (\mathbf{x}_i - \hat{\mu}_k) (\mathbf{x}_i - \hat{\mu}_k)', \qquad k = 1, \ldots, c, \tag{10}$$

where $\hat{P}(k \mid \mathbf{x}_i)$ is simply (7) with parameter values replaced by their estimates.

For estimating the mean and variance–covariance matrix of a single normal density the maximum likelihood equations would be

$$\hat{\mu} = \frac{1}{n} \sum_{i=1}^{n} \mathbf{x}_i, \tag{11}$$

$$\hat{\Sigma} = \frac{1}{n} \sum (\mathbf{x}_i - \hat{\mu}) (\mathbf{x}_i - \hat{\mu})'. \tag{12}$$

So we see that equations (9) and (10) are closely analogous to equations (11) and (12) except that each sample point is weighted by the estimated posterior probability. In the extreme case where this is unity when $\mathbf{x}_i$ is from component k and zero otherwise, then $\hat{p}_k$ is simply the fraction of samples from component k, $\hat{\mu}_k$ is the mean vector of these samples, and $\hat{\Sigma}_k$ their variance–covariance matrix. More generally $\hat{P}(k \mid \mathbf{x}_i)$ is between zero and one, and all observations play a role in the estimates.

The appearance of the estimated posterior probability in equations (8), (9) and (10) means that, unlike equations (11) and (12), they do not give the parameter estimates explicitly (since $P(k \mid \mathbf{x}_i)$ is a complex function of the parameters and so these now appear on both the right and left hand sides of equations (8), (9) and (10)). Consequently they have to be solved by some form of iterative procedure, the simplest of which is that suggested by Hasselblad (1969) and Wolfe (1970). This method involves obtaining initial estimates of all the parameters, which are then used to obtain initial estimates of the posterior probabilities, (7); these are inserted into the right-hand side of equations (8), (9) and (10) to give revised estimates of p_k, μ_k and Σ_k and the process is repeated until some convergence criterion is satisfied. Such a procedure is extremely easy to implement on a computer. The properties of this algorithm have been studied in detail by Dempster *et al.* (1977).

Initial estimates for the parameters may be obtained by a variety of methods, of which perhaps the most useful is the initial application of some form of cluster analysis to the data. (Clustering techniques are described in Everitt, 1980.)

A problem which has often been considered in respect of the maximum likelihood estimation of the parameters in a normal mixture is that of singularities in the likelihood surface, that is, points where the likelihood becomes infinite. The reasons why such points occur are discussed by Day (1969) and Everitt & Hand (1981). One way of overcoming this problem is to assume that each component density in the mixture has the same variance–covariance matrix.

5

Numerical examples

To illustrate the maximum likelihood estimation procedure outlined in the previous section we shall apply it to the data shown in Table 1 which gives the murder/manslaughter and rape rates for 16 cities in the USA. Since in this case the data involve only two variables, they may be plotted as shown in Figure 1, and such a diagram is likely to be of great help in the interpretation of the results obtained from fitting finite mixture densities, as we shall see later.

Table 1. City crime data

	Murder/Manslaughter	Rape
1. Atlanta	16.5	24.8
2. Boston	4.2	13.3
3. Chicago	11.6	24.7
4. Dallas	18.1	34.2
5. Denver	6.9	41.5
6. Detroit	13.0	35.7
7. Hartford	2.5	8.8
8. Honolulu	3.6	12.7
9. Houston	16.8	26.6
10. Kansas City	10.8	43.2
11. Los Angeles	9.7	51.8
12. New Orleans	10.3	39.7
13. New York	9.4	19.4
14. Portland	5.0	23.0
15. Tucson	5.1	22.9
16. Washington	12.5	27.6

Source: United States Statistical Abstract (1970); per 100 000 population.

Let's begin by fitting a two-component bivariate normal mixture using the algorithm described in the previous section. Starting values for the parameters were obtained from a 'k-means' clustering procedure (see Everitt, 1980, Ch. 3), and the final parameter values were obtained after 12 iterations of the estimation algorithm. (In this example we have assumed that the correlation between the two variables, murder rate and rape rate is the same in each group.) The results are shown in Table 2.

The final parameter estimates given in Table 2 may now be used to find estimates of the posterior probabilities of each city belonging to each of the component densities in the mixture. These are given in Table 3. The maximum posterior probability for each town can be used to partition the towns into two groups as shown. Here the two groups differ predominantly on the murder/ manslaughter rate, with those in the first group having very high rates.

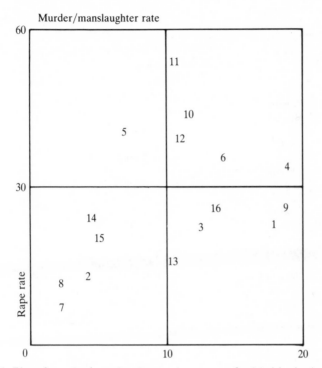

Figure 1. Plot of murder/manslaughter and rape rates for 16 cities in the USA.

Table 2. Results of fitting a two-component bivariate normal mixture to the city crime data using maximum likelihood

Starting values for the parameters	Final values for the parameters
$p=0.438$	$p=0.386$
$\hat{\mu}_1'=(13.99, 27.57)$	$\hat{\mu}_1'=(14.40, 27.97)$
$\hat{\mu}_2'=(6.46, 28.54)$	$\hat{\mu}_2'=(6.83, 28.21)$
$\hat{\sigma}_1=2.94,\ \hat{\sigma}_2=11.67$	$\hat{\sigma}_1=3.00,\ \hat{\sigma}_2=11.68$
$\hat{\varrho}=0.76$	$\hat{\varrho}=0.70$

Iterative algorithm took 12 iterations to converge.

Next a four-component bivariate normal mixture was considered for the data and parameter estimates obtained, again by the iterative algorithm described previously. (As before the correlation between the two variables was assumed to be the same for each of the four component densities.) The results are shown in Table 4. Here the estimated posterior probabilities divide the data as shown in

Table 3. Estimated posterior probabilities of each city in Table 1 belonging to each of the two components of the mixture density fitted in Table 2

	P (component 1)	P (component 2)
1. Atlanta	1.00	0.00
2. Boston	0.00	1.00
3. Chicago	0.91	0.09
4. Dallas	1.00	0.00
5. Denver	0.00	1.00
6. Detroit	0.78	0.22
7. Hartford	0.00	1.00
8. Honolulu	0.00	1.00
9. Hoiston	1.00	0.00
10. Kansas City	0.00	1.00
11. Los Angeles	0.00	1.00
12. New Orleans	0.01	0.99
13. New York	0.54	0.45
14. Portland	0.00	1.00
15. Tucson	0.00	1.00
16. Washington	0.95	0.05

On the basis of these probabilities the two groups consist of the following cities:

Group 1. 1, 3, 4, 6, 9, 13, 16.
Group 2. 2, 5, 7, 8, 10, 11, 12, 14, 15.

Table 4. Results of fitting a four-component bivariate normal mixture to the city crime data using maximum likelihood

Starting values for the parameters	Final values for the parameters
$\hat{p}_1=0.188$, $\hat{p}_2=0.250$, $\hat{p}_3=0.438$	Same as starting values
$\hat{\mu}_1'=(17.13, 28.53)$	
$\hat{\mu}_2'=(11.62, 26.85)$	
$\hat{\mu}_3'=(5.93, 23.37)$	
$\hat{\mu}_4'=(8.30, 46.65)$	
$\hat{\sigma}_1=2.20$. $\hat{\sigma}_2=9.12$	
$\varrho=0.98$	

In this case the iterative algorithm converged after just one iter.tion; the estimates given by the k-means algorithm coincide with the maximum likelihood estimates.

Figure 2. It is clear that in this case, the effect of requiring equal correlation for each component has 'imposed' a structure on the data in which the murder rate and rape rate for cities within the same group lie almost perfectly on a straight line. It would be interesting to compare this result with that obtained by allowing

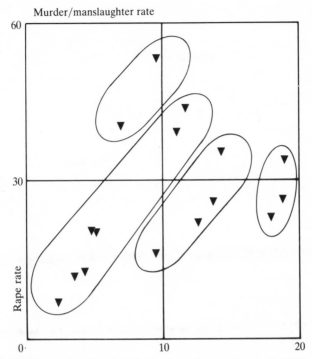

Figure 2. Four groups of cities given by estimated posterior probabilities found after fitting four-component bivariate normal mixture to city crime data.

the within group correlations to differ. In this case, however, this was not possible because with so few observations problems were encountered with singularities in the likelihood surface.

As a further example of the use of finite mixtures of normal components, we shall briefly describe an investigation carried out by Powell *et al.* (1979) with 86 aphasic cases. Each patient was described by four scores arising from the administration of the *Minnesota Test for the Differential Diagnosis of Aphasia*. The four scores measured auditory disturbance, visual and reading disturbance, speech and language disturbance, and visuomotor and writing disturbances. For these data a four-component mixture density was found necessary (using the likelihood ratio test described in the final section). Figure 3 gives the means on each of the variables for each of the four components in the mixture. (The means here are the mean error score expressed as a percentage of the maximum possible number of errors.) The finding that a four-component mixture was sufficient to describe these data, implying that aphasic subjects fall into essentially four groups, contradicts a claim by Schuell (1965), that such subjects are best described in terms of seven categories, and the reasons for this disagreement are discussed in detail by Powell *et al.* (1979).

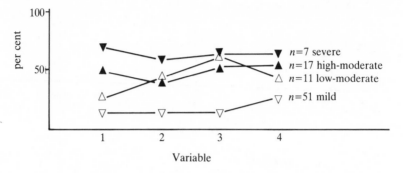

Figure 3. Mean error scores for the four variables for each of the four components of the normal mixture density fitted to the data on aphasic patients. (Taken from Powell *et al.*, 1979.)

FINITE MIXTURE MODELS FOR CATEGORICAL DATA

The finite mixture densities described in the previous section provide models for the presence of groups in a set of data provided that the variables are measured on an interval scale. However, in many areas of the social and behavioural sciences, variables are frequently measured only on an ordinal or nominal scale. Examples of such variables might be a rating scale for anxiety, marital status and assessing the presence or absence of some symptom. The latter type of variable is particularly common in an area such as psychiatry where clinicians may rate patients for the presence or absence of hallucinations, depression, anxiety, etc. For data involving such *binary variables*, finite mixtures of normal components will clearly not provide realistic models for the presence of groups and, consequently, we are led to consider other possibilities. The most common is to assume that within each group in the data the d binary variables are independent and that the observed associations amongst the variables are generated by the presence of the groups. If we do assume this, the next question is what is the probability density function of the variables within a particular group? To answer this question let us begin with an example in which there are three binary variables, x_1, x_2 and x_3, and that within a particular group, j, the probabilities of a positive response for each of the variables are θ_{j1}, θ_{j2}, and θ_{j3}. Assuming that the three variables are independent of one another within this group we can now find the probability of observing any value of the vector $\mathbf{x}' = (x_1, x_2, x_3)$. For example

$$P\{\mathbf{x}' = (0 \quad 1 \quad 1)\} = (1 - \theta_{j1})\, \theta_{j2}\, \theta_{j3}$$

or

$$P\{\mathbf{x}' = (1 \quad 0 \quad 0)\} = \theta_{j1}\, (1 - \theta_{j2})(1 - \theta_{j3}).$$

Both of these may be rewritten in the form

$$P\{\mathbf{x}'=(x_1, x_2, x_3)\}=\theta_{j1}^{x_1} (1-\theta_{j1})^{1-x_1} \; \theta_{j2}^{x_2} (1-\theta_{j2})^{1-x_2} \; \theta_{j3}^{x_3} (1-\theta_{j3})^{1-x_3}$$

$$=\prod_{l=1}^{3} \theta_{jl}^{x_l}(1-\theta_{jl})^{1-x_l}. \tag{13}$$

This is known as a *multivariate Bernoulli density* and is extended to the d-dimensional situation in an obvious fashion:

$$P\{\mathbf{x}'=(x_1 \; x_2 \; \ldots \; x_d)\}=\prod_{l=1}^{d} \theta_{jl}^{x_l}(1-\theta_{jl})^{1-x_l}. \tag{14}$$

These density functions will now be the components of the mixture, which consequently takes the form

$$P(\mathbf{x}; \Theta)=\sum_{j=1}^{c} p_j \prod_{l=1}^{d} \theta_{jl}^{x_l}(1-\theta_{jl})^{1-x_l}, \tag{15}$$

where $p_1, \ldots, p_{c-1}$ are the mixing proportions and $\Theta=(\theta_1, \ldots, \theta_c)$ where $\theta_i'=(\theta_{11}, \theta_{12}, \ldots, \theta_{1d})$.

The parameters in (15) may be estimated by maximum likelihood, and it is relatively simple to show that the estimation equations take the form

$$\hat{p}_k=\frac{1}{n}\sum_{i=1}^{n}\hat{P}(k\,|\,\mathbf{x}_i), \qquad k=1, \ldots, c-1, \tag{16}$$

$$\theta_k=\frac{1}{n\hat{p}_k}\sum_{i=1}^{n}\mathbf{x}_i \; \hat{P}(k\,|\,\mathbf{x}_i), \qquad k=1, \ldots, c, \tag{17}$$

where $\mathbf{x}_1, \ldots, \mathbf{x}_n$ are the n sample values of the d-dimensional vector $\mathbf{x}$ and $\hat{P}(k|\mathbf{x}_i)$ is the estimated posterior probability given by

$$\hat{P}(k\,|\,\mathbf{x}_i)=\frac{\hat{p}_k \displaystyle\prod_{l=1}^{d} \hat{\theta}_{kl}^{x_{il}} (1-\hat{\theta}_{kl})^{1-x_{il}}}{P(\mathbf{x}_i; \hat{\Theta})}. \tag{18}$$

Equations (16) and (17) are of exactly the same form as those for normal mixtures and may be solved using the same iterative algorithm; some numerical examples will be described in the next section.

The model for group structure in binary data described above is perhaps more familiar to psychologists under the name *latent class analysis*, a technique which has been developed primarily by Green (1951), Gibson (1959) and Lazarsfeld & Henry (1968). These authors consider a variety of ways in which the parameters of the model can be estimated concentrating in the main on techniques equivalent to the method of moments. However, these do not appear to be as convenient for general use as the maximum likelihood procedure outlined above, although they may be of some use in providing initial estimates for the iterative algorithm used.

The extension of (15) to categorical data in which some of the variables have more than two categories is relatively straightforward and is described in Everitt (1984).

Numerical examples

As a first example we shall consider the data shown in Table 5. These arise from four machine design subtests given to 137 engineers, with each test scored 1 if the engineer scores above the subtest mean, and 0 if below the subtest mean. (The data were originally collected by Schumacher *et al.*, 1953.) The iterative algorithm for finding maximum likelihood estimates was applied to these data assuming the mixture density given by (15) with $c=2$, that is, a two-group or two-class model. Initial estimates were obtained from a technique due to Anderson (1954). The results are summarized in Table 6. It is clear that in one group the engineers have high probabilities of scoring above average on each of the four tests, in the other rather low probabilities. The two classes could perhaps be labelled 'creative' and 'non-creative'.

A further example of the application of the latent class model is provided by the investigation described in Aitkin *et al.* (1981). They analysed data from questionnaires containing 38 binary items given to 468 primary school teachers. Their main aim was to examine the data for the existence of distinguishable teaching

Table 5. Machine design data

Response pattern				Observed frequency
Variable 1	Variable 2	Variable 3	Variable 4	
0	0	0	0	23
1	0	0	0	8
0	1	0	0	6
0	0	1	0	5
0	0	0	1	5
1	1	0	0	9
1	0	1	0	3
1	0	0	1	2
0	1	1	0	2
0	1	0	1	3
0	0	1	1	14
1	1	1	0	8
1	1	0	1	3
1	0	1	1	8
0	1	1	1	4
1	1	1	1	34

Table 6. Results of fitting a two-component multivariate Bernoulli mixture to the machine design data using maximum likelihood

Starting values for the parameters	Final values for the parameters
$\hat{p}=0.52$	$\hat{p}=0.47$
$\theta'_1=(0.73, 0.75, 0.77, 0.74)$	$\theta'_1=(0.66, 0.69, 0.84, 0.81)$
$\theta'_2=(0.08, 0.19, 0.11, 0.23)$	$\theta'_2=(0.26, 0.32, 0.06, 0.16)$

The algorithm took 143 iterations to converge.

styles. Two- and three-class models were fitted by means of the maximum likelihood procedure described previously. Parameter estimates for each model are given in Table 7. For the two-class model a number of response probabilities show large differences between the classes, indicating systematic differences in behaviour on these items for teachers in the two latest classes. For the three-class model the response probabilities for classes 1 and 2 are very close to those for the corresponding classes in the two-class model, and the response probabilities for class 3 are mostly between those for classes 1 and 2. Thus class 3 is to some extent intermediate between classes 1 and 2. The detailed interpretation of these classes is given by Aitkin *et al.*, but the identification of class 1 with a 'formal', and class 2 with an 'informal', teaching style is very clear.

DETERMINING THE NUMBER OF COMPONENTS IN A MIXTURE

In the previous sections it has been implicitly assumed that c, the number of components in the mixture, is known before the estimation of parameters is attempted. In many cases this will be so, since the decision to fit a mixture distribution will be based upon theoretical knowledge of the application at hand, for example, the known existence of two or more species, the presence of males and females, etc. However, in other cases where mixture densities are being used as models for the *possible* existence of groups, questions as to the appropriate value of c, and in particular whether $c=1$, become of considerable interest and importance. Several methods have been proposed which may be helpful in such situations, but here we shall concentrate on a technique particularly associated with maximum likelihood estimation, namely a *likelihood ratio test*.

Likelihood ratio test for number of components in a finite mixture

Suppose we wish to test the hypothesis that $c=c_0$ against $c=c_1$, where c is the number of components in the mixture. The ratio of the likelihood of the observations under the two hypotheses is given by

$$\lambda = \mathscr{L}_{c_0} / \mathscr{L}_{c_1},$$

where $\mathscr{L}$ is given by equation (3), with the maximum likelihood estimates substituted for the parameters.

Table 7. Two- and three-latent-class parameter estimates $(100 \times \theta_{jl})$ for teacher data

Item	Two-class model		Three-class model		
	Class 1	Class 2	Class 1	Class 2	Class 3
1. Pupils have choice in where to sit	22	43	20	44	33
2. Pupils sit in groups of three or more	60	87	54	88	79
3. Pupils allocated to seating by ability	35	23	36	22	30
4. Pupils stay in same seats for most of day	91	63	91	52	89
5. Pupils not allowed freedom of movement in classroom	97	54	100	53	74
6. Pupils not allowed to talk freely	89	48	94	50	61
7. Pupils expected to ask permission to leave room	97	76	96	69	95
8. Pupils expected to be quiet	82	42	92	39	56
9. Monitors appointed for special jobs	85	67	90	70	69
10. Pupils taken out of school regularly	32	60	33	70	35
11. Timetable used for organizing work	90	66	95	62	77
12. Use own materials rather than textbooks	19	49	20	56	26
13. Pupils expected to know tables by heart	92	76	97	80	75
14. Pupils asked to find own reference materials	29	37	28	39	34
15. Pupils given homework regularly	35	22	45	29	12
16. Teacher talks to whole class	71	44	73	37	62
17. Pupils work in groups on teacher tasks	29	42	24	45	38
18. Pupils work in groups on work of own choice	15	46	13	59	20
19. Pupils work individually on teacher tasks	55	37	57	32	50
20. Pupils work individually on work of own choice	28	50	29	60	26
21. Explore concepts in number work	18	55	14	62	34
22. Encourage fluency in written English even if inaccurate	87	94	87	95	90
23. Pupils' work marked or graded	43	14	50	16	20
24. Spelling and grammatical errors corrected	84	68	86	64	78
25. Stars given to pupils who produce best work	57	29	65	30	34
26. Arithmetic tests given at least once a week	59	38	68	43	35
27. Spelling tests given at least once a week	73	51	83	56	46
28. End of term tests given	66	44	75	48	42
29. Many pupils who create discipline problems	09	09	07	01	18
30. Verbal reproof sufficient	97	95	98	99	91
31. Discipline – extra work given	70	53	69	49	67
32. Smack	65	42	64	33	63
33. Withdrawal of privileges	86	77	85	74	85
34. Send to head teacher	24	17	21	13	28
35. Send out of room	19	15	15	08	27
36. Emphasis on separate subject teaching	85	50	87	43	73
37. Emphasis on aesthetic subject teaching	55	63	53	61	63
38. Emphasis on integrated subject teaching	22	65	21	75	33
Estimated proportion of teachers in each class	0.538	0.462	0.366	0.312	0.322

Wilks (1938) showed that under certain regularity conditions $-2 \ln \lambda$ is asymptotically distributed as chi-square with degrees of freedom equal to the difference in the number of parameters between the two hypotheses. Consequently values of $-2 \ln \lambda$ can be used to test hypotheses about c. Wolfe (1970) suggests a series of tests, the first of which consists of testing H_0: $c=1$ against H_1: $c=2$: if H_0 is rejected by the likelihood ratio test, a test of H_0: $c=2$ against H_1: $c=3$ is performed, and so on, until a value of c is found which gives a non-significant result. Some examples are given in Everitt (1980).

Some authors, for example, Wolfe (1971), and Binder (1978) have pointed out that in the context of fitting finite mixtures, there are a number of difficulties with Wilks' likelihood ratio test, and a number of simulation studies have indicated that a slightly amended test will give more satisfactory results: see, for example, Everitt (1981) and Aitkin *et al.* (1981).

SUMMARY

Finite mixture densities provide useful models for the existence of distinct groups of observations in data. Maximum likelihood estimates of their parameters may be found via the iterative algorithm described earlier in this chapter. This algorithm appears to be fairly successful in most cases, although it can occasionally be rather slow to converge. Since in mixtures with a moderate number of components there may be a large number of parameters to estimate, it is likely that large samples will be needed. Assessing the number of components in the mixture appropriate for a particular data set may be difficult, but the likelihood ratio test described earlier is, in general, helpful.

References

AITKIN, M., ANDERSON, D. & HINDE, J. (1981). Statistical modelling of data on teaching styles. *Journal of the Royal Statistical Society, Series A, 144*, 419–461.

ANDERSON, T.W. (1954). On estimation of parameters in latent structure analysis. *Psychometrika, 19*, 1–10.

BINDER, D.A. (1978). Bayesian cluster analysis. *Biometrika, 65*, 31–38.

CASSIE, R.M. (1954). Some uses of probability paper in the analysis of size frequency distributions. *Australian Journal of Marine and Freshwater Research, 5*, 513–522.

CHARLIER, C.V.L. (1906). Researches into the theory of probability. *Lunds Universitets Arskrift, Ny foljd*, Afd. 2.1, No. 5.

DAY, N.E. (1969). Estimating the components of a mixture of normal distributions. *Biometrika, 56*, 463–474.

DEMPSTER, A.P., LAIRD, N.M. & RUBIN, D.B. (1977). Maximum likelihood from incomplete data via the EM algorithm. *Journal of the Royal Statistical Society, Series B, 39*, 1–38.

EVERITT, B.S. (1980). *Cluster Analysis*, 2nd ed. London: Heinemann Educational Books.

EVERITT, B.S. (1981). A Monte Carlo investigation of the likelihood ratio test for the number of components in a mixture of normal distributions. *Multivariate Behavioural Research, 16*, 171–180.

EVERITT, B.S. (1984). A note on parameter estimation for Lazarsfeld's latent class model using the EM algorithm. *Multivariate Behavioural Research, 19,* 79–89.

EVERITT, B.S. & HAND, D.J. (1981). *Finite Mixture Distributions,* London: Chapman and Hall.

GIBSON, W.A. (1959). Three multivariate models: factor analysis, latent structure analysis and latent profile analysis. *Psychometrika, 24,* 229–252.

GREEN, B.F. (1951). A general solution for the latent class model of latent structure analysis. *Psychometrika, 16,* 151–166.

HALD, A. (1952). *Statistical Theory with Engineering Applications.* New York: John Wiley & Sons.

HARDING, J.P. (1949). The use of probability paper for the graphical analysis of polymodal frequency distributions. *Journal of the Marine Biological Association of the U.K., 28,* 141–153.

HASSELBLAD, V. (1969). Estimation of finite mixtures of distributions from the exponential family. *Journal of the American Statistical Association, 64,* 1459–1471.

KENDELL, R.E. (1969). The continuum model of depressive illness. *Proceedings of the Royal Society of Medicine, 62,* 335–339.

KENDELL, R.E. & GOURLAY, J. (1970). The clinical distinction between psychotic and neurotic depressions. *British Journal of Psychiatry, 117,* 257–260.

KILOH, L.G. & GARSIDE, R.F. (1963). The independence of neurotic depression and endogenous depression. *British Journal of Psychiatry, 109,* 451–463.

LAZARSFELD, P.F. & HENRY, N.W. (1968) *Latent Structure Analysis.* Boston: Houghton Mifflin Co.

PEARSON, K. (1894). Contribution to the mathematical theory of evolution. *Philosophical Transaction,* A, *183,* 71–110.

PILOWSKY, I., LEVINE, S. & BOULTON, D.M. (1969). The classification of depression by numerical taxonomy. *British Journal of Psychiatry, 115,* 927–945.

POWELL, G.E., CLARK, E. & BAILEY, S. (1979). Categories of aphasia: a cluster analysis of Schuell test profiles. *British Journal of Disorders of Communications, 14,* 111–122.

RAO, C.R. (1948). The utilization of multiple measurements in problems of biological classification. *Journal of the Royal Statistical Society, Series B, 10,* 159–203.

SCHUELL, H. (1965). *Differential Diagnosis of Aphasia.* Minneapolis: University of Minnesota.

SCHUMACHER, C.F., MAXSON, G.R. & MARTINEK, H. (1953). *Tests for Creative Ability in Machine Design.* Annual report, Project ONR458. Armed Services Technical Information Agency 21 284.

WILKS, S.S. (1938). The large sample distribution of the likelihood ratio for testing composite hypotheses. *Annals of Mathematical Statistics, 9,* 60–62.

WOLFE, J.H. (1970). Pattern clustering by multivariate mixture analysis. *Multivariate Behavioural Research, 5,* 329–350.

WOLFE, J.H. (1971). A Monte Carlo study of the sampling distribution of the likelihood ratio for mixtures of multinormal distributions. *Technical Bulletin, STB72-2,* Naval Personnel and Training Research Laboratory, San Diego, California, USA.

7

Sample Size and Power

the late BERNARD R. SINGER with A. D. LOVIE and P. LOVIE

In baiting a mouse-trap with cheese, always leave room for the mouse.
(Saki, The Infernal Parliament, *The Square Egg*, 1924)

CHOOSING THE SAMPLE SIZE OR THE FINAL NUMBER OF OBSERVATIONS

There is little doubt that at the present time the usual experiment is carried out largely in ignorance of its total cost in terms of time, effort, materials and observations. Very few would build a house with no idea of the amount of materials and labour needed, yet an analogous situation so frequently happens in scientific research. If the materials are insufficient when building a house, it may be too late to find similar ones at a suitable time and the prices may have risen in the interval. If there is too much material it may be troublesome to dispose of it. In an experiment, the observations which are more than necessary may not be of use to anyone else and the time or money expended might have been better employed elsewhere. Again, if we find that insufficient observations were used, it may not be possible to duplicate the precise conditions of the experiment or even to repeat it.

At least of equal importance is the fact that if we ignore the sample size we may fail to detect effects or differences due to our treatments which are actually present. It is simply not true that large differences will be readily detected and that this is not a problem. A 'clear' difference will not always lead to a significant result even with a so-called 'reasonable' sample. The fact is, typical experimenters have little or no idea of the chances they have of detecting a true and noticeable difference or correlation following from the treatments. An understanding of the ability of the *power* of statistical tests to detect such effects should be an essential part of the training of every scientific researcher.

Let us illustrate these points with a numerical example. Some American researchers find that there is a large difference between the times taken to solve certain problems when a new method of training (A) is used compared with traditional method (B). Two independent groups of children are used in the experiment; one group is trained with method A and the other with method B. After the training, the children are each given intelligence type problems to solve.

129

The average solution time for group B is 12 minutes but for group A it is 8 minutes. The variability of the two groups is similar and gives a standard deviation of 5.

A research group in Britain are very impressed with this large difference of 4 minutes between the two methods and wish to apply the new technique A to children in England. They feel that there may be some small variation with a sample from a different nationality and decide to repeat the basic experiment with English children. With such a large difference in solution time they expect similar findings but decide to use a 'reasonable' sample of 30 children under each of the two methods A and B. They choose a non-directional (i.e. two-tailed) test at the 1 per cent level. After applying Student's t test for independent samples they find to their astonishment that there is not a significant difference between the sample means at the 1 per cent level.

Another group in Scotland are also impressed with the American findings and independently of the researchers in England carry out an experiment with many more children who are readily available in nearby schools. Using 100 children with each method they find a significant difference using Student's t test beyond the two-sided 1 per cent level. The American findings are thus confirmed with a large number of Scottish children.

The question must now be asked: why did not the English experiment show significance when the original results were so impressive? Again, why did the experiment in Scotland confirm the original experiment in contrast with the English study? Experienced researchers will reply at once that there were many more children in the Scottish experiment and this would improve the chances of showing a significant difference. This is perfecly true, but the English experiment used 60 children in all to confirm a very large difference between the training methods. Many researchers in the social sciences would use two samples of 30 in each for even moderate differences and our English group have therefore employed a common sample size.

The fact is, the English researchers did not know the power of Student's t test used to assess their finding; that is, they did not know the ability of the test to detect differences at the chosen significance level. Had they known this they would probably not have used only 30 children in each group with a 1 per cent level, since in contrast to the American data their ability or *power* of finding significance was too low. The chances of not obtaining significance were 33 per cent or only 1 out of 3. Conversely their chances of finding significance at the 1 per cent level were 67 per cent or 2 out of 3 (i.e. power is equal to 67 per cent). Not a very powerful test! With a mean difference of 4 minutes and a standard deviation of 5, they would need about 48 children in each group to obtain significance at the 1 per cent level with a 90 per cent chance of success (i.e. with power equal to 90 per cent). With 58 children in each, they would have had a 95 per cent chance of obtaining significance.

But what about our successful Scottish group? Surely they should be pleased with their findings? Yes, if you ignore the fact that they used far more children than were really necessary. With 88 children in each sample the power would be 99.5 per cent and the chance of finding a significant difference was at least 995 out of 1000. With 76 children in each, the power would be 99 per cent and thus the chance of wrongly rejecting the null hypothesis would be equal to the chance of wrongly accepting it. Even with 58 children under each method, the chance of failing to obtain significance would be only 5 per cent with power of 95 per cent. In other words, our successful group had a very good chance of obtaining significance at the 1 per cent level with 84 fewer children than were actually used!

SAMPLE SIZE, POWER AND EFFECTS

Experimenters often wish to know the minimum number of observations required in order to show that there are real effects or differences resulting from the treatments used. For reasons of time or economy the number of subjects may be limited and, in consequence, the researcher is often unwilling to use more than are really necessary. On the other hand, even for quite large differences or effects it might not be possible to demonstrate them at an acceptable statistical level with a sample that is in fact too small for the purpose.

GENERAL METHODS

For all statistical tests we need to have two different kinds of information when selecting the number in the sample. The first kind is common to every test whatever its nature and is concerned with how we choose the size of the alpha (α) and beta (β) errors in an experiment. The second kind of information depends upon the test chosen and is concerned with finding the *effect size* or the result of the treatments applied; parts of it apply to all tests and parts vary with the test to be used.

Choosing the α and β errors

We need to know the size of the two different risks we are willing to take in relation to the data. We commit an α or Type I error when we claim significance but there is no difference and the null hypothesis is true. The less familiar Type II (β) error occurs when we fail to reject the null hypothesis when it is in fact false and there *is* a difference (or effect).

Selecting the α level gives us little trouble since there are certain conventional significance levels such as 5 and 1 per cent. The task of selecting the size of the β error is not so simple since we do not have at present generally acceptable levels for it. Cohen (1977) has suggested a β level which is four times larger than the α level. In other words, we tolerate an error of 20 per cent for β compared with an error of 5 per cent for α. That is, the error of wrongly rejecting the null hypothesis is considered to be four times more serious than the error of failing to detect an effect when the null hypothesis is not true.

If we use this suggested convention, it gives us a power of 0.80 for $\beta=0.20$ since $1-\beta$ is equal to the power (i.e. ability) of the test to detect differences or effects that exist. This is often put in percentage terms and we say, for example, that a test has an 80 per cent power. Such a test has an 80 per cent chance of showing the effect to be significant at the chosen α level.

Many researchers would not feel content with such a relatively low power and would prefer to use a much higher one, say 95 per cent, to correspond roughly to an α level of 1 per cent (remember $1-\beta=0.96=1-(4\times0.01)=1-(4\times\alpha)$). This is perfectly acceptable, if we are prepared to obtain large samples. For example, if we expect a medium effect (see the next section) and require power of 95 per cent for an α level of 1 per cent, about 144 subjects will be needed in each group if a two sample t test is to be used. However, for the same medium effect size with $\alpha=0.05$ and power $1-\beta=0.80$, only 60 will be needed in each treatment for a two-tailed t test. Some would feel that even this is too demanding and would use a 10 per cent α value to give a subject requirement of only 50 in each treatment.

We can summarize our remarks on the choice of α and β levels as follows. A suggested convention is to use $\alpha=5$ per cent for $\beta=20$ per cent or a power of 80 per cent. The consequences of departure from this suggestion might be an unacceptably high α level or a large subject requirement. If, however, you find a high effect size, as we shall see in the next part, you may be able to choose with greater freedom.

Finding the effect size

The effect size is a measure or indicator of the influence of the treatment or treatments used in the experiment. The greater the effect of the treatment, the larger the effect size. The actual method of calculating it depends on the statistical method. In this chapter we shall be concerned mainly with a measure known as d. This is an indicator of the effect of different treatments on the means of different samples when the sample variability is taken into account. For example, if we have two unrelated samples of equal size from populations with means μ_{max} and μ_{min} and common variance σ^2, d is defined as

$$d=\frac{(\mu_{\text{max}}-\mu_{\text{min}})}{\sigma}. \tag{1}$$

It should be noted that:

(i) we are only interested in effect sizes under an alternative hypothesis of a difference between means;
(ii) in practice, we often need to estimate d using sample values.

We can see from equation (1) that the greater the difference between the means, the greater the value of d, but that d decreases as the standard deviation becomes larger for a fixed difference between the means.

Cohen (1977) suggests that the range of values corresponding to a small, medium or large effect of a treatment depends on the field of experimentation and that only experience in one's own research area can given possible values. In his own field of research in the clinical, personality and testing areas of psychology, Cohen suggests a value of $d=0.20$ for low effect size, $d=0.50$ for medium effect size and $d=0.80$ for large effect size. Some might find these values on the low side; in some biological and chemical disciplines, they might be much higher. Clearly, the researcher's own experience must modify these tentative suggestions.

How do we determine the value of d? Three possible ways are:

(a) *Previous research.* Here we simply examine previous reports in that area of experimentation and determine from them the values for μ_{max}, μ_{min} and σ. Clearly we cannot hope that our estimated value of d will be an accurate measure of the effect size for that type of experimental research, but it will give an approximate idea of it.

(b) *Pilot study.* This entails carrying out a small experiment with a few subjects in order to obtain estimates of the means and variances. This method has the advantage that it is more likely to represent the experimental conditions under which the full scale research will be carried out.

(c) *Assumption.* If previous work has not been undertaken in the area and a pilot study is ruled out, a particular effect size can be assumed. The sample size for the chosen α and β levels is then calculated on the basis of this value of d.

We summarize the methods for selecting sample size by the following suggested steps:

1. Choose your Type I error level α.
2. Choose your Type I error level β.
3. Calculate the effect size.
4. Using the above three values, calculate n, the size of each sample, using the methods given later. If the sample size required is unreasonably large, it may be necessary to modify your α and β choices.

TWO SAMPLE t TEST

Approximate methods

These methods are suitable in situations where the samples are from normal populations with equal variances. They can be used for both one- and two-tailed tests. Neither method is reliable when both the sample sizes and the variances are very different. However, if the variances σ_1^2 and σ_2^2 are reasonably similar, the common standard deviation may be found from $\sigma = \sqrt{\{(\sigma_1^2 + \sigma_2^2)/2\}}$; if the sample sizes are different, the harmonic mean $2n_1n_2/(n_1+n_2)$ of the individual sample sizes can be used.

The sample size procedure, which is due to Neyman *et al.* (1935), can be found in Snedecor & Cochran (1967); the method for estimating power is given in Dixon & Massey (1983) and Cohen (1977).

Estimating the sample sizes required

Suppose we wish to find the sample sizes needed to give a two-tailed test with power 95 per cent if $\alpha=0.01$ and $d=0.85$.

Step 1

Calculate a tentative sample size n_1 (to one decimal place) using

$$n_1=2(z_{1-\alpha}+z_{1-\beta})^2/d^2, \tag{2}$$

where $d=$ the calculated effect size from $(\mu_{max}-\mu_{min})/\sigma$ and $z_{1-\alpha}$ and $z_{1-\beta}$ are the values of the normal deviates for the α and β levels, respectively. Note that for a two-tailed test, the value obtained is $z_{1-\alpha/2}$.

In our case $n_1=2(2.576+1.645)^2/(0.85)^2=49.273$.

Therefore $n_1=49.3$ (to one decimal place).

Step 2

Determine the number of degrees of freedom associated with the test. For two independent samples of equal size this is $f=2n_1-2$, where n_1 is taken from step 1 but the value is rounded *upwards* to the next whole number.

Thus, n_1 is rounded to $n_1=50$ and we obtain $f=2(50)-2=98$.

Step 3

Take the value of n_1 from step 1 (to one decimal place) and multiply it by $(f+3)/(f+1)$ to give the final sample size n. Round *upwards* to the next whole number.

In our example, with $n_1=49.3$ and $f=98$ we have

$$n=\frac{f+3}{f+1}\times n_1=\frac{98+3}{98+1}\times49.3$$

$$=\frac{101}{99}\times49.3=50.3.$$

Therefore $n=51$ (rounded upwards).

Estimating the power of the test

Suppose we have two samples each of size 30, what is the power of a two-tailed test if $\alpha=0.01$ and the effect size $d=0.80$?

Calculate

$$z_{1-\beta}=\frac{d\sqrt{2n}}{2+\{1.21\,(z_{1-\alpha}-1.06)\}/(n-1)}-z_{1-\alpha}, \tag{3}$$

where d is the effect size, n is the sample size and $z_{1-\alpha}$ and $z_{1-\beta}$ are the normal deviate values for α and β.

In our example

$$z_{1-\beta} = \frac{0.80\sqrt{2(30)}}{2+\{1.21(2.576-1.06)\}/29} - 2.576 = 0.427.$$

The area under the normal curve to the left of $z_{1-\beta} = 0.427$ is the power of the test; the power of this particular test is therefore 66.5 per cent.

We cannot consider this test to be a powerful one of the effect size $d=0.80$. If we had added only 8 subjects to each sample we would have increased the power to 80 per cent for the 1 per cent α level. With 48 subjects in each treatment we would have a power of 90 per cent. Using the 5 per cent level, our power would have been 86 per cent with $d=0.80$ (two-tailed) for $n=30$ and with 48 subjects we would have the high power of 97 per cent for the experiment.

Both methods can be adapted easily for use with the related samples t test and the non-parametric equivalents of the independent and related samples t tests, the Mann–Whitney and Wilcoxon signed ranks tests. The steps outlined above are followed exactly, except that the effect size d in equations (2) and (3) is multiplied by the appropriate value as shown in Table 1.

Table 1. Multipliers of d

Test	Multiplier
*Related samples t	$1/\sqrt{1-r}$
Mann–Whitney	$\sqrt{3/\pi}$
*Wilcoxon signed ranks	$\sqrt{6/\pi(1-r)}$

*Note that if the correlation is unknown and cannot be estimated, r is assumed to be 0.5.

As an example, for a two-tailed Wilcoxon test for $\alpha=0.01$, $d=0.80$ and 30 pairs of observations where the correlation is unknown

$$z_{1-\beta} = \frac{d\sqrt{(12n/\pi)}}{2+\{1.21(z_{1-\alpha}-1.06)\}/(n-1)} - z_{1-\alpha}$$

$$= \frac{0.8\sqrt{\{12(30)/\pi\}}}{2+\{1.21(2.576-1.06)\}/29} - 2.576$$

$$= 1.575$$

The power of the test is therefore 94.2 per cent.

Non-centrality and the two sample *t* test

So far we have dealt with the power and effective sample sizes of two sample tests, both parametric and non-parametric, through approximations of the appropriate tests and sampling distributions. The advantages of such an approach are two-fold. First, parametric and non-parametric tests can be dealt with under the same system by simple transformations. Further, the need for special, and hence relatively inaccessible, tables is avoided since only standard tables of the normal distribution are required.

The disadvantages of the methods are that they generate only approximate answers when more exact ones are possible, and power and sample sizes are calculated from different formulae. However, the problem can be approached more directly through the use of so-called non-central distributions, which are the sampling distributions for tests where a null hypothesis of equality (homogeneity) of the population parameters is considered false. Under these circumstances the sampling distribution will be shifted by an amount determined by the alternative hypothesis. The size of the shift is represented by the *non-centrality parameter*, denoted either by δ, λ or ϕ depending upon the textbook. We will use ϕ in this and the succeeding section.

Further, the non-centrality parameter is related to the effect size d, in that it is also defined as a function of the expected difference in parameter values under the alternative hypothesis. Note that the variance of this shifted distribution will have to be estimated, a point that will be discussed at greater length in the section on the analysis of variance. Finally, since the following analysis for the two sample t test is readily available in many texts, including fairly elementary ones (see, for example, Howell, 1982), the coverage will be brief and designed as an introduction to the more extensive treatment in the next section.

In a study of age differences in verbal ability, two groups of 20 people were asked to define a word by choosing from a list of definitions. The score used was the number of correct definitions. Group A had a median age of 18 years, group B one of 60 years, with an equal but small spread of ages in both groups.

The average score out of 40 words was 25 correct for Group A and 28 for Group B, rounded to the nearest integer. The variances for the two groups were 11 and 13 respectively, again rounded to the nearest whole number. The pooled variance is 12. Our H_0 is that $\mu_A = \mu_B$ or that $\mu_A - \mu_B = 0$. For our alternative hypothesis, we suggest that $\mu_A < \mu_B$, that is, the 60-year-old group will perform more effectively than the 18-year-olds.

The non-centrality parameter ϕ is defined as

$$\frac{\mu_A - \mu_B}{\sigma\sqrt{(1/n_A + 1/n_B)}}, \tag{4}$$

where σ is the common or pooled standard deviation, and n_A and n_B are the sample sizes for groups A and B.

Assume that our α is 0.05, that the difference or shift $(\mu_A - \mu_B)$ under the alternative hypothesis is 8 correct definitions and that σ is effectively estimated by $\sqrt{12}$, or 3.5. Thus

$$\phi = \frac{8}{3.5\sqrt{(1/20 + 1/20)}}$$

$$= 7.2.$$

From tables of the non-central t distribution (see, for example, Winer, 1971, or Howell, 1982), with d.f. $= 38$ and our α of 0.05, we find that a ϕ of 7.2 has a power in excess of 0.99. Lowering the size of the expected difference under the alternative hypothesis will push down the power, as will a decrease in the size of the α error. Note that when dealing with a two-tailed test (i.e. the direction is not specified), the α level of such a test is twice the α level of the one-tailed one.

Effective sample sizes can also be estimated from the non-centrality formula. For instance, if we require a power of 0.80 for an alternative hypothesis of a difference of 3 correct definitions and an α of 0.05, ϕ is 2.8 (Howell, 1982). Substituting this in the formula for ϕ, and assuming equal numbers of readings in each group, we have

$$2.8 = \frac{3}{3.5\sqrt{(1/n_A + 1/n_B)}},$$

so n_A and $n_B = 21$. Thus, for a smaller expected alternative hypothesis, our present sample size is probably adequate for a power of 0.80.

Other related tests for which power calculations, non-centrality parameters and tables are available include t tests for correlated samples (Cohen, 1977; Howell, 1982) and F tests for two variances (Dixon & Massey, 1983).

ANALYSIS OF VARIANCE

This section will cover the determination of power and sample size for one and two factor designs, with and without interaction present in the latter case. Some consideration will also be given to whether the factors are fixed, random or mixed, that is, whether we have instances of ANOVA Models I, II, or III. It is important to introduce these latter considerations since they determine the *precise* form of the non-centrality parameters for the various F tests. The non-central F distribution is used to describe the situation when the null hypothesis of equality, or homogeneity, of the parameters is considered to be false. The non-centrality parameter has the property of shifting the central (or null hypothesis) F distribution in accord with the detailed form of the alternative hypothesis. Such a distribution, therefore, needs to be specified when calculating the power of the various F tests.

One factor ANOVA for independent groups (fixed effects)

(Here, as with the other designs in this section, we are assuming that there are equal numbers of readings associated with each level of the factor.)

The determination of specific alternative hypotheses is more difficult for factorial designs than for simple two sample experiments, mainly because of the large number of different patterns of parameters even for the single factor case. Consequently, researchers often have to entertain a series of simplified alternative hypotheses, ones which reduce, for example, the number of values which have to be entered in the appropriate tables (see Cohen, 1977, for the more complex case).

One heuristic is to assume a simple relation between the average ANOVA effect size and the error mean square. Other related ones include the patterning or grouping of the means themselves (see Cohen, 1977, for more on this latter rule of thumb). An even simpler move is to assume a specified constant distance between the means, where such a constant is larger than might be expected under a null hypothesis of homogeneity (equality) of the parameters.

Although such simplications are necessary in the interests of mathematical and computational ease, it should not be forgotten that the researcher's own background knowledge or theoretical expectation should be incorporated into the form of the alternative hypothesis since the power of the test (and the related decisions on expected sample sizes) is only meaningful in the light of the specified alternative hypothesis. Put another way: users should always be aware of the precise form of the alternative hypothesis and its substantive implications, *even if they are using simplifying assumptions, such as equal distance between means, to help in arriving at an alternative hypothesis.*

The non-centrality parameter (ϕ) for the single factor design is

$$\phi = \sqrt{\frac{n \sum \tau_i^2}{I \sigma_e^2}}, \tag{5}$$

where n is the number of readings per level, τ_i is the effect ($\mu_i - \mu$) of level i, I is the number of levels of the factor and σ_e^2 is the mean square error.

A possible simplification here is that

$$\frac{\sum \tau_i^2}{\sigma_e^2} = 1,$$

that is, the mean of the squares of the effects (τ_i) is a simple function of the error mean square. Thus, (5) now becomes $\phi = \sqrt{(n/I)}$ (see Odeh & Fox, 1975, for more on this).

An example is as follows: in an experiment on solving anagrams of differing lengths (see Bourne *et al.*, 1971), four lengths of anagram, from 3 to 12 letters, were chosen with equal frequency solutions and common transition probabilities for these solutions. Independent groups of 10 subjects were assigned to each of these four levels and an average solution time obtained for each of the 40 subjects. For a significance level of 0.01 and a power of 0.80, with the alternative hypothesis that the error mean square is four times the size of the average effect size squared, are 10 readings per level enough? ϕ now becomes $\sqrt{(n/4)}$ and, from the tables compiled by Tiku (1967) (see Cohen, 1977; and Howell, 1982), ϕ is approximately equal to 2.2 for 3 and 36 d.f. for the treatment factor and error respectively.

Thus, solving (5) for n under the alternative hypothesis we have $n=19$. Consequently, 10 subjects are not sufficient to achieve a power of 0.80 under the alternative hypothesis. What power do we actually have? Again the Tiku tables, which list a limited range of ϕ, d.f. and power values, are of help here, although the more extensive charts in Odeh & Fox (1975) are more generally useful. So the ϕ value for our actual experiment is $\sqrt{(10/4)}$ or 1.58, which corresponds to a power of 0.45, for the given α and d.f. – not a particularly impressive result.

How would the power alter if we changed the α level and/or the alternative hypothesis? If α was set at 0.05, the power of our experiment against the original alternative hypothesis now rises to 0.71. Further, if we suggested that the average effect was a different function of the error mean square, say,

$$\sum \tau_i^2/\sigma_e^2=2,$$

then the ϕ for the experiment is

$$\sqrt{(2n/I)} \quad \text{or} \quad \sqrt{(20/4)}=2.24,$$

and the power increases to 0.82, as would be expected from accepting a larger effect size under the alternative hypothesis. Of course, how *realistic* such an alternative hypothesis might be is open to question.

Other simplifying rules mentioned earlier include assuming an equal distance between the parameters under the alternative hypothesis. This leads to the possibility of the *constant* effect size being a function of the error mean square, which in turn implies a simplification of the formula for the non-centrality parameter. For example, if the square of the constant effect τ_i^2 satisfies the relationship $\tau_i^2=2\sigma_e^2$, then $\phi=\sqrt{2n}$ (see Odeh & Fox, 1975).

Of course, the discussion so far has treated the mean square error as a nuisance parameter, to be bypassed by these simplifying assumptions. If, however, the experimenter, in the interests of specifying a reasonable alternative hypothesis and hence a more realistic estimate of the power of any tests, is unable to subscribe to any of these assumptions, then the error variance may have to be dealt with more directly. This follows because the provision of a specific alternative hypothesis, based perhaps on experience with the area or from a knowledge of the background literature, could suggest a more complex pattern of effects. This, in turn, might rule out the simple relationships between τ_i and σ_e^2 mentioned earlier and hence imply that the fuller equations for the non-centrality parameter should be employed, for example, equation (5).

Estimating the σ_e^2 term now becomes something of a problem. The simplest solution is to use the observed error mean square as an estimate under the alternative hypothesis. Unfortunately, there is evidence to suggest that the sample sizes commonly used to estimate σ_e^2 are too small, perhaps by as much as a half. What one now needs is a routine to provide better estimates of what are bottom line sample sizes. Several suggestions have been made recently (see Wilcox, 1984, for an up-to-date review). The most useful move is to implement a two-stage sequential scheme of the kind described in Chapter 8 on ranking and selection. This routine tests whether the sample size used in estimating the error mean square is large enough for a given power and, if not, how many extra observations are needed. Wilcox (1984) also provides some computer simulations on the robustness of the various parameter estimators used in this sequential routine.

A further problem in estimating power for the linear hypotheses assumed here is the type of structural model, whether Type I or II for single factor independent group designs. For fixed effects, the approach outlined so far, that is, the one leading to a non-central F distribution, is appropriate. For random effect models, however, the approach outlined in Winer (1971) leads to a solution based on the central F distribution. Here the usual F value under the null hypothesis of zero effects is weighted by a joint function of the level sample size and observed F ratio (Winer, 1971, p. 246).

Two-factor ANOVA for independent groups (fixed effects)

Here the extra complication is the possible existence of an interaction. Odeh & Fox (1975) consider three approaches for two-factor designs. Two of these specify null and alternative hypotheses about the main effects, the third about the interactions. We will deal with only two of the situations. Again simplifications relating the effects to the error mean square are introduced to ease some of the problems with calculating the non-centrality parameter.

Let us examine a more complex version of our anagram experiment to illustrate certain of the procedures. Our first factor is, as before, anagram length with four levels of the variable. The second factor is subjects' verbal IQ, which has three levels: low, middle and high. Separate groups of 10 subjects are assigned to the 12 cells of the design.

The first analysis concerns the main effects only and assumes that there is no interaction. The non-centrality parameter for, say, factor 2 is defined as

$$\phi = \sqrt{\frac{In \sum \gamma_j^2}{J \sigma_e^2}},$$

where n is the number of observations per cell, γ_j is the main effect, I, J are the number of levels of the first and second factors and σ_e^2 the (augmented) error mean square. (Note that in this case, the error mean square has been pooled with the interaction mean square, as have their respective degrees of freedom.)

Again, as with the single factor case, certain simplifying assumptions may be made about the alternative hypotheses. These include equal (constant) distances between ordered means, or a simple relationship between the average main effect size squared and the error mean square. For example, if we could assume in our experiment that $\Sigma\gamma_j^2/\sigma_e^2 = 1$, (6) would become

$$\phi = \sqrt{(4n/3)}.$$

If we require a power of 0.80, with an α level of 0.05, either the Tiku (1967) tables or the more extensive ones by Odeh & Fox (1975) yield a ϕ of 1.8 with degrees of freedom of 2 and 114, or more generally, $(J-1)$ and $(IJn-I-J+1)$. Note that these are the degrees of freedom for the F test on factor 2.

Thus $1.8 = \sqrt{(4n/3)}$ and n is, therefore, about 3. The experimental sample is more than adequate against such an alternative hypothesis. Of course, other simplifying rules to ease the development of alternative hypotheses are possible.

When interactions are to be tested, an appropriately modified version of (6) is given by

$$\phi = \sqrt{\frac{n \sum_i \sum_j \tau\gamma_{ij}^2}{\{(I-1)(J-1)+1)\} \sigma_e^2}} \tag{7}$$

where $\tau\gamma_{ij}$ is the interaction effect. Note that the d.f. for ϕ are now those for the interaction and error terms. In our example, these are $(I-1)(J-1)=6$ and $IJ(n-1)=108$ (or ∞).

If we assume that

$$\sum_i \sum_j \tau\gamma_{ij}^2/\sigma_e^2 = 3,$$

then (7) becomes

$$\phi = \sqrt{(3n/7)}$$

or, for a power of 0.9 and an α of 0.01, $2.0 = \sqrt{(3n/7)}$, or $n = 10$ (rounded upwards), which is the number of readings that we have already taken.

So far we have assumed that the two factors are fixed, hence a non-centrality parameter has had to be estimated. If, however, we have random factors then, as Winer (1971, p. 334) shows, the distribution of F under a general alternative hypothesis for the main effects, for example, that $\sigma_{\tau_i}^2 > 0$, is a multiplicative function of the appropriate *central* F distribution. Here the weighting is by a parameter, say θ, which equals 1 when $\sigma_{\tau_i}^2 = 0$ and is greater than 1 when $\sigma_{\tau_i}^2 > 0$. This parameter can be estimated from the observed F ratio for the effect.

If we have model III, that is, mixed effects, then Winer (1971, pp. 334–5) points out that a non-central F distribution may be used to evaluate power, providing that the highly restrictive assumptions attached to such models can be accepted or proved.

References

BOURNE, L.E., Jr, EKSTRAND, B.R. & DOMINOWSKI, R.L. (1971). *The Psychology of Thinking*. Englewood Cliffs: Prentice-Hall.

COHEN, J. (1977). *Statistical Power Analysis for the Behavioral Sciences*, rev. ed. New York: Academic Press.

DIXON, W.J. & MASSEY, F.J., Jr (1983). *Introduction to Statistical Analysis*, 4th ed. New York: McGraw-Hill.

HOWELL, D.C. (1982). *Statistical Methods for Psychology*. Boston: Duxbury.

NEYMAN, J., IWASZKIEWICZ, K. & KOLODZIEJCZYK, S. (1935). Statistical problems in agricultural experimentation. *Journal of the Royal Statistical Society Supplement*, 2, 114.

ODEH, R.E. & FOX, M. (1975). *Sample Size Choice*. New York: Marcel Dekker.

SNEDECOR, G.W. & COCHRAN, W.G. (1967). *Statistical Methods*, 6th ed. Ames, Iowa: The Iowa State University Press.

TIKU, M.L. (1967). Tables of the power of the F test. *Journal of the American Statistical Association*, 62, 525–39.

WILCOX, R.R. (1984). A review of exact hypothesis testing procedures (and selection techniques) that control power regardless of the variances. *British Journal of Mathematical and Statistical Psychology*, 37, 34–48.

WINER, B.J. (1971). *Statistical Principles in Experimental Design*, 2nd ed. New York: McGraw-Hill.

8

Ranking and Selection of Populations

ALEXANDER D. LOVIE

George the First was always reckoned
Vile, but viler George the Second;
And what mortal ever heard
Any good of George the Third?
When from earth the Fourth descended
(God be praised!) the Georges ended.

Walter Savage Landor

CHOOSING THE SITE AND CLEARING THE GROUND

Although analysis of variance (ANOVA) and related techniques, for example, multiple regression, have proved a boon to the users of large, complex experimental designs, they have one major drawback: their pronouncements are too global. An omnibus test like ANOVA, for instance, performs all possible comparisons (or contrasts) *simultaneously* on the levels of a factor (or the combinations of levels for a particular factor interaction) and is, therefore, unable to pinpoint the locus of a significant comparison. A related problem is that a worker might want to run an experiment in a systematic way so as to ensure reasonably unambiguous inference by, for example, fully crossing the factors, but is only interested in making selected comparisons between the various means, etc. ANOVA alone has little to offer such an experimenter since the output of the analysis is on too large a scale.

There is, of course, an extensive range of recent methods whose task is to solve certain of these problems. Under the collective name of simultaneous multiple comparisons, these include so-called planned or *a priori* comparisons and *post hoc* or *a posteriori* comparisons. The former are selected comparisons decided on before the experiment and would not normally be linked to, or justified by, an overall analysis such as ANOVA. Such contrasts usually form a tiny subset of the possible comparisons and are normally suggested (and hence justified) by the *substantive* content of the work. For example, in a study of the effect of age on a simple motor skill, a selective planned comparison between the averages of the youngest and oldest subjects would be worth making since most studies suggest the existence of a large difference between such groups on such tasks.

143

Traditionally, there are said to be two important differences between tests *a priori* and *a posteriori*. First, the former are said to be more powerful than the latter, that is, they have a higher probability of correctly rejecting a null hypothesis of no difference. Second, *post hoc* tests can be performed on any of the possible comparisons while *a priori* tests are restricted to independent, that is, orthogonal, contrasts. Not everyone agrees, however, on the validity of such distinctions (see, for example, Myers, 1979, on this matter). It is still possible, nevertheless, to classify the methods into those that offer alternatives to such global analyses as ANOVA, and those that supplement such methods.

The disadvantages of such methods include the following. First, they are usually limited to contrasts between a small class of parameter estimates, usually means. Second, the fact that we normally make inferences about these estimates on the basis of null hypotheses of no difference reduces the power of such tests when compared with ones which incorporate any assumed or expected differences. In other words, such traditional multiple comparisons form unnecessarily *indirect* tests of collections of parameter estimates which are in fact assumed to show some differences, either because the substantive context of the experiment or because tests such as ANOVA have given support for the existence of signficant or important differences. Demonstrating the existence of a difference by showing that no differences are *not* the case seems a particularly convoluted form of inference when differences can be legitimately expected. The rest of this chapter describes a class of direct methods for evaluating such expected differences for many different parameters.

One further point: since we are concerned with evaluating the truth of non-trivial partitions of the collection of parameters, we are faced with decision-making problems more akin to testing the alternative hypothesis than with those determining the value of null hypotheses of no difference. However, our interest is in non-homogeneous hypotheses, that is, with ones asserting a particular pattern of *differences*, so there is only one kind of error (analogous to the classical Type II or β one) that needs to be considered, since if all the parameters are in fact equal then *any* of them could be selected as largest (or smallest) and hence no consideration of Type I (α) errors need be included. In other words, when testing for the largest of an ordered collection of means, you need only worry, when asserting that a particular population has the highest mean, that it is in fact some other population that has this largest value. This error is analogous to the β one in classical significance testing in that it is associated with an alternative hypothesis of a difference. Therefore, the power $(1-\beta)$ of the selection is a measure of the correctness of the choice since power is the probability of correctly *rejecting* a null hypothesis of homogeneity or equality of the population parameters. This is a necessary consequence of (a) concerning oneself with hypotheses that assert a difference, (b) wishing to demonstrate the truth of such hypotheses, and hence (c) selecting only a subset from the existing collection.

That a considerable amount of work has been driven by the needs of applied areas may be seen from these last remarks. The methods will, therefore, be of interest to psychologists and other social scientists wishing to determine the best psychotherapeutic treatment, the best teaching method, the most comfortable seating arrangement, the most effective advertising campaign, etc.

FOUNDATIONS, WALLS AND ROOF

The range of configurations of population parameters that can be considered is almost as extensive as the number of parameters themselves. For example, we can ask which is the highest mean or variance, which two (or more) means are larger or smaller than a control, which is the largest regression parameter for a series of bivariate linear regression equations. Notice again that we are interested in non-homogeneous, unequal arrangements of parameters. Notice, too, that the techniques are *not* concerned with *estimating* such values, rather the issue is to *identify* them using a decision procedure which will yield as high a probability of correct selection as the various determinants of the selection process allow. Consequently, many of the routines assume that the relevant parameters are known. Where they are estimated, then the traditional versions rather than any novel ones are used.

However, since there are many possible configurations, or patterns of relationships, in a number j of population parameters, the routines for identifying the one of interest must take this complexity into account. The way chosen here is to proceed via the 'indifference and preference zone' route (see Gibbons *et al.*, 1977, 1979, for more detail). This means constructing two areas or zones within which either the configuration of interest does not exist (the IZ or indifference zone) or the one where the configuration does (the PZ or preference zone). If you were interested, for example, in establishing that a given population parameter, θ_j say, was the highest parameter of an ordered collection of parameters $(\theta_1 \leqslant \theta_2 \ldots \theta_{j-1} \leqslant \theta_j)$, then an intuitively attractive way of establishing a PZ and IZ would be to look at the difference between the largest and the next largest, that is, $(\theta_j - \theta_{j-1})$. If this distance (which we will call δ) is *strictly less than* some critical or threshold distance $\delta^\star$, that is, $\delta < \delta^\star$, then we would be indifferent between the two parameters, that is, at least either (or both) could be the highest. If, however, $\delta \geqslant \delta^\star$, then we would select θ_j as the highest. In general, ranking and selection procedures are much more concerned with the construction of the PZ than the IZ since only the former contains the exemplars of the assumed difference.

Notice that since the two parameters have been ordered, that is, $\theta_j > \theta_{j-1}$ then in drawing up the PZ and IZ there are certain inadmissible areas or values of $(\theta_j - \theta_{j-1})$. Specifically this means that θ_j can *never* be less than θ_{j-1}, hence the difference(s) can never be negative. In this case, therefore, the lower boundary of the IZ is where $\theta_j - \theta_{j-1} = 0$, and the IZ/PZ boundary is where $\theta_j - \theta_{j-1} = \delta^\star$.

Of course, when drawing up PZ and IZ for the sample, the rest of the parameters $(\theta_1$ to $\theta_{j-2})$ are ignored since the selection procedure is only concerned with choosing the largest parameter, hence we are interested exclusively in the relationship between θ_j and θ_{j-1}. However, the PZ will contain configurations where $\delta > \delta^\star$ is still true but where many different patterns of configurations of relationships between the *other* parameters are also true. It turns out that this has practical implications for the methods. Consequently, the probability of making a correct selection (called $P(CS)$) is often calculated from a baseline configuration called the 'least favourable configuration' (LFC). For the example discussed earlier, the LFC is that $\theta_1 = \theta_2 \ldots = \theta_{j-1} > \theta_j$, that is, that all the parameter values are the same except θ_j. This simplest configuration, however, still allows the selection of θ_j as the largest. In general, the $P(CS|LFC)$ represents the minimum $P(CS)$ for that selection routine, that is, for choosing the largest parameter. Bearing in mind the discussion of Type I errors earlier, the P value has a minimum of $1/j$, that is, the probability of a random choice. Consequently, for $j=2$, the minimum value of P is 0.5. However, for most practical selection procedures, we would want to work with probabilities of correct selection ≥ 0.75. Other situations require the determination of different LFCs, IZs and PZs.

For selection procedures based not on distances or differences between parameters but on ratios, for example, choosing the smallest variance (see later worked example), the IZ and PZ are bounded, unlike those for the selection of means. This would also be true for selections of binomial parameters (π) based on differences or distances since such proportions can only take on the range of values 0 to 1.

The procedures themselves normally yield both confidence statements and confidence intervals based on the difference between the selected parameter and the true value. These statements and intervals can in turn be related back to the PZ and IZ to answer such questions as: is the selected value nearer the true value than the next highest one (however 'next' is defined)? The determinants of the confidence intervals and statements include the number of populations, the size of the parameter of interest, the value of any other relevant parameters of the population (so-called nuisance parameters), the sample size(s), and the probability of correctly selecting the parameter (usually under the LFC).

In other words, if the problem is to select the highest parameter (θ_j) as being the true highest (say θ), then confidence statements of the form ($\theta_j - \delta \leq \theta \leq \theta_j$) can be made for the $P^\star$ confidence level, where $P^\star$ is defined as the probability of a correct selection conditional upon the LFC. Other variants on the same confidence statement can be constructed, for example, $0 \leq \theta - \theta_j < \delta^\star$ is an equivalent version. In words, this states that the difference between the selected largest value θ_j and the true largest value lies between zero and the critical or threshold value, the latter $\delta^\star$ being the difference between the largest and next largest parameter. As before, such a statement is made with $P^\star$, the probability of correct selection. If δ is less than or equal to this threshold, then one can, of course, assert that the selected value θ_j is the true highest one, θ, rather than the next lowest, with probability $P^\star$ of having made the correction selection.

The width of this confidence statement is a function of the value of pairs of

$(\delta^\star, P^\star)$ for differing sample sizes n. These pairs can be used to generate operating characteristics of $\delta^\star$ versus $P^\star$ (analogous to power function curves) which, in turn, can help to produce the confidence statements. Clearly the trade-offs between these quantities $(\delta^\star, P^\star$ and $n)$ can be used for a variety of purposes. For example, it might be possible to determine what size n should be for a given value of $P^\star$ and/or $\delta^\star$, or if the common sample size is fixed (or known) then a value of $\delta^\star$ could be determined for a fixed value of $P^\star$. Analogous relationships can also be seen when determining the power of a test (see Ch. 7 by Singer *et al.*).

Confidence intervals can also be drawn up for θ; thus, with probability $P^\star$, θ lies in the interval $(\theta_j, \theta_j + \delta^\star)$ – again, a further development from the earlier confidence statement. The general forms of these confidence statements and intervals need to be modified for the particular parameters and selection routines although they are more or less suitable in their present form, for example, for choosing the best (or worst) means or best variances or regression values.

Finally, the means for determining sample sizes are also different for different selection problems.

The philosophy associated with subset (or subset-like) selection procedures, for example, the best two or more means or variances, the largest number of means better than a control, is determined by the choice of the subset size, that is, is the subset predetermined or random? This in turn is a function of the kind of question asked of the data. If the experimenter is interested in a fixed number of parameters then the analysis uses the IZ/PZ approach. This follows because prior knowledge of the number of parameters, combined with the fact that in such circumstances the more complex subset problems can usually be reduced to the simpler one of the relation between two key parameters, mean that a threshold value $\delta^\star$ can normally be determined.

For the case where the subset size forms a random variable, however, the approach is more complex since it is not usually possible to determine the value of $\delta^\star$ and hence an IZ. Here an interval (hopefully short) is erected around a given key or 'tagged' parameter *estimate*, usually the largest or smallest. Values outside this interval are usually taken to be worse or inferior to at least one member (and implicitly to most of the values) within the interval. Here the emphasis is on *observed* estimates of the parameters and hence with predetermined common sample sizes. Gibbons *et al.* (1977) refer to this as a screening or elimination procedure since it is often augmented or aided by the experimenter's own knowledge, which can be used to choose as small an initial subset as possible. Moreover the outcome of the statistical method is to exclude even more members of this first subset.

Ranking or ordering methods also depend upon the IZ/PZ approach in so far as an ordering of the population parameters implies that the pairwise difference should either equal or exceed a designated threshold $\delta^\star$. In other words, if we have, say, an ordered set of means: $\mu_1 \leqslant \mu_2 \ldots \mu_{k-1} \leqslant \mu_k$ then $\mu_2 - \mu_1 = \delta_1$, $\mu_3 - \mu_2 = \delta_2, \ldots, \mu_k - \mu_{k-1} = \delta_{k-1}$ is a true order if $\delta_1 \geqslant \delta_1^\star$, $\delta_2 \geqslant \delta_2^\star, \ldots, \delta_{k-1} \geqslant \delta_{k-1}^\star$.

It is usual to simplify this by designating a common constant $\delta^\star$. Further, as with the selection procedures, there are different routines depending upon whether one knows, or has to estimate, the parameters which form part of the process, for example, the population variances which are used in the ranking and selection of means.

WORKED EXAMPLES (A). SELECTING PARAMETERS

Which is the largest mean? Or: Pin-ball wizard (from Lindgren & Berry, 1981).

(*Note that the various tables with letter codes cited in the worked examples are those of the tables in the back of Gibbons et al. (1977) where routines for table interpolation may also be found.*)

The players of TV computer games sometimes assert that the position of the games paddle with respect to the screen influences success. In a simple experiment using a pin-table simulation, separate groups of 20 subjects were asked to play a game for a fixed length of time with the paddle in one of three positions: centre, far left, medium left. Summary data on their scores are as shown in Table 1.

Table 1

Paddle position	n	Mean	Variance
Centre	20	40.78	32.30
Far left	20	48.53	33.25
Medium left	20	50.50	20.50

Question: Does the medium left paddle produce the highest mean score?

Answer: This will be in the form of a confidence statement, with a particular level of the probability of a correct selection ($P^\star$), based on the distance between the true highest mean and our selected value. A complication here is that we have had to estimate the variances. We, however, make the simplifying assumption that the variances are equal and hence can be pooled to provide us with an estimate of the (common) population variance. A further simplification is that we assume normal populations.

The task is somewhat eased, however, because we have equal n. So our confidence interval is based not only upon $P^\star$ but also upon a common n.

There is a complex relationship between n, $\delta^\star$, $P^\star$ and σ (population standard deviation) in the determination of the width of the confidence statement, so we can designate an expression for $\delta^\star$. This equals $\tau\sigma/\sqrt{n}$ where τ is the standardized version of $\delta^\star$, thus $\tau = \delta^\star\sqrt{n}/\sigma$. (Note that τ can also be used to determine common sample sizes for a given $P^\star$, since $n = (\tau\sigma/\delta^\star)^2$.)

So for $P\star$ equal to 0.90 (tabulated $P\star$ values usually range from 0.75 to 0.999), the confidence statement $(\mu_j - \delta\star \leqslant \mu \leqslant \mu_j)$ is calculated in the following steps:

(a) Calculate a pooled variance estimate:

$$s^2 = \frac{\sum ns_j^2}{\sum n} = \frac{20\ (32.30 + 33.25 + 20.50)}{60}$$

$$= 28.68$$

(b) Substitute for s, n and τ in the formula for $\delta\star$. (Note that values of τ can be obtained from Table A.1 and involve j and $P\star$. For $j=3$ and $P\star = 0.90$, $\tau = 2.23$.)

(c) Thus

$$\delta\star = \frac{2.23\ \sqrt{28.68}}{\sqrt{20}} = 2.67.$$

Therefore, for a $P\star$ of 0.90, the largest observed mean (50.50) is 2.67 units distant from the true largest mean. This is more than the distance between the largest and next largest mean $(50.50 - 48.53) = 1.97$. The conclusion that the largest observed mean is the true largest does not, therefore, seem to be supported here.

However, if one had chosen a $P\star$ of 0.75, with a tabulated value of τ of 1.43, then $\delta\star$ becomes 1.71, less than the distance between the largest and the next largest mean. However, if one asserts, on the basis of this evidence, that the largest mean is the true largest mean then one does so with a lower probability of making the correct selection than the earlier analysis ($P\star$ of 0.75 as against one of 0.90).

One can see how important is the value of the common sample size in determining the width of the interval. By how much, therefore, should our original n of 20 be increased so that one could select the largest mean as the true largest with our original $P\star$ of 0.90? To answer this we need only specify an acceptable $\delta\star$ and then solve for n in the formula $(\tau\sigma/\delta\star)^2$. Choosing a value for $\delta\star$ less than the distance between the largest and next largest mean (1.97), say 1.70, gives

$$n = \left(\frac{2.23\ \sqrt{28.68}}{1.7}\right)^2 = 49.$$

In other words, we would need over twice the number of readings per sample to select the largest mean as the true largest with a $P\star$ of 0.90.

Finally, it is now possible to test how close the *lowest* mean is to the true lowest mean, since it is almost exactly the same routine as that for the highest one. In the original version of our example, a $\delta\star$ of 2.67 with a $P\star$ of 0.90 was calculated. If we were to select the lowest observed mean (40.78) as the true lowest, then it

6

should be within (or no more than) 2.67 of the true lowest value. Consequently, since the difference between this mean and the next largest (48.53−40.78) is 7.75, so, with a probability of a correct selection of 0.90, we can assert that the lowest mean is the true lowest.

It is worth repeating just how important is the sample size in all these procedures. In particular, the larger the sample the more stable the estimates of both the parameter(s) under investigation and the so-called 'nuisance parameters' (means and variances respectively in our current example). Further, unless the sample sizes are large, then the selection rule could be based on different parameter estimates for repeats of the experiment. In addition, small unbalanced sample sizes mean that both individual and pooled estimates are subject to considerable instability and extra variation *within* the experiment. The latter problem and the adjustments necessary to cope with it are covered in our next worked example.

Which is the highest mean (unequal n)? Or: Who is this sitting beside me?

In a study reported by Mazur (1977), psychologists photographed pairs of unrelated males sitting on park benches in three cities, San Francisco, Tangiers and Seville. From the developed pictures, average inter-trunk distances were measured in inches for all pairs. A summary data set for all three groups is shown in Table 2.

Table 2

Place	n (pairs)	Mean	SD
San Francisco	35	28	10
Tangiers	25	35	10
Seville	22	33	7

Notice that we do not have a common n. The way to proceed here, therefore, is to calculate a common value, called n_0 from these unequal numbers which can be used to compute $\delta^\star$ for the selection of means. The formula for n_0 is

$$\sum n_j^{1/2}/j.$$

For our example

$$n_0 = (\sqrt{35} + \sqrt{25} + \sqrt{22})/3 = 27.1.$$

For the calculation of $\delta^\star$ we need to produce a pooled variance estimate, as before:

$$s^2 = \{(35 \times 100) + (25 \times 100) + (35 \times 49)\}/82 = 9.2,$$

so that

$$\delta^\star = \frac{\tau\sigma}{\sqrt{n}} = \frac{2.23\sqrt{9.2}}{\sqrt{21.1}} = 1.3.$$

The highest mean (35) is, therefore, 1.3 inches from the true highest, with a $P^\star$ of 0.90. Since the difference between the highest and next highest observed means is 2 inches, we can conclude that we can select the highest as the true highest with a good probability of correct selection.

What would be the case if our $P^\star$ was increased to 0.99? Using Table A.1 we compute a new $\delta^\star$,

$$\delta^\star = \frac{3.6\sqrt{9.2}}{\sqrt{27.1}} = 2.1,$$

which is a little larger than the difference between the largest and the next largest mean.

What is the smallest variance (n equal and unequal)?

Using the last two examples, we can ask which sample has the smallest variability? The critical value $\delta^\star$ separating the PZ from the IZ here is not the distance between the two smallest variances, as with the examples on means, but their ratio – the same statistic used in the conventional two sample F test. The PZ for such a ratio will, of course, have a lower limit of 1.00 and be otherwise unbounded.

Gibbons *et al.* (1977) point out that if one defines δ as the ratio not of the two variances, but of the standard deviations, that is, σ_2/σ_1, where $\sigma_1 \leq \sigma_2 \ldots \sigma_{j-1} \leq \sigma_j$, then the reciprocal of δ (called Δ) is now an upper bounded function, $0 \leq \Delta \leq 1$. (Note that standard deviations rather than variances are used, since only the former is scaled in the units of the original data, and hence may be intuitively more meaningful. Note too that the reciprocal can be re-expressed as the ratio of the smallest to the next smallest standard deviation.)

We can also designate a quantity $\Delta^\star$ which is the critical value of Δ, usually under some least favourable configuration. As will be recalled this provides a lower bound to the probability of a correct selection.

As with the selection of means, there are complex trade-offs between $\Delta^\star$, $P^\star$ and sample size (or more precisely, degrees of freedom) to be exploited. Consequently, one can recast the selection procedure in terms of acceptable degrees of freedom (ν) for a given $\Delta^\star$ and $P^\star$ (see Table G.1). Gibbons *et al.* (1977) point out, however, that one would not normally require a very high value of $P^\star$ (say 0.975 or more) since $\Delta^\star$ and $P^\star$ are directly related.

Finally, the routines are a little different if one knows or has to estimate the nuisance parameters μ_j (the population means), or has equal or unequal degrees of freedom. The assumptions, as before, are that the populations are normally distributed and that the μ_j are equal.

One selection procedure, therefore, is to choose the σ_j with the lowest value (usually σ_1 in an ordered collection), calculate Δ (note that $\Delta \leq \Delta^\star$), and use the tables to calculate ν (and, from this, a common sample size) for a given value of $P^\star$

(usually $\geqslant 0.75$). One can then construct a confidence interval around the lowest value (or make a confidence statement about it). Notice of course that one could use such a procedure prior to an investigation to determine a sample size, or even an acceptable value of $\Delta^\star$. Indeed, Gibbons *et al.* (1977) view such tables as useful planning aids for any experimenter.

In our first example on TV games, with a common n (20), the v is $(n-1)$ or 19. The ratio of the next smallest to the smallest standard deviation (Δ) is $4.53/5.70=0.79$. For $j=3$, $\Delta^\star=0.79$ and a $P^\star$ of 0.75, a minimum v is 23, a little larger than our observed value of 19. In other words, a common sample size of 20 is not large enough to allow us to select the smallest variance as the true smallest, even with a $P^\star$ value as low as 0.75.

The second example on the inter-trunk distances of the parkbench pairs has 7 and 10 as its lowest and next lowest standard deviations. This produces a Δ of $7/10=0.7$. Since the samples are unequal we need to compute a standard common sample size. As before this is n_0 or 27.1. Using Table G.1 we can see that $\Delta^\star$ of 0.7, with j (number of groups) of 3 and n_0 of between 21 and 31 produces a probability of correct selection ($P^\star$) between 0.9 and 0.95. There is, therefore, more evidence here to suggest that the smallest variance is the true smallest, although a few more observations might be advisable to achieve a $P^\star$ of 0.95.

What is the highest binomial parameter (π)? Or: What's eating you?

In a study from *Science News* discussed by Gibbons *et al.* (1977), three separate groups of 500 people, obese, normal weight, and elderly, were blindfolded and given strained bananas to taste. The proportions of successful identification of the food by each group are as follows:

Obese	0.69
Normal weight	0.41
Elderly	0.24

Does the obese group have the highest sensitivity? Gibbons *et al.* (1977) pointed out that with equal n, the selection procedure is fairly straightforward, particularly for $n \geqslant 10$. Here the LFC (from Gibbons *et al.* 1977) is

$$\pi_1 = \pi_2 = \ldots = \pi_{j-1} = 0.5 - \delta^\star/2 \text{ and } \pi_j = 0.5 + \delta^\star/2,$$

where $\delta^\star$ is a critical value of $\pi_j - \pi_{j-1}$.

The form of LFC is not dependent upon n, provided that $n \geqslant 10$ and $j \geqslant 2$. As can be seen, the LFC implies a range of $\delta^\star$ values symmetric about 0.5 (or, more precisely, values of π_j and π_{j-1}, are symmetric around 0.5).

In our example, δ is $0.69-0.41=0.28$. If we assume that $\delta^\star \geqslant \delta$, then Table E.1 gives $\delta^\star$, $P^\star$ pairs for different values for j (2, 3, and 10) and n. For the nearest lower value of $\delta^\star$ (0.25 here), one needs an n of 52 for a $P^\star$ of 0.99, so our sample sizes are clearly more than adequate for our selecting the obese value as the highest.

A $P^\star=0.99$ confidence statement would, therefore, make π_3 (obese) lie some 0.25 units from the true mean with $n=52$, where the confidence statement is of the usual form $0<\pi_j-\pi<\delta^\star$, where π is the true largest value. This implies an interval of width $(\pi, \pi + \delta^\star)$.

However, since our n is much larger than 43, the table shows that we would produce a much shorter width interval, with only a small drop in $P^\star$, even with a tabled value of n very near our own figure of 500 (tabled value of n for $P^\star=0.9$, $j=3$, and $\delta^\star=0.01$, is 498). This would yield an interval of length $(\pi, \pi+0.01)$ for $P^\star$ of 0.9, which is much smaller than our observed $\pi_3-\pi_2$ or $0.69-0.41=0.28$.

The tables can also be used to test for the smallest π by symmetry, since if there are only two outcomes (traditionally called success and failure), and if π is the probability of success, then $(1-\pi)$ is the probability of failure. Therefore, the largest and next to largest values of $(1-\pi)$ can now be fed into the routine since they are, in fact, the smallest and next to smallest values of π.

Finally, since the n is fixed and equal in our example, so the selection rule 'choose the highest observed π as the true highest π' can be restated as 'choose the population with the highest frequency of the selected event as the true highest π'. If, however, n is not equal for each proportion then one uses the conventional n_0 formula to estimate an average or constant n for the results. However, the selection rule would relate only to the π values in this latter case.

What is the best treatment (level) in a multi-factor design of computer-aided instruction and study time (two factors with equal readings per cell)?

In an experiment on computer assisted learning, four programmes were investigated with three lengths of study time (see Mendenhall *et al.* 1981). Table 3 shows the structure and achievement test results for the two factor (4×3) design.

Table 3

		Study time			
		1	2	3	Σ
CAI	1	61 49	77 61	90 86	424
programme	2	72 65	84 72	109 86	502
	3	54 53	69 53	78 79	386
	4	59 63	96 83	110 95	506
	Σ	476	595	747	1818

The selection procedures, as before, allow one to trade off sample sizes (or ν, degrees of freedom), number of levels, $\delta^\star$, $P^\star$ and the size of level means. An ANOVA of the data is shown in Table 4.

Both main effects are significant at well beyond the 0.01 level. The interaction

Table 4

Source	SS	d.f.	MS	F-ratio
CAI programme	1755.2	3	585.1	10.34
Study time	4612.8	2	2306.4	40.75
Interaction	337.5	6	56.3	0.99
Error	679.0	12	56.6	
Total	7384.5	23		

is non-significant and, for the selection procedure, its MS is pooled with that for the error to give

$$\text{Pooled MS} = 56.47 = s^2.$$

The routine first checks if the sample sizes are large enough for us to decide that the largest level mean for a particular factor is the true largest. If they are, then the routine stops and the selection can be made with an appropriate $P\star$. If not, then the routine says how many more readings are needed. Technically, such a two-stage or sequential process should be performed on a randomly chosen sample from the original data. (Note such a two-step routine is sometimes used for selecting a largest mean when the σ^2 are unknown and based on only a small n.) However, since we have only a small amount of data in the example, we will proceed as if this were a subset of a larger set of values.

For either factor, select the largest level mean as the true largest level mean if the number of readings on which each mean is based is greater than M, where

$$M = \left(\frac{2s^2 h^2}{\delta^{\star 2}}\right)^+$$

and s^2 is the error (or pooled) residual mean square or variance, h is a joint function of the number of levels, the appropriate degrees of freedom for s^2 and $P\star$, and a^+ signifies the smallest integer larger than a. For example, if $a = 3.3$, then $a^+ = 4$, $a = 3.5$, $a^+ = 4$, etc. As before, $\delta\star$ stands for the minimum difference between the largest and next largest mean consonant with a pre-selected value of $P\star$.

For the CAI programme factor, the levels means (in order) are 64.3, 70.7, 83.7, and 84.3. From Table A.4, h is 2.21 for four levels, 18 degrees of freedom and a $P\star$ of 0.95. Only $\delta\star$ remains to be chosen. There is, however, a problem here since the two largest means are very close. So I have chosen a largish value of $\delta\star$ (12) to see how these two largest values compare with the next largest one. So

$$M = \left(\frac{2 \times 56.47 \times 2.21^2}{12^2}\right)^+ = 4,$$

which is a little less than six, the number of readings for each marginal level mean.

Consequently, we can conclude that the two largest means are nearer the true largest than the third. However, which of these two largest (83.7 and 84.3) is nearer the true largest cannot be decided here since if we substitute 0.5 for $\delta^\star$ in the formula for M, we get $M=2207$, somewhat larger than six!

The analysis should, however, enable us to say how many more readings per level we would need before we could conclude that the largest mean was the true largest. This is M − (number of readings for each level mean) or, $2207-6=2201$. Further, since this would need to be a multiple of the number of levels of the other factor (to preserve the equal number of readings per cell), that is, a multiple of 3, so the additional number of readings per mean would be 2199, or 733 more readings for each cell. Clearly there are economic reasons (as well as the more mundane substantive ones) for not bothering to differentiate between the two largest means! Moreover, the difference between the smaller of the three means and the smallest mean, 63.3, is less than 12 points, so it would not be possible to conclude that the smallest observed mean was the true smallest.

A similar analysis could be used on the other factor, study time, to demonstrate whether or not there are enough readings to enable us to assert that the largest mean, $747/8=93.4$, is the true largest.

If we are interested in the best interaction, however, the picture is somewhat more complex, with few easily available treatments or tables. Nevertheless, recent work suggests that a PZ can be erected for many two factor fully crossed designs, based on the difference between the largest and next largest interaction effect (see Gupta & Panchapakesan, 1979). There is, however, no general treatment for higher order interactions.

Finally, notice that our analysis of the factor CAI programme could, because of the pattern of mean values, be treated as an example of *subset selection*, for example, which are the *two* largest means of the four? Aspects of this part of selection will be dealt with next.

WORKED EXAMPLE (B). SUBSET SELECTION

As was pointed out earlier, methods of subset selection are conditioned by choice of subset size; that is, is it predetermined (the best four treatments) or random (the worst collection of means)? Variants on this theme include the set of treatments different from a control.

It should be noted that the two main references for this chapter, Gibbons *et al.* (1977) and Gupta & Panchapakesan (1979), differ over the exact definition of what constitutes a subset selection procedure. The former treat only the random size subset as a true subset selection problem, while the latter lump both random and predetermined subset sizes together, even though each requires a different approach. This chapter follows the latter reference. However, readers interested in the complexity of the various arguments should consult Gibbons *et al.* (1977, pp. 296–301).

Selecting *k* means from *j* where the factor is display complexity

In Winer (1971) the following ordered means (based on 10 readings per mean) for a single factor design (display complexity) with six levels are given:

Levels	1	2	3	4	5	6
Means	10.0	11.0	12.0	18.0	19.0	21.0

Which are the best three means from the six? The distance measure for the selected subset is the difference between the smallest mean of this subset, say μ_{j-k+1}, and μ_{j-k}, the largest of the *excluded* means. In other words $\delta=\mu_{j-k+1}-\mu_{j-k}$. Under an LFC which states that all the means in the subset are the same and that the lower valued means in the excluded part are also equal, $\delta=\delta^\star$, and so a PZ is established.

Unfortunately, the tables for this procedure assume that certain parameters are known, specifically σ^2, and not estimated from the data. Consequently, I have assumed a σ^2 of 18.00 (see the example in Winer, 1971, p. 179) and a σ of 4.25. The formula for a minimum *n* for a specified $\delta^\star$ is as follows:

$$n=\left(\frac{\tau\sigma}{\delta^\star}\right)^2.$$

This is the same expression as the case for a single best mean, with a known variance.

Let us make $\delta^\star$ equal 5, while τ, from Table N.1 with a $k=3$ and a $P^\star$ of 0.95, is 3.48. The minimum common *n* is, therefore: $(3.48\times4.25/5)^2$ or 9 (to the nearest integer). Consequently, we have a big enough *observed* common $n(10)$ to allow us to select as the best subset of three means the three largest, with a critical distance function $\delta^\star$ of 5 and a probability of correct selection $(P^\star)$ of 0.95.

WORKED EXAMPLE (C). SELECTING THE BEST *k* MEANS GREATER THAN A CONTROL

As Gibbons *et al.* (1977) point out (pp. 247–249), the decision that a mean lies above a comparison or control value implies *two* PZs, one above (larger means) and one below (smaller means) the IZ around the control value. Consequently, since the decision *larger*, and hence the value of $\delta^\star$, is based on the distance between the means and the control, so the statement defining the PZ for larger must take into account the PZ for smaller. This should, therefore, avoid a mean being misclassified as larger simply on the basis of its distance from the control.

The larger and smaller PZs and the IZ for a single mean and control are, therefore, defined thus:

$$\text{Decide larger if} \quad \mu\geqslant\mu_0+\delta_2^\star$$
$$\text{Be indifferent if} \quad \mu_0-\delta_1^\star<\mu<\mu_0+\delta_2^\star$$
$$\text{Decide smaller if} \quad \mu\leqslant\mu_0-\delta_1^\star$$

where μ is the selected mean, μ_0 is the control mean, and $\delta_1^\star$ and $\delta_2^\star$ are the critical distances for the boundaries of the smaller and larger PZs.

One control and three experimental conditions

Winer (1971), in his discussion of the so-called Dunnett test for comparing all means with a control, examines a study which contains the following results for a control and three experimental conditions (taken originally from Dunnett):

	Control	1	2	3
Means	50	61	52	45

Which means are greater than the control?

There is a common n of 3 and a pooled s^2 of 19.00. Since the common variance has had to be estimated, as has the standard or control value, Gibbons *et al.* (1977) recommend a two-stage process, as with our two-factor worked example. This consists of selecting a random sample, size n, of readings which are used to estimate σ^2. To see if more readings are necessary for the second stage, a quantity N is calculated, that is, the total number of readings to select the number of means. Thus $N-n$ is the expected number of readings for the second stage. Of course, n might be large enough to obviate the need for a second stage so:

$$N \geqslant \text{maximum} \left(n, \frac{8s^2 h_v^2}{(\delta_1^\star + \delta_2^\star)^2} \right).$$

In their discussion about the selection of suitable $\delta^\star$ values Gibbons *et al.* point out (1977, pp. 254–255) that $\delta_1^\star$, and $\delta_2^\star$ need not always be symmetric about the control value, since the real-life consequences for means judged greater than a control could often be different for ones judged to be less by about the same amount. However, there is little to guide us with the present example, so I have chosen equal values of $\delta^\star$ of 10. The quantity h_v, which is a function of the degrees of freedom of the pooled variance, is given in Table M.3. For the example, v is $4 \times 2 = 8$ or, more generally, (number of conditions+standard)$\times (n-1)$. If $P^\star$ is set at 0.95, then $h_v = 2.51$. Thus $N \geqslant$ (3 or $(8 \times 19) \times 2.51$) or $N \geqslant$ (3 or 19). Clearly our initial (and only) sample size is much too small for us to conclude, with a $P^\star$ of 0.95 and a large $\delta^\star$ of 10 that, say, condition 1 (and all conditions with means $\geqslant$ its mean) is larger than the control. We need a minimum of $(19-3) = 16$ more readings (and stability of our σ^2 estimate) before we can proceed further.

WORKED EXAMPLE (D). SUBSET SELECTION – RANDOM SIZE SUBSET

Does my sample contain the single best value?

Here the PZ/IZ approach cannot be used since the number of means, and hence the pattern of their differences, cannot be predetermined. In general, one hopes that the size of the subset is dependent not only upon the total number of means, the common sample size and $P^\star$ but also the true configuration of the popula-tions. Consequently, as Gibbons *et al.* (1977, pp. 297–8) point out, the choice of a subset for a given configuration is determined by its size if two procedures which lead to a common $P^\star$ also generate different subset sizes.

The approach adopted here is to tag one of the populations as 'best' under a given configuration. Gibbons *et al.* (1979) point out that such an approach also allows one ultimately to select the single best population without involving the IZ/PZ concept (see Gupta & Panchapakesan, 1979, and Gupta & Huang, 1981, for more details of the non-indifference zone orientation).

Testing the temperature

In a study by Woods & Holland (1966), five separate groups of 10 rats were offered the choice between two temperatures of water. The factor is variation in the two temperatures and the dependent variable is the percentage of time spent by the animal in the *warmer* of the two (note that the data reported had been arc-sine transformed). The ordered means and other information is as shown in Table 5.

Table 5

	1	2	3	4	5
Means	20.1	40.4	55.1	61.1	64.2
	$s^2 = 136.89$	$n = 10$			

What is the *smallest* size subset that we can choose so as to ensure, with a given probability $(P^\star)$, that it contains the highest mean? This involves choosing a mean as a tagged value (here the highest one), and setting up a closed, non-empty interval around this tagged value. As with most of the examples so far, the assumption is that the underlying populations are normal with a common variance.

The interval is thus:

$$I = \left(\bar{x}_j - \frac{\tau\sigma}{\sqrt{n}}, \ \bar{x}_j \right)$$

where $\bar{x}_j$ is the tagged mean and τ is the same as in Table A.1. For a mean, say $\bar{x}_k$, to be included in the subset then

$$\bar{x}_k \geqslant \bar{x}_j - \frac{\tau\sigma}{\sqrt{n}},$$

that is, the lower bound of the interval.

For our example,

$$I = \left(64.2 - \frac{3.05 \times 11.7}{10}, \ 64.2 \right)$$

for $j=5$ and $P^\star=0.95$, that is, 52.92 to 64.2. This yields a subset of size three, that is, the means 55.1, 61.1 and 64.2.

Gibbons *et al.* (1977) present further results for subsets of a fixed size which have a given $P^\star$ of containing the highest value and a routine for selecting a subset of means larger than a control (Chapter 13).

WORKED EXAMPLE (E). RANKING POPULATIONS

In this final section of worked examples I will recycle the last set of results. Here the question is: 'Is the observed rank order of means the true ranking?' An IZ/PZ approach is used and the simplifying assumption is made that it is possible to determine a common threshold distance, $\delta^\star$, between adjacent pairs of ordered means, that is, for all the observed pair-wise distances, δ_j, $\delta_j \geqslant \delta^\star$.

As with other IZ/PZ formulations, it is possible to trade-off $\delta^\star$, $P^\star$ and n when asserting that the observed order is the true one. Also slightly different routines may be pursued if the nuisance parameter (here the variance) is either known or estimated, for example, a fixed size or two-stage sampling programme.

For simplicity, let us assume that the estimated variance 136.89 is a good approximation to the true value. An expected n for a given $\delta^\star$, $P^\star$ pair can, therefore, be given by the formula

$$n=\left(\frac{\tau\sigma}{\delta^\star}\right)^2.$$

Table P.1 gives $P^\star$ values for given j and τ pairs. However, it may be necessary to interpolate τ for a standard value of $P^\star$. In our example, if we set $\delta^\star$ as 3 and with a $P^\star$ of about 0.9 (in fact 0.906) and j of 5, we have τ of 2.8. So

$$n=\left(\frac{2.8\times11.7}{3}\right)^2=119.$$

Clearly, our available sample size of 10 is quite inadequate for us to decide that the observed ranking is the true one, although a $\delta^\star$ of, say, 8 yields an n of 17, much nearer to our observed value of 10.

Other routines available will allow us to order variances or to partition the set of values into disjoint or overlapping subsets which are ordered between the subsets. The problem with the latter methods, however, is that $P^\star$ is not controlled.

OTHER METHODS NOT TREATED HERE BUT AVAILABLE FROM THE REFERENCES

It is clear from our extended treatment that most of the routinely available methods are parametric, that is, they make quite strong assumptions about the form of the parent populations ordered or selected. These are usually taken to be normally or binomially distributed. There are, however, some results for other distributions, for example, exponential and gamma distributions, and the related Poisson distribution. Here a gamma or exponential parameter may be selected as best. Such distributions are often thought to model reaction or processing times in skilled performance and many branches of cognitive psychology.

There are also non-parametric methods for selecting the best percentiles, or order statistics, of a population. Here the median would be viewed as the 50th percentile and hence is a useful non-parametric analogue of the mean. Gibbons *et al.* (1977) also consider the selection of certain paired-comparison parameters.

It is also clear that our treatment has emphasized univariate methods, although mention was made of methods to select correlations and regressions. There are, in addition, procedures for selecting multivariate means and multiple correlation coefficients.

Finally, although following Gibbons *et al.* (1977) I have not discussed estimation problems for ranking and selection, it is possible to use any order information to improve the estimation of many parameters or quantities such as means and percentiles (see Gupta & Panchapakesan, 1979, Ch. 21).

FINAL REMARKS

Except for the one study by Reading (1975), which anyway only discusses the case of means with known variances, there have been few attempts to marry selection procedures and multiple comparison tests. However, it is worth looking briefly at the relation between the two since I will be arguing in Chapter 9 of this book that one strand in the selling of new statistics is that new improves on the old.

In general, multiple comparison tests tend to be of the shotgun or blunderbuss variety, that is, they are designed to throw up every possible significant contrast, whether they make sense or not. The Newman–Keuls test, for instance, is specifically sold as a way of performing *all* pair-wise comparisons between means. Of course, such a procedure is justified since the H_0s usually entertained by such procedures are those of homogeneity of the parameters under examination. Such an *unstructured* approach to data snooping can have certain advantages in highlighting surprising or unexpected findings, particularly in complex designs where a simple eyeball of the data often yields only a confused and uncertain picture of the results.

However, where differences or heterogeneity of effects might either be expected or sought, such techniques tend to be less useful than the ranking and selection ones covered in this present chapter. Certainly, to make proper use of such methods, the experimenter needs to be structured in his or her thinking. But this is usually justified either because an omnibus test such as ANOVA has indicated that an H_0 of homogeneity can be rejected, or because the literature has strongly suggested where such differences might lie. In this sense, therefore, the methods in this chapter would tend to encourage a more self-conscious and planned exploration of data and hence a more systematic growth of knowledge.

Further, for the applied experimenter looking for the best or worst of a set of treatments, the present techniques offer a much more direct and powerful means of establishing such values than multiple comparisons. And, of course, the range of parameter types which can be evaluated is much larger than with multiple comparisons, as I hope has been demonstrated by the examples in the chapter.

Perhaps the best way of summarizing the methods is that they offer a richer and more flexible set of methods than have hitherto been available and, apart from the extreme empiricism of the blunderbuss, can be shaped to answer most questions of detail about a collection of results. The task confronting the experimenter, therefore, is in translating hypotheses into a form suitable for ranking and selection routines.

Finally, it is worth pointing to a connection between ranking and selection and the earlier chapter on outliers. This is via the notion of *slippage tests*, that is, tests of the hypothesis that one of a collection of populations has moved or 'slipped' to either the right or left of the other populations. This will often show itself, in a univariate sample, as a cluster of results somewhat apart from the bulk of the data. Such data can often be treated as outliers and their influence assessed accordingly. However, a test of slippage may also reduce to a form of selection test since the parameters of such a population are likely to be the best, or worst, of the collection of populations. Gibbons *et al.* (1977) have considered the case of slippage in their treatment of paired-comparisons (p. 215), even going so far as to develop a *least favourable slippage configuration* (LFS), parallel to the LFC. Although they point out that the two are not necessarily identical for the same situations, the notion of slippage provides a conceptual link, however informal, between this chapter and the earlier one (Chapter 3) on outliers.

References

It is clear that I have depended very heavily for this chapter on three major books and papers. I will, therefore, list these with comments and then follow them with additional references and the papers and books providing the data sets.

Main references
GIBBONS, J.D., OLKIN, I. & SOBEL, M. (1977). *Selecting and Ordering Populations: A New Statistical Methodology*. New York: Wiley.
   Comprehensive and relatively accessible treatment. Many references and useful tables. Likely to become the standard applied text.
GIBBONS, J.D., OLKIN, I. & SOBEL, M. (1979). An introduction to ranking and selection. *American Statistician, 33*, 185–195.
   Brief but useful introduction of the field emphasizing IZ/PZ approach. Should be read in conjunction with the first reference.
GUPTA, S.S. & PANCHAPAKESAN, S. (1979). *Multiple Decision Procedures: Theory and Methodology of Selection and Ranking Populations*. New York: Wiley.
   Complex, high powered and high level treatment. Many references. De-emphasizes IZ/PZ approach. No tables. Should be read as an advanced alternative to Gibbons *et al.*

Additional references

DUDEWICZ, E.J. (1980). Ranking (ordering) and selection: an overview of how to select the best. *Technometrics, 22,* 113–119.

GIBBONS, J.D. (1982). Methods for selecting the best process. *Journal of Quality Technology, 14,* 80–88.

GUPTA, S.S. & HUANG, D.Y. (1981). *Multiple Statistical Decision Theory: Recent Developments.* Lecture Notes in Statistics, number 6. New York: Springer-Verlag.

MILLER, R.G. (1981). *Simultaneous Statistical Inference,* 2nd ed. New York: McGraw-Hill.

MYERS, J.L. (1979). *Fundamentals of Experimental Design,* 3rd ed. Boston: Allyn & Bacon.

READING, J.C. (1975). A multiple comparison procedure for classifying all pairs of M means as close or distant. *Journal of the American Statistical Association, 70,* 832–838.

References for worked examples

LINDGREN, B.W. & BERRY, D.A. (1981). *Elementary Statistics.* New York: Macmillan.

MAZUR, A. (1977). Interpersonal spacing on public benches in 'contact' vs 'noncontact' cultures. *Journal of Social Psychology, 101,* 53–58.

MENDENHALL, W., McCLAVE, J.T. & RAMEY, M. (1981). *Statistics for Psychology,* 2nd ed. North Scituate: Duxbury.

WINER, B.J. (1971). *Statistical Principles in Experimental Design,* 2nd ed. New York: McGraw Hill.

WOODS, P.J. & HOLLAND, C.H. (1966). Instrumental escape conditioning in a water tank. *Journal of Comparative and Physiological Psychology, 62,* 403–408.

9

Getting New Statistics into Today's Crowded Syllabuses

ALEXANDER D. LOVIE

THERE *IS* LIFE AFTER 1940

I recently received a complimentary copy of the second heavily revised edition of a statistics book intended for beginning psychology students. No names, no pack drill but on p. viii of the preface I read (and this in a text published in 1981 not 1881) that, in order to make the book 'as up-to-date and modern as possible', more coverage of descriptive statistics 'in particular a new chapter covering correlation' (!), had been provided. The writers then go on to list other 'up-to-date' topics such as significance levels, experimental design, the analysis of repeated measures, factor interaction and non-parametric analysis of variance. Closer reading of the new chapter on correlations (as descriptive measures, note) reveals such modern wonders as scattergrams (but no mention of outliers) and the Pearson product moment correlation!

The attitude to statistics displayed by this book is no more than a more extreme version of the one found in most recent introductory statistics texts for psychologists and other social scientists (the very limited number of Bayesian treatments I exclude from this list; see, for example, Phillips, 1973; and Novick & Jackson, 1974; also Pitz, 1982). Put succinctly this states that statistics for social science died around 1940. Or put another way: the bulk of the contents of the average introductory statistics text could have been written over 40 years ago.

LAG TIME COWBOY JOE

Why should this be? There is, of course, the obvious point that for most social scientists, statistics=mathematics=turn off. Consequently, the textbook writer, even if he or she were personally committed to the subject, is likely either to have been badly taught or, fearing the real or apparent problems of students, has fallen back on the tried and tested. There are, however, deeper reasons than this; reasons concerned with the relationship betwen statistics and social science. First of all, let me repeat a point that I made in the Introduction to this book: statistics is a branch of *applied* mathematics. In other words, it is driven by (and its form shaped by) its clients in a reflexive relationship of some subtlety. In particular,

163

the client poses the problem in his or her terms. The statistician's role, although rarely formalized, is nevertheless crucial in that he or she translates this problem into more or less mathematical form, usually as a *model*.

This model can either be completely novel (very rare) or one drawn from the available literature, or a mixture of the two. In turn, the statistician will negotiate with the client over the value and relevance of this model to the client's problem. However, as Baskerville, in a recent review of the statistical consultancy literature, has written: 'An analysis that is too far beyond the accepted procedures of inference in a particular discipline may be viewed sceptically by clients' (1981, p. 122).

Such an interaction, which usually provides the motor for statistical advance, is difficult to capture in a textbook, but it does demonstrate that statistics progresses. Therefore, the success of any substantive discipline in incorporating the fruits of this advance into itself is directly related to the recent existence of such an interaction between the field and statistics. If, as in most psychological and social science research, such an interchange has never taken place then the expected payoff in the form of new methods cannot happen. Put more simply, if the social sciences are not prepared to use statisticians on a regular basis then the new statistical ideas developed from statistician/client interactions in other fields will not be taken up so readily.

Of course, one clear implication of statistics as an applied subject is that if you buy *statistical* method X, then you also buy the *substantive* context in which method X was developed. It is, however, the strength of statistical analyses, as R. A. Fisher pointed out many years ago, that they readily generalize to other areas where uncertainty and variability has to be described and dealt with. Nevertheless, the relative rarity of creative client/statistician interchanges within the social sciences means that any new methods take that much longer to pass to us and, because of their somewhat tailored nature, are not always properly used. There is, in other words, a trade-off between the general and the specific in statistics that we, as potential and actual users, should be aware of.

A further aspect of the time-lag for those who do not pursue joint ventures with the statistical fraternity is to risk being unable to communicate with them (and hence benefit from their advances) or indeed to interest them in social science problems. Being actively involved in trying out new methods and new approaches should, however, encourage a more active interaction. And this means learning (and, for some of us, teaching) new material. Which is where we go next.

NEW WINE IN PARTLY NEW BOTTLES

Although the attractions of swift and revolutionary change are many and varied, for example, instant disposal of dead wood, they rarely commend themselves to the teachers of a particular subject who, not unnaturally, do not like to think of themselves as standard bearers for obsolescent ideas and practices. Of course, change is necessary but a gradualist position still yields the advantages of reasoned and planned progress with the new seeming to grow out of and improve on the old. If even a slight feeling of uncertainty about statistics is engendered by such a gradualist attitude then some recognition of the dynamic nature of the subject would be attained and appropriate action taken, as would, of course, be normal for, say, the neuropsychologist after a particular breakthrough in neurophysiology. Building on the old by showing how the earlier methods can be improved on should help break down the barriers to new material. It should also maintain the flow of new material since with the barriers gone and a justifiable unease with the present methods established, the transfer of new material should be ensured. This should not, therefore, be viewed as a one-off, one-shot attempt at breaching the dam to new material but a long-term project to ensure that the flow of ideas and procedures *never* ceases.

How should these rather abstract notions be translated into specific teaching programmes, at least for the topics covered in this book? This I will now consider in some detail.

A SELECTION OF THIS NEW WINE

Pictures and EDA

Most conventional texts include sections on graphical methods – scattergrams, histograms, graphs, etc. – together with the division (sometimes explicit sometimes not) between *descriptive* and *inferential* statistics. John Tukey's Exploratory Data Analysis (EDA) emphasizes an informal, *pictorial* approach to data. The clear implication here is that pictures do not merely represent the data in an alternative form. Rather they serve *both* descriptive and inferential purposes in that hypothesis seeking (one of the major characteristics of EDA) consists of drawing pictures thàt emphasize both surprising and important aspects of the data. In other words, they not merely present the data in a different, more compact form but the form positively *aids* subsequent hypothesis detection/ confirmation. Of course, even in conventional statistical treatments it is impossible to separate description and inference when, for example, the calculation of means and variances seems to figure so prominently in both. However, it is over the role and importance of pictures that EDA and more conventional texts differ. Consequently, it is worth pointing out not only how much extra information an EDA picture conveys (a stem-leaf plot, for example, is like a histogram in that it shows where the data are grouped and the form of this group, but in addition it lists the actual data and their frequency if repeated), but that it is legitimate to draw conclusions (however tentative) from such a representation. Perhaps, even in the conventional framework, people were tempted to draw conclusions from histograms and all that Tukey has done is to legitimize this. However, the stress in most texts on *formal* methods of hypothesis evaluation would certainly have discouraged such a move. Thus Tukey (and EDA) is somewhat more revolutionary than is realized. Thus in order to make full use of EDA and to extract the maximum from its pictures, it will be necessary at some early stage to emphasize the differences in attitude between the passive description of data on the one hand and the active exploration of data plots on the other. Perhaps the best way is the indirect one of encouraging users and students to draw preliminary conclusions from plots and then go on to use such findings in a formal, confirmatory mode.

It is also worth pointing out the parallels between the kinds of informal inference possible with certain EDA graphs and their more formal (and more familiar) analogues. A clear example is the EQQ (Empirical Quantile Quantile) plot (Chambers *et al.*, 1983), where the ability of people to decide whether a data plot is above, below or coincident with the diagonal datum line parallels whether there is a difference in measures of location (means, medians, etc.) between the two samples. This is, of course, an informal analogue of, say, a *t* test or a Mann–Whitney *U* test.

EQQ plots, in addition, provide quick tests of the homogeneity of variance assumption made by many tests. Such a portmanteau plot is useful since it allows many of the more important aspects of *formal* inference (assumptions, direction of difference, basis of differences, size of difference, etc.) to be demonstrated in an *informal*, graphical fashion.

Robustness

The value of robust measures should be much easier to sell if robustness is defined as resistance, that is, relative lack of sensitivity to outliers. It is easy to construct samples which demonstrate the instability of, say, means in the presence of atypical values, compared with medians or biweight measures of location. Of course, the value of such a criterion of robustness for choosing between measures of, say, spread (scale) and location needs justifying, otherwise one is caught in an uncomfortably tight circular justification for robust over non-robust measures. Here, invoking EDA is again useful because an explorer obviously needs a collection of resistant measures since, by definition, one has little prior knowledge of the territory one is moving into. Too constrained (parametrically speaking) a set of assumptions may lead the explorer into drawing wrong conclusions when the data are noisy or heavily contaminated.

Outliers

The centrality of EDA for much modern statistics can be clearly seen both in the recent rebirth of an interest in graphical methods and in the study of robustness. This also applies to the justification for much modern work including the study of outliers.

In a sense, much EDA has been outlier inspired, in that studies of robustness grew out of the inadequate performance of least square estimators in the face of deviant values (and, more generally, the failure of all estimators that treat each observation as being equally important). This, in turn, illustrates the tailward direction that much recent statistics has taken, that is, towards an interest in the edges or tails of distributions and samples. Placing some emphasis on outliers in teaching should motivate much learning about EDA and provide a way into many modern statistical approaches. A considerable body of recent work on regression for example, is concerned with detecting and dealing with lack of fit, one of whose causes (and signs) is the presence of outliers (see, for example, Cook & Weisberg, 1982).

The well-known collection of scattergrams compiled by Anscombe (1973), all of which yield the same r^2 but which are all obviously different, shows in part just how sensitive least squares estimators (here product-moment correlations) are to the presence of outliers. A useful teaching device would be to compute least squares estimators with and without outliers in many situations, both univariate and multivariate, and then to introduce the notion of robust estimators for such situations, including robust regressions. Here one could motivate the teaching of such neglected measures as medians by pointing to their advantages over means in the presence of outliers, that is, by building *rationally* on the known and accepted.

In general, it should be possible to tie up outliers, graphical methods and robust measures into a viable package designed to represent data, first for informal inference then for more formal procedures. This both unifies and motivates the teaching of this recent material.

Counts and models

The other chapters, although not part of an explicit EDA package, can still be sold as improvements on the old. For example, the one on the analysis of counts or frequencies improves on the old chi-square analysis of such data in that it replaces the somewhat informal approach of goodness-of-fit and contingency tables with the more modern and more rigorous philosophy of the generalized linear model. Thus, the analysis of multi-indexed counts can be linked conceptually with the analysis of factorial designs and certain multivariate techniques. Hence, the decomposition of relatively strong data into the effects of factors and their interaction, so familiar to users of ANOVA, is now paralleled by the decomposition of counts. Further, the approach pursued in Chapter 4 whereby models are developed and tested sequentially on the data, from the most to the least saturated, reveals how many contemporary data analysts approach model building. Although this is becoming a familiar strategy to the users of multiple regression packages, for example, interactive SPSS and BMD, it is rarely used in experimental or survey studies. Perhaps teaching the analysis of counts by means of such a flexible, model building approach might ease the introduction into statistics courses of regression analysis and a more dynamic attitude to ANOVA. Further, the emphasis on a *model* (usually a linear one) (a) underlines the centrality of such a concept to modern statistics and (b) points to the unity of conception and analysis in multiclassified, multivariate and multifactor data sets. Many psychological texts, for example, Cohen & Cohen (1975), Edwards (1979) and Myers (1979) have all pointed to the common basis of such techniques as regression and ANOVA. This can now be done for counts with multi-indexed designs.

Mixture designs

Mixture designs are more difficult to relate to elementary work in statistics. However, for those with an interest in multivariate statistics, Chapter 6 offers the mathematical basis for the sampling distributions of certain classificatory techniques, for example, discriminant functions and some types of clustering methods. The increasing introduction of multivariate teaching into psychology and other social sciences should benefit from the extra formalism of the processes of inference offered by the study of mixtures.

Comparative studies

Comparative studies, on the other hand, have long featured in the social sciences, for instance, in the fields of training and learning and in the study of ageing and change in general. Further, continuing criticism of repeated measures designs has meant that some people are now looking towards more sophisticated methods of analysing such sequential designs. Studies of cross-over and switch-back designs, and their associated ANOVAs, have shown that more realistic linear models can be developed for repeated measures. So teaching such methods should build on current repeated measure ANOVAs, with their questionable assumptions about the structure of the relevant variance–covariance matrices.

Comparative studies also allow us to extend more formal analyses into less formally controlled situations, for example, human and animal field studies, survey analysis and observational studies of all kinds. Thus some of the more exciting areas can now be analysed by more than informal, subjective methods.

Further, the use of comparative studies would facilitate interdisciplinary work between social scientists, since much interesting research takes place at the borders of our respective areas. It might, in addition, unify and simplify the various extant analyses, since such techniques as causal modelling, particularly by means of path analysis, have much in common (analytically at least) with ANOVA and regression.

In general, therefore, comparative studies remind us that few if any organisms operate outside a context, be it intellectual, historical or physiological. Until fairly recently there were few techniques to enable us to make provision for this frame of reference effect. Now we have much less excuse for ignoring the relativity of much psychological and social science data.

Power and sample size

The study of power and sample size builds on a variety of currently available methods and teaching. Like ranking and selection techniques, for example, considerations of power emphasize the Type II (β) error and with it the form of the alternative hypothesis. This oddly neglected aspect of classical inference (odd because most users are substantively only concerned with H_As) is now emerging as the more interesting of the two hypotheses. More speculatively, this could also make hypothesis testing a little easier to teach since it can now be seen more as a test of a hypothesis of interest (H_A), rather than one of a hypothesis (H_0) that by convention is of no serious concern to anyone.

Further, the question of how many readings to take is of practical interest to many workers, although rarely dealt with in elementary texts. This, in turn, means that although the material in Chapter 7 is somewhat novel, the questions it tackles are of sufficient relevance to form part of a sensible teaching programme.

Ranking and selection

The ranking and selection material, on the other hand, can be sold as an improvement on existing methods. At the risk of repeating this material, the currently available methods, so-called individual or multiple comparisons, provide only indirect tests of non-homogeneous hypotheses. Such tests are also less powerful in detecting true differences than the appropriate selection routines. Further, the range of parameters that can be evaluated by these newer methods is much larger than individual comparison tests. In addition, the ability to order a collection of parameters is not open to multiple comparison tests, unlike these newer methods. Of course, certain of the advantages of selection and ranking methods can only be realized if one has some idea as to how certain non-homogeneous alternative hypotheses might reveal themselves in the patterning of the parameters. Since this implies that experimenters have to think seriously about their science and how it might translate into patterns of data, there are advantages in emphasizing the alternative hypothesis over and above the demands of the statistical methods themselves.

To summarize so far, I have emphasized the value of an easier transfer of recent statistics into social science and that this can be facilitated by showing how the new builds upon and improves the old. The problem, of course, is that something has to go, given that time and syllabuses are always limited.

CHANGING THE GUARD

It should follow that if statistics is a branch of applied mathematics, then the world view implied by and investigated by such techniques should in part at least determine what methods are in and what are out of favour. Of course, there has to be a rather more reflexive relationship between *zeitgeist* and statistics than I have implied. However, the long lasting advantage enjoyed by ANOVA over simple two-sample tests in psychology for instance does imply a move from a less to a more complex world view (see Lovie, 1979, for a review of this change). The long-term survival of *t*- and Wilcoxon tests, therefore, on any thing other than pedagogical grounds, is now in question. Even the dominance of ANOVA is now being challenged by various multivariate and time-series methods (see O'Hare, 1983, for a recent comment). Such changes in analysis clearly reflect changes in methods (more field, less laboratory orientated) and concepts (less positivist and mechanistic, more cognitive). So our traditional emphasis on ANOVA will have to diminish.

There are other pressures for change and, in certain hopeful cases, simplification in our teaching. For example, the growth in EDA should increase our coverage of more informal means of inference and reduce our reliance on the 'sanctification' role of traditional inference to quote Tukey (1970). Indeed, a more widespread acceptance of EDA might encourage an increasingly creative approach, with statistics and substantive invention advancing hand in hand together with a more modest defence of our hypotheses (because they are explicitly perceived as being based on *informal* analyses) – in short, a riskier but more interesting route to follow.

Further, a recognition of the unity behind ANOVA and regression (and eventually log-linear models) should reduce the need to teach basically the same concepts on separate occasions, thus simplifying and unifying both the teaching and hopefully the *language* of these seemingly disparate areas.

In conclusion, therefore, I would suggest the regular overhaul of statistics teaching by people who are sensitive to changes in both statistics *and* social science, since there is little fun in peddling a cure for no known disease. Such people would encourage *creative dissatisfaction* among the current ranks of statistics users, thus helping to transfer new methods into our discipline or, even better, encourage useful interactions between social scientists and statisticians which might eventually produce new and valuable methods.

COMPUTERS WITH EVERYTHING

Although I have concentrated on the various topics in this book as exemplars for my remarks on teaching new statistics, there is one large outside area which should be discussed, however briefly. This is the impact of computers on statistical methods and statistics teaching. Clearly, the provision of increasingly sophisticated packages is of vital importance for many of the topics covered in this text. For example, the analysis of log-linear models is crucially dependent on the correct software, as are many of the robust (jackknives, biweights) and quasi-robust (bootstrap) methods covered in Chapter 2. No doubt this will continue to be the case, although the increasing power and falling cost of the microprocessor will mean a movement of influence away from the large mainframe towards the mini- and the microcomputer. This should also encourage the proliferation of package standards (bad) and package contents (good).

There is an increasing tendency, therefore, to let the hardware (and the software) take the strain: what the Dutch statistician van der Geer rightly called 'the mindless use of canned packages' (1971). What we increasingly need is a useful set of can-openers for these packages, since as the old computer adage has it 'garbage in, garbage out'. My rather obvious teaching advice is 'learn it in the small, trust it in the large'; that is, learn how to perform and interpret statistical calculations on small data sets either by hand (or by hand calculator), so that one can come to trust the computer to deal with large data sets. The computer is an aid to thought not a substitute for it. However, in order to resist the pressures (which are very seductive at times, particularly if you have masses of data and a friendly computer), then one has to work harder at understanding the purposes, processes and results of any statistical analysis.

Of course, the value of computers in statistics teaching goes beyond the number crunching package. In particular, the provision of good graphical facilities on even the most modest of microcomputers opens up interesting possibilities for both static and dynamic displays. Recent reviews of computer-driven graphical methods include ones by Gentleman (1977), Everitt (1978), Fienberg (1979) and Wainer (1981). Although EDA has taken up such opportunities with alacrity (see, for example, McNeil, 1977, or Velleman & Hoaglin, 1981), I think that we have scarcely started to exploit this increasingly accessible facility.

One final point is that the newish interdisciplinary topic of statistical computation (see Kennedy & Gentle, 1980, also the regular section in the *American Statistician* devoted to the area) can encourage the teaching of both statistics and computing in the social sciences. For example, Efron's bootstrap for the distribution of the correlation coefficient (versions of which can be run on a microcomputer) may be used to illustrate (fairly) simple computing routines and the importance of simulations for modern statistics (see Diaconis & Efron, 1983). More generally, so-called randomization tests (see Edgington, 1980) provide many useful examples for the joint teaching of computing and statistics.

CONCLUSIONS

This chapter has travelled much further and has indulged in more speculation than any of the other parts of the book. The message, however, is simple and clear: statistics is a vital and advancing topic, flexible enough to follow (and aid) all the twists and turns of our subject. Thus, it is well worth psychology and the social sciences in general learning new tricks and not to be afraid to dump the old ones. Further, since the future of much statistics lies in the marriage between itself and computing, so it is vital for both teachers and researchers to climb as fast as possible on to this particular bandwagon.

References

ANSCOMBE, F.J. (1973). Graphs in statistical analysis. *American Statistician*, 27, 17–21.
BASKERVILLE, J.C. (1981). A systematic study of the consulting literature as an integral part of applied training in statistics. *American Statistician*, 35, 121–123.

CHAMBERS, J.M., CLEVELAND, W.S., KLEINER, B. & TUKEY, P.A. (1983). *Graphical Methods for Data Analysis*. Belmont, Calif.: Wadsworth.

COHEN, J. & COHEN, P. (1975). *Applied Multiple Regression/Correlation Analysis for the Behavioural Sciences*. Hillsdale: Erlbaum.

COOK, R.D. & WEISBERG, S. (1982). *Residuals and Influence in Regression*. London: Chapman Hall.

DIACONIS, P. & EFRON, B. (1983). Computer-intensive methods in statistics. *Scientific American, 248*, 96–108.

EDGINGTON, E.S. (1980). *Randomization Tests*. New York: Marcel Dekker.

EDWARDS, A.L. (1979). *Multiple Regression and the Analysis of Variance and Covariance*. San Francisco: Freeman.

EVERITT, B. (1978). *Graphical Techniques for Multivariate Data*. London: Heinemann.

FIENBERG, S.E. (1979). Graphical methods in statistics. *American Statistician, 33*, 165–178.

GENTLEMAN, J.F. (1977). It's all a plot (using interactive computer graphics in teaching statistics). *American Statistician, 31*, 166–175.

KENNEDY, W.J. & GENTLE, J.E. (1980). *Statistical Computing*. New York: Marcel Dekker.

LOVIE, A.D. (1979). The analysis of variance in experimental psychology: 1934–1945. *British Journal of Mathematical and Statistical Psychology, 32*, 151–178.

McNEIL, D.R. (1977). *Interactive Data Analysis*. New York: Wiley.

MYERS, J.L. (1979). *Fundamentals of Experimental Design*, 3rd ed. Boston: Allyn and Bacon.

NOVICK, M.R. & JACKSON, P.H. (1974). *Statistical Methods for Educational Psychological Research*. New York: McGraw Hill.

O'HARE, D. (1983). Action research – toward a multi-variable future. *Bulletin of The British Psychological Society, 36*, 201–202.

PHILLIPS, L.D. (1973). *Bayesian Statistics for Social Scientists*. London: Nelson.

PITZ, G.F. (1982). Applications of Bayesian statistics in psychological research. In: G. Keren (ed.), *Statistical and Methodological Issues in Psychology and Social Sciences Research*. Hillsdale: Erlbaum.

TUKEY, J.W. (1970). Analyzing data: sanctification or detective work? *American Psychologist, 25*, 83–91.

VAN DER GEER, J.P. (1971). *Introduction to Multivariate Analysis for Social Science*. New York: Freeman.

VELLEMAN, P.F. & HOAGLIN, D.C. (1981). *Applications, Basics and Computing of Exploratory Data Analysis*. Boston: Duxbury.

WAINER, H. (1981). Graphical data analysis. *Annual Review of Psychology, 32*, 191–241.

Index